M000282683

SINNERS

SINNERS

JESUS AND HIS EARLIEST FOLLOWERS

Greg Carey

BAYLOR UNIVERSITY PRESS

© 2009 by Baylor University Press
Waco, Texas 76798

All Rights Reserved. No part of this publication may be reproduced, stored
in a retrieval system, or transmitted, in any form or by any means, elec-
tronic, mechanical, photocopying, recording or otherwise, without the prior
permission in writing of Baylor University Press.

Cover Design by Stephanie Blumenthal
Cover Art: *Jesus and Veronica*. Paintings by Niccolo Frangipane
(1560–1600). The Granger Collection, New York. Used by permission.

Library of Congress Cataloging-in-Publication Data

Carey, Greg, 1965-
Sinners : Jesus and his earliest followers / Greg Carey.
p. cm.
Includes index.
ISBN 978-1-60258-146-3 (pbk. : alk. paper)
1. Jesus Christ--Character. 2. Jesus Christ--Example. 3. Sin--Christianity
--History of doctrines--Early church, ca. 30-600. 4. Jesus Christ--Friends
and associates. 5. Bible. N .T.--Criticism, interpretation, etc. I. Title.

BT604.C37 2009
232.9'04--dc22

Printed in the United States of America on acid-free paper with a minimum
of 30% pcw recycled content.

CONTENTS

PREFACE

The title of this book, *Sinners: Jesus and His Earliest Followers*, aims to
be provocative. In Christian contexts one often hears that Jesus, being
divine, did not commit sin. This is a theological claim, grounded in centuries of doctrine and tradition. To place Jesus' name among "sinners"
strikes at the heart of Christian reverence for him. I do not intend to
demean Jesus.

But I do mean to make a point. In their own historical contexts,
in their own times and places, people knew Jesus and his earliest followers as sinners. That is, Jesus and the first generations of Christians
frequently violated conventional social norms. What is more, they provoked hostility, sometimes violence, as a result. Jesus' cross, which was
a sign of a publicly sanctioned execution, stands as a primary symbol
for this movement. This book traces several of the ways in which Jesus
and his earliest followers stepped across normal lines of propriety and
elicited responses ranging from suspicion to outright resistance.

In contrast, people today generally associate Christianity with
respectability. Virtues like compassion, justice, or grace rank far below
respectability on the public radar. If people think well of Christians, they
envision nice people who uphold basic moral standards. Or sometimes,

they also conjure self-righteous preachers who castigate other people while hoarding skeletons in their own closets. For the sake of grace, let us not name names. The point is, in many respects mainline Christianity has rendered itself harmless through its respectability. Moreover, mainline Christianity *clings* to its respectability with all its might; this diminishes both the churches and the world. This book aims to introduce deviance and transgression as ways in which early Christians understood themselves and as consistent with how their ancient neighbors saw them. I believe their witness offers both a challenge and some hope to our church and world today.

A book like this requires a word about methodology. This book is deeply engaged with concerns far removed from the world of the first generations of Christians. As a professional biblical scholar, I must ask how texts produced by ancient people may prove relevant for contemporary audiences. I understand this as the basic question of how to read the Bible theologically. It is a tough problem, and I do not have a systematic solution. However, I find that the most compelling interpretations of Scripture honor the ancient contexts in which it was written while bringing the Bible into conversation with today's living questions. As a result, this book is largely historical. I will devote most of my attention to understanding how the first generations of Christians shaped their identity through, and with, the texts they produced. In many respects, their cultures were not our culture, and the issues they faced were not our issues. Yet I find that how they imagined themselves and their relationship to their own world challenges and informs how contemporary Christians—and others—come to terms with our own times and places.

My primary focus involves how early Christians came to understand their collective identity within their larger societies. When I discuss Jesus, I mean Jesus as he was remembered by those first generations of followers who produced our earliest Christian literature. From a literary perspective, Jesus is a character in the Gospels of Matthew, Mark, Luke, and John. Mark's Jesus and John's Jesus hardly amount to the same character: They talk about different things; they sound different; and they do different things. Although I claim a personal interest in the real, flesh and blood historical Jesus, that is not the focus of this book. Likewise, when I discuss other early Christian literature my main question involves how, say, 1 Corinthians reflects the process of early Christian self-definition—not so much why or how an author like the Apostle Paul wrote this letter (though questions like that are important for this book). Throughout the book I have sought to maintain this focus on early Christian identity in a pagan world.

Sinners explores several dimensions of early Christian deviance and transgression. Chapter 1 investigates the "sinful woman" of Luke 7:36-50. It introduces the idea that "sin" is as much a social as a theological concept. Although many of us could agree that some things—such as cruelty to children—simply violate God's will (theological sin), I want us to consider how societies identify, or label, particular groups of people or behaviors as sinners and sinful (sin in a sociological sense). In this light, we might consider the stigma our society attaches to the homeless or to persons on welfare. This is an important concept: Although today we may not consider some behaviors of early Christians to be "sinful," we must appreciate how and why their neighbors did.

Chapter 2 considers a striking phenomenon in the Gospels. Jesus' opponents apparently criticized him for keeping company with sinners and tax collectors. Guilt by association, we might call it, and Jesus accepts this stigma. Remarkably, not only does Jesus keep company with sinners, he accepts them with open arms. No Gospel traditions depict Jesus criticizing these sinners or calling them to repentance.

Chapter 3 takes on one of the common things for which Christians praise Jesus and twists it into something else. Jesus is often credited for transgressing Israel's purity laws by associating with lepers, touching menstruating women and corpses, and blessing Gentiles. On the contrary, it is far from obvious that Jesus is violating Jewish law on any point—in fact, that suggestion leads to Christian anti-Semitism. Moreover, in these stories it is not Jesus who takes on impurity; rather, impure people impose themselves on Jesus. If Jesus is a hero of these stories, it is not because he reaches out to the unclean but because of how he responds to them.

Chapter 4 shamelessly plays on lyrics from an old country song. I investigate how Jesus, his disciples, and Paul, among others, dealt with conventional assumptions concerning masculinity. Jesus and Paul conform to some expectations. For example, they work in public and demonstrate skill in public speaking. On the other hand, neither man marries, establishes a household, or contributes to a particular village or city. Instead, they travel and build networks of relationships. Moreover, the Gospels and Paul's letters reflect some self-awareness of the tension created by their "imperfect" masculinity.

Chapters 5 and 6 both dwell upon the matter of Jesus' crucifixion. Chapter 5 emphasizes that Jesus did not die simply as an innocent victim. On the contrary, the Gospels reveal that Jesus met his fate precisely because he initiated conflict with Jewish and Roman authorities. Although Jesus did not initiate anything like a revolt, he did create dangerous public disturbances in Jerusalem during a holy festival. This is why he died. Chapter 6 explores what Jesus' death must have meant to the first generations of Christians. Paul refers to this as "the scandal of the cross"— What were the implications of worshiping someone who had been executed by crucifixion, one of the most horrific, shameful modes of execution available to the Romans? Yet worship him, they did.

Between Chapters 5 and 6, I have inserted an Interlude. I am no expert on Christian doctrine, so I keep this discussion brief. In this reflection I problematize the traditional understanding of Jesus' sinlessness. For one thing, no human being totally avoids contamination with sin. We are all, Jesus included, born into webs of oppression and exclusion, on which we rely for our survival. Second, I suggest that this can be good news for Christian theology. Rather than portray Jesus as being untouched by sin (except as its victim), we might conceive of the incarnation as God's full investment in the human condition, including its moral brokenness. But the real energy for this excursus lies beyond doctrine. The confession of Jesus' sinlessness, I believe, contributes to Christian "respectability." We understand righteousness in terms of avoiding sin rather than doing justice and pursuing mercy. Here I draw on the teachings of German martyr Dietrich Bonhoeffer, who maintained that in times of crisis followers of Jesus must act, even if it means incurring guilt.

Chapters 7 and 8 bring the book toward its conclusion by engaging how early Christians interacted with their neighbors. Chapter 7 explores four early Christian texts—Luke and Acts (understood as one story), 1 Corinthians, 1 Peter, and Revelation. With the exception of Revelation, all of these texts express concern about how Christians may appear in the sight of their neighbors—respectability, if you will. Revelation does not. At the same time, all four texts also celebrate early Christian distinctiveness, or deviance, within their cultural contexts. That tension between respectability and deviance animates the chapter. Chapter 8 imagines the other side of the equation: how those Jews and pagans who did not follow Jesus would have evaluated those who did. This chapter underscores early Christian deviance by attempting to understand what motivated people to oppose the movement.

The Epilogue brings things home, first by rehearsing the book's overall arguments, and then by imagining what it might mean for contemporary Christians to take on a sinner consciousness. Can we imagine a church animated more by solidarity than respectability, more by doing righteousness than by maintaining a righteous appearance?

When I began this project, I knew it emerged from my faith heroes. These are typically people whose devotion to the gospel has made them sinners in their own time and place, whose faithfulness not only inspires but intimidates me. Bonhoeffer not only disobeyed orders to cease teaching and writing, he actively participated in the anti-Hitler movement. Clarence Jordan founded a racially integrated farming community in 1940s Georgia and continued to preach for peace and justice despite harsh resistance even from the state government. Who can forget his peanut ad, "Help us ship the nuts out of Georgia"? Fannie Lou Hamer not only sang her way through Mississippi voter registration drives, she sang the night of her vicious beating in jail. Ed King pretty much forfeited his future in Mississippi Methodism while his activism included interracial visits to worship services at white Jackson congregations. With heroes like these, it is only a short hop to an appreciation for Jesus and the first Christians as "sinners."

That is the academic part. This project has led me to look into my own life in a new way. Having grown up white and male in Alabama,

I have enjoyed the privilege of rarely having to explain myself. Yet one experience did set me apart from most of my friends, and I suppose it runs deeper even than I have come to appreciate by this time. My parents divorced when I was young. When my mom and I returned to north Alabama, she raised me as a single parent. Her home religious culture did not reject her for this, but it never fully accepted her divorce as okay. Moreover, she experienced discrimination, patronization, and mistreatment as a divorced woman, the likes of which I am still coming to appreciate. I have been blessed to see my mom, Barbara Akin Pace, meet and marry a wonderful man, Dewey Pace.

In the meantime, although my Dad was succeeding in business, he was also living as an alcoholic. I had no idea, until Dad entered treatment during my senior year in college. I have experienced the rare joy of watching his personal transformation, even to have presided over his wedding to my stepmom, Diane Carey, a skilled and compassionate educator and counselor, and my dear friend.

Because I have had the opportunity to reflect, I suppose I have always identified with people who, like my parents and me, did not follow the prescribed path in every respect. That is not necessarily a virtue. But looking back, I see why I have gravitated toward *Sinners*.

I dedicate this book to my Dad, George Walter Carey, Junior, in celebration of over twenty years of sobriety and with gratitude for the person he is and continues to become.

THANKS

I have benefited from many opportunities to develop the ideas for this book, ranging from classrooms at Lancaster Theological Seminary, academies and retreats for youth, an adult education curriculum developed by Lancaster Seminary, and quite a few local church presentations. I am particularly indebted to the trustees and administration of Lancaster Seminary, who provided a sabbatical leave that allowed a focused opportunity for writing and research. Tim Van Meter, now at the Methodist Theological School in Ohio, Jacquie Church Young, and Courtney Harvey have administered Lancaster's youth ministry program, Leadership Now: Spiritual Formation with Youth, where much of this material has taken form. I am grateful to those spectacular young people as well. Likewise, Bruce Epperly and David Mellott of Lancaster Seminary's Continuing Education program have allowed me to try out these ideas in an adult education curriculum. Charles Melchert has allowed me to present some of this material in a Lancaster Seminary Doctor of Ministry seminar, and he has provided invaluable constructive criticism. Rachel Gawn, faculty secretary at Lancaster, has helped with countless details, including effective editorial review.

Courtney Harvey has reviewed parts of the manuscript, as have two alumni of Lancaster Seminary, David de Jesus Bowles and Jennifer Williams. So has Anna Fuller, who brings so much joy to my life. I have benefitted greatly from their wisdom. The Rev. Dr. Lyle Weible, formerly Conference Minister for Penn Central Conference of the United Church of Christ, has volunteered help for this book, and Professor Luke Timothy Johnson, R. W. Woodruff Professor of New Testament and Christian Origins at Emory University's Candler School of Theology, has responded to my random suggestions with characteristic wisdom and insight. I am further grateful to the anonymous reviewers of Baylor University Press, and to Carey Newman. As an editor, Carey helped me imagine what a book like this might actually look like. As a visiting professor, long ago back at the Southern Baptist Theological Seminary, Carey helped me imagine myself as a New Testament scholar—a brand new idea for me at that time. His friendship and encouragement have never wavered.

Erin Summers Carey and Emily Hope Carey are gracious enough to call me Dad in public. They have put up with a lot for this project to reach completion, and they have supported my work on it throughout. Thanks, E and Em!

Chapter 1

"HOW DO YOU KNOW SHE'S A (SINNER)?"

The woman walks into the room, but we do not know her. Immediately we hear that she is a "sinner." She walks over behind Jesus, who is reclining beside the table, opens an expensive jar, and bathes his feet with her tears and her hair. Then she kisses his feet, anointing them with ointment (Luke 7:36-50).

But she is a sinner. This identity is the third thing we learn about her: she is a woman; she is from the city; and she is a sinner. The host of the dinner, Simon, will not say it aloud, but he, too, knows she is a sinner. Jesus divines Simon's thoughts, and he scolds his host, but he does not correct Simon's appraisal of the woman's identity, not at all. Instead, Jesus agrees that her sins are many. Case closed. This woman is a sinner.

Luke's story leaves us with an information gap. How do we know she is a sinner? How do the narrator, Simon, and Jesus possess this information? What leads them to this shared assessment? What has she done?

COMIC (AND SERIOUS) DETOURS

These questions recall a famous scene from the film *Monty Python and the Holy Grail*. Sir Bedevere arrives in a village where he encounters a mob. The residents confront him with a defendant and an accusation:

> *A witch! A witch! A witch! We've got a witch! A witch!*

An inquiry is in order. Wise Bedevere will not go for just any lynch mob accusation:

> *How do you know she is a witch?*

This line of questioning elicits multiple responses. The woman looks like a witch, but then again that is because her neighbors have dressed her up for the role, including placing a carrot over her nose.

> *And the hat—but she is a witch!*

The villagers bring more evidence. Apparently the woman has also transformed a poor villager into a newt. He looks fine now, of course. Reluctantly, he confesses:

> *I got better.*

How fortunate! Unfortunately for the alleged witch, the evidence against her mounts. Because witches are made of wood, because wood floats, and because ducks also float, witches and ducks must weigh the same. It makes sense to weigh the woman against a duck, right? Amazingly, on the scales the woman and duck balance one another. The mob shouts the verdict:

> *A witch!*

A hilarious scene, but it raises serious questions. Witchcraft accusations have led to the deaths of quite a few persons. Looking at the trial records, modern historians have wondered how such charges emerged—not to mention how they were substantiated. What kind of person is liable to be called a witch? What does one have to do? How do societies apply the label *witch* to someone?

It happened in New England. Historians have reconstructed some of the social processes by which people recognized women, and some men, as witches. Carol F. Karlsen notes that the New England witch trials reflected "an ideology of womanhood" that supported the kind of society Puritans were trying to create.[1] "Accusers denounced witches for behaviors and emotions that were widespread among the colonists, not least of all among the accusers themselves."[2] If the accusations were mundane, then how were prospective witches selected as defendants? Women who deviated or challenged the norms of feminine behavior were far more likely to face witchcraft charges. Naturally, as witchcraft trials grew more common, New England women grew cautious. Many began stifling their outspoken criticisms of the religious and political leadership.[3] Thus, witchcraft allegations performed a social function by protecting the social and religious order at that time.

Research in sociology and cultural anthropology illuminates our understanding of witchcraft accusations. Witchcraft reveals other dimensions of communal life such as family organization, social structure, and individual psychology.[4] For example, in New England many witchcraft cases pitted adolescent girls as accusers against middle-aged women defendants. This pattern likely reflects tensions between younger and older women, possibly as a result of the parenting customs of the day and the relations between older and younger women.[5] Moreover, most accused witches already had records or reputations of antisocial or criminal behavior.[6] Once again, there are ties between labeling individuals as "witches" and methods of social control. As James M. Morone puts it, "The witchcraft frenzy came, in part, from an urge to force secular problems into a moral frame." The New Englanders tried to "pin social tensions on hidden, immoral victims."[7]

Witchcraft accusations surface primarily in certain kinds of societies. Witchcraft requires proximity and rivalry. Where people live close to one another, where the means for negotiating conflict are unclear or weak, and where people routinely compete with their neighbors for vital social and material resources, witchcraft accusations are likely to flourish. By placing one's adversary at a disadvantage, witchcraft accusations provide one means of social control.[8]

Labels like "witch" and "witchcraft" or ("sinner" and "sin") reflect the values, anxieties, and power relations of particular societies. They may or may not indicate a person's moral guilt or innocence. And they certainly do not demonstrate that the witch or sinner is especially guilty in comparison with his or her neighbors. They do, however, reveal something about how the accused relates to the social order and concerns of their day.

This detour into witch accusations bears implications for the woman in Luke 7. Because labeling persons as witches involves complex social processes, those processes also reveal the core values and pressing concerns of societies. What lessons does the pattern of witchcraft allegations hold for a similar phenomenon: the labeling of sinners? By what processes do societies label people as sinners?

Accusations of sin often reflect other social agendas. Their roots may lie so deep as to prevent their observation. For example, the prominent Southern Baptist spokesperson Al Mohler recently articulated a new sin, "the sin of delaying marriage." Scripture makes clear, Mohler argued, that marriage is one of the primary means by which people grow in holiness. Mohler maintained that because men are called to lead, they should pursue that calling through marriage. There they can cultivate their leadership in their relations with their wives and children. "The longer you wait to get married," he argued, "the more habits and lifestyle patterns you will have that will be difficult to handle in marriage."[9]

It is unclear to me how the Bible specifies that people ought to marry early in life. Presumably, some have strong theological convictions that lead to this opinion. Yet we might also ask: What values are at stake for those who advocate early marriage and thereby stigmatize single adults? Here we might reflect for a moment on the political and religious divisions so prominent in the United States. The religious right insists that it represents traditional—in their view, biblical—family values. They support legislative action, even a constitutional amendment, to define marriage in a particular way. Visit a local Christian bookstore, and you will be amazed by the evangelical market for books on parenting and family life. Pay careful attention, and you will also find a movement within some evangelical circles to promote large families. Is the Christian right making babies to extend their political influence through coming generations? Evangelicals have long insisted that the Bible teaches people to avoid sexual intimacy until marriage. The longer people remain single, the more likely they are to engage in premarital sexual intimacy, perhaps distancing themselves from evangelical communities. In short, the invention of a new sin, the sin of delaying marriage, resonates with broader social stresses and political goals. This new sin represents an attempt to promote some social values—large, patriarchal, sexually pure evangelical households—over their alternatives.

We can learn quite a lot from witchcraft accusations and Christian right rhetoric. Labeling of sins and sinners demands a complicated process. It does involve the moral standards of particular communities. But labeling also reflects the stresses that threaten those communities, their struggles to define themselves or affect the social worlds they inhabit. The New England women accused as witches failed to conduct themselves as their community wished middle-aged women to behave. They experienced conflict with the younger generation of women, perhaps reflecting deeper stresses in New England social arrangements. Some probably had engaged in witchcraft—some, at least, confessed to it— but their accusations and convictions reveal how other forces made such charges both likely and deadly. In a similar fashion, the contemporary religious right upholds well-defined sexual standards. Some believe that the promotion of early marriage will foster those standards. But early marriage also relates to larger stresses within the political culture of the United States. On the one hand, the Christian right claims that it has attained significant influence in public affairs—and it wants more. But on the other hand, the Christian right sees secularism as an ever-present threat, and sexuality as the ground on which the struggle for cultural power will be won or lost. Dig a little, and we will see it: deep roots sustain both witchcraft accusations and the sin of delaying marriage. So it is in every society.

SINNERS IN JESUS' WORLD

When Luke describes someone as a sinner, what exactly is that supposed to mean? What did it mean in Jesus' day? Several understandings of sinners have emerged in the life of the church and in biblical scholarship, so perhaps a brief review is in order.

Some would equate "sinners" with bad people. That is, sinners were people who routinely did bad things. In the case of the woman who anoints Jesus, her wicked deeds would be public knowledge. This understanding also tends to associate her sins with her sexual history, though Luke does not indicate that this is the case.[10] Luke tells the story so that we do not know what the woman's sins are. The behavior we do see—her shameless and elaborate adoration of Jesus—makes it difficult to regard her as a "bad person" in some simple sense. She is not malicious, antisocial, or cruel. But she is a sinner. Seeing her as a bad person does not account for Luke's portrait of her.

1. At the other end of the spectrum, some think theologically. Because according to Paul and many other biblical writers all people have sinned, then "sinners" really indicates everyone. Thus, the woman is indeed a sinner in that she has failed to live up to God's standards. But so are we, and so is everyone else. Whatever its theological merits, this approach does not help us understand Luke' story. No one in the story, including Jesus, does anything but reinforce the impression that the woman's "many" sins mark her off from her neighbors. After all, why would Luke identify her—and others in the Gospel as well—as a sinner, if the category did not set her apart?

2. Some historians have introduced a social resolution for this question. The sinners in ancient Judaism were simply ordinary people, the *am ha'arets* (or, "people of the land"). Because they were uneducated—and unconcerned—about such things, one could not expect such commoners to observe the details of the

law.[11] In this view, the woman is a sinner not because she is mean or cruel but because she does not live up to the highest standards of her religious culture. This account also has its problems. It depends on rabbinic writings that were produced long after the time of Jesus, when conditions in Judaism had changed dramatically. And it assumes that the Pharisees, whose ideological descendants likely did produce those later rabbinic writings, had enough authority to label anyone who failed to live up to their standards as sinners. But we have no evidence that most Jews of Jesus' day regarded ordinary people as sinners. Instead, our best evidence suggests that most people in Galilee and Judea observed the basics of the law insofar as they could. Religious specialists may have looked down on commoners, but they would not have excluded them from the covenant people, nor would they have called them sinners.[12]

3. Most historians today understand sinners to indicate simply unfaithful Jews, the "wicked" in the eyes of those who followed God's law. Not bad people in the ordinary sense; the sinners are those who separate themselves from Judaism by disregarding the law of Israel. We encounter this view not only in later Jewish rabbinic literature but also in works that appeared before or around the career of Jesus.[13] This view distinguishes sinners from the righteous as "a matter of fundamental loyalty and life-orientation."[14] In contrast to the other options, this view corresponds to our evidence from the time of Jesus and before, and it poses no obvious problems for interpreting the story of the woman who anoints Jesus. Simply, a sinner was someone who habitually transgressed the law of Israel.

Yet even this resolution, like all of the others, raises a problem. Each interpretation takes the sinners label at face value. Each takes for granted that sinners represented an easily identifiable group of people in the time of Jesus. Or worse, each assumes that everyone would have agreed in identifying the sinners in their neighborhood. They attach a simple moral value to the category of sinners. But as Elisabeth

Schüssler Fiorenza observes, sinner could include any among a host of marginal people, many of whom were excluded from social and economic benefits.[15] Naming sin and sinners is far more complicated than these approaches suggest.

COMPLICATING SIN AND SINNERS

Concerning the woman from Luke 7, consider how much Luke does not tell us. Luke does not disclose the nature of her sins, why she arrives at a formal meal unaccompanied by a man, or whether she comes to Jesus seeking forgiveness or giving thanks for the forgiveness she has already received.[16] Almost always, church study groups who pore over this passage find themselves frustrated by the same omissions.

Ever creative, Christian tradition has assigned the woman an identity and a history. As Barbara E. Reid notes, "It is curious that although the text does not say what sort of sins the woman had committed, much attention has been given to speculation on the nature of her sinful past."[17] Indeed. Popular traditions associate the woman with Mary Magdalene, who appears in the verses immediately following the sinner's story. But these traditions make several imaginative leaps. Luke never tells us who this woman is, and so many readers have identified the sinner as Mary. Luke describes Mary as a woman from whom Jesus had expelled seven demons. Luke also relates that Jesus and his followers rely on her and other women for support (8:2-3). These traditions identify the woman who anoints Jesus with Mary because the anonymous woman is a sinner, whereas Mary had required exorcism. The identification also presumes that the woman's sins, and Mary's, must be sexual. Thus, in popular tradition Mary Magdalene is a former prostitute who found redemption in the company of Jesus. The best-selling novel *The DaVinci Code* and many other popular sources further suggest that she may even have been Jesus' lover. F. Scott Spencer gets it just right: "this supposedly 'loose' woman has suffered from some rather 'loose' interpretation."[18] A little voyeuristic curiosity can go a long way.

But Reid insists, first, that we do not know the nature of the woman's sins.[19] Moreover, the perception that she is a sinner misses the point. Kathleen E. Corley, for example, interprets the accusation not as a reflection of the woman's actual moral status, but as an invective against a woman who is "out of place." When she comes to Jesus while he reclines at the table, she is entering space often reserved for men. During the time of Jesus women were more frequently present at public meals than in the not-too distant past, yet some continued to exclude them. Those who resent her presence could label her a sinner, perhaps even a prostitute. This represented common slander against a woman out of place.[20] According to Reid, the woman had been a sinner (one possible translation) but had already received forgiveness. By calling her a sinner, Jesus' host—like many traditional interpretations—misses the point. Luke's story, Reid says, is not about her sinfulness but about her lavish love for Jesus.[21]

Even if we emphasize the woman's great love, three times the story insists on her sinful identity. Luke's story depends on her label as a sinner. If Luke does not emphasize her commonly known identity, then there is no controversy between Jesus and Simon, his host. Luke makes a big deal of the woman's identity as a sinner, and we have much to learn from it. As Patrick Mullen puts it, "not only was the woman a sinner; in light of her many sins she must have been accomplished in her transgressions."[22]

Let us suppose, for the sake of argument, that the woman's sins *did* involve her sexual history. We do not know this, but it is possible. After all, (traditionally male) commentators have assigned her this history for a simple reason: when patriarchal cultures mention "disreputable" women, they almost always imply sex. Why, one may ask, would we expect Luke to be any different? Although Luke's description of her conduct—she unbinds her hair and wipes Jesus' feet with it—would not necessarily have carried sexual connotations in that historical context,[23] they can be understood that way.

Again, we do not know this woman's history because Luke chooses not to disclose it. For the sake of our discussion let us explore the possibility that her sin is sexual. What can we learn from her? If this woman were a prostitute, as tradition has it, what can she teach us?

Prostitutes have long held the public imagination—among both men and women. In contemporary media their image tends to be glamorized. Those of us from a certain generation might recall Miss Kitty from the television series *Gunsmoke*. No one ever called her a prostitute, but there she was, all dressed up in that bar and vulnerable to the men who came through. Miss Kitty reflected all the qualities pop society imposes on prostitutes. She was sexy, sophisticated, and good hearted—virtuous, even. Even more striking, she was her own woman. She possessed self-determination. Things have not changed much since the *Gunsmoke* era. Even today Heidi Fleiss, "the Hollywood Madam," appears regularly on our television screens as a slick, sophisticated, and successful businesswoman. Somehow our pop culture has turned prostitution into something "naughty" rather than something dangerous and abusive.

Unfortunately, the Bible offers little help in correcting this image. Language about prostitution in Scripture and in ancient Judaism and Christianity seems imprecise at best, including any kind of illicit sexual activity.[24] Hosea describes his wife Gomer as a "wife of prostitution." Although the book does not directly call her a prostitute, it attributes her sexual behavior to her moral corruption and promises her corporal punishment, including her sexual humiliation.[25] The apocryphal book Sirach testifies to the prostitute's alluring appeal. The language, "Do not *give yourself* to prostitutes, or you may lose your inheritance" (9:6), suggests the prostitute's initiative rather than the prospective john's sexual acquisitiveness. When the book of Revelation condemns Rome as Babylon the Great Prostitute, her attributes include luxurious garments, a haughty disposition, and an insatiable desire for blood.

Miss Kitty aside, we all know better. Few, if any women choose prostitution from a range of viable life alternatives. One cross-cultural study revealed that 92 percent of prostitutes desired to leave prostitution, whereas two thirds met the diagnostic criteria for posttraumatic stress disorder.[26] Prostitution is not naughty; it is deadly. If the woman who anoints Jesus is a prostitute, her transgression does not outweigh her victimization.

Thus, even the traditional interpretation of the woman's story under-mines a straightforward understanding of sin and sinners. This tradition identifies the woman's sin as prostitution. Yet would that render her a villain or a victim?

We still do not know how people came to regard this woman as a sinner. Ancient villages were quite small, so that people's lives were open to one another. Whatever her misdeeds, they were open knowl-edge to her neighbors. By contrast, the woman's history is closed to us. All we can say is that Luke introduces her as a sinner, which makes her one who habitually lives outside of Israel's covenant with its God.

SIN: ABSOLUTE AND CONTEXTUAL

We have all experienced sin. We have observed how cruel human beings can be to one another in a variety of contexts. This includes individual sins that anyone would condemn in any context, such as neglecting or abusing children. And it includes systemic structures of sin, in which the true nature of sin proves difficult to name. It is one thing to spot an individual real estate agent steering minority families from white neighborhoods, but much more difficult to explain why neighborhoods remain as segregated as they are. To what degree are some neighbor-hoods segregated as a result of the individual decisions of racist hom-eowners and real estate agents, and to what degree do deeper conditions underlie such patterns? Surely it is some of both.[27] Most all of us would condemn neglect of children; most of us would condemn unfair hous-ing patterns; but it is easier to blame an individual act we can see than systemic patterns that require deep levels of analysis.

Although we acknowledge the theological reality of sin, we also recognize how profoundly notions of "sin" are tied to particular cultural moments. In sociological terms, we have been talking about "labeling" and "deviance." Simply, deviance involves any behaviors that trans-gress generally accepted social norms. For example, we might consider drinking beer among Southern Baptists and Roman Catholics. (I have done both.) Among Southern Baptists in those cultural pockets where Baptists represent a large percentage of the population, beer drinking represents a deviant behavior. If a person, especially a young person, drinks beer, her behavior elicits prayers from her peer group. The old joke is that although Protestants may not recognize the Pope, two Baptists will not recognize one another in a liquor store. Not so, of course, among Roman Catholics in most of the world, for whom drinking is one of life's pleasures. From a social point of view, sometimes beer drinking counts as sin and sometimes it does not.

Deviance is not necessarily immoral. What may represent deviant behavior in one social context may seem heroic in retrospect. Sociologists Rodney Stark and William Sims Bainbridge note the power of deviance to counter social norms:

> although religion may generally function to support the moral order, clearly it does not always do so. Often enough, religious organizations and movements challenge the prevailing secular culture, and in so doing can be seen as a source of deviant behavior rather than as a source of social control.[28]

Along these lines, we might consider those nineteenth century activists for women's rights. Branded as "unwomanly" in their own time by many, today they provide the subjects for countless admiring books and articles. Not only did they open the path for women's access to the vote and the pulpit, their activism was an essential contribution to the antislavery struggle. Their examples show how one epoch's deviance can provide another's virtue.

Labeling and deviance have a complicated relationship. Labeling is the process by which society imposes identities on individuals and groups, usually according to one characteristic they are presumed to possess. When we think of labeling, usually negative values come to mind. When persons acquire negatively valued labels, stigmatization occurs: that is, the person generally faces suspicion or discrimination on account of this deviant trait.

The complication involves which comes first, labeling or deviance. Social scientists hotly contest this topic. For example, consider a boy who lives in a crime-ridden neighborhood and whose father has been convicted of several crimes. The child is likely to be labeled a delinquent, at least a potential delinquent, and the burden to prove otherwise rests on his shoulders. Indeed, he might even follow expectations and take that identity on himself. Does this label make it more likely that the boy will engage in delinquent behavior? Alternatively, would such delinquent behavior reflect more his social disadvantages than the label attached to him? That is, does labeling cause delinquency?[29]

My limited personal experience has borne out the significance of labeling and deviance. For example, I can now appreciate my mother's heroism as she raised me by herself in a small city in the South. The religious and cultural value system there imposed heavy stigma on divorced women. No one cared how she became a single parent, but people certainly made assumptions about her and about me, a weight I have only come to appreciate in adulthood.

I also recall the unanimous testimony offered by a group of high school students at Lancaster Seminary's Youth Leadership Academy. We were studying the woman in Luke 7, and I asked the students to identify groups labeled as sinners in our own society. I expected to hear about racial and sexual minorities, welfare mothers, the homeless, promiscuous youth, and immigrants—and I did. But they began somewhere else, with the category, *youth*. The group identified the countless ways in which adults treated them with suspicion and prejudice. Sure enough, I have worked among young people in a poor urban community whose every move was regarded as threatening. I recall one woman sharing her fear of driving through such neighborhoods: "Why do they have to stand on the corner threatening?" As if poor urban kids had somewhere else to be! Such is the effect of labeling.

We know this pattern in U.S. history. Society has its ways of labeling certain groups in ways that serve some political or economic interests at the expense of others. In his fascinating study, *Hellfire Nation: The Politics of Sin in American History*, political scientist James A. Morone has documented this process in cases like the stereotype of the welfare queen.[30] During the 1980s opponents of welfare, then known as Aid to Families with Dependent Children, began rallying around the image of the shiftless woman who preferred drawing welfare checks to going out and working to support her children. One popular image had the woman sitting on the sofa watching television and eating potato chips. And that was the optimistic view. Another image involved her sexual promiscuity. Why worry about pregnancy when more kiddies bring bigger government checks? Lazy or promiscuous, the welfare queen had one more attribute: few people would say it in public, but she was black.

By this point in our study we know to regard such images with suspicion. Sure enough, the image did not match the facts. Most women on welfare have always been white. Birth rates among black teens had consistently fallen, not risen, during the time of these debates. And if the welfare queen was scorned for failing to support her own children, even those who resented welfare would admit that children of single mothers are generally better off if their moms stay at home.

All this, Morone argues, reflects that the real agenda in the 1980s welfare debates—and the debates as they play out today—did not involve what was best for the economy, what was best for society, or what was best for children. The welfare queen was not about an aid system that people felt was unfair. At its heart it was about controlling sexuality. Advocates of welfare reform did not hide this agenda; they simply associated it with the implicit accusation that going on welfare was sinful. One advocate spied the "ultimate goal" as "to promote marriage and family formation," whereas another aimed at "reducing illegitimacy and fostering moral . . . renewal." Though it greatly misrepresented reality, the welfare queen stereotype contributed to debates about sexual morality.[31]

Now, when we think about the woman in Luke 7, she comes thrice labeled: she is a sinner. But we have learned, however, that her label does not *necessarily* indicate a pattern of immoral behavior. Instead, it indicates that she does not conform to some expectations of her particular cultural environment. Even if she has such a pattern of behavior, we still may not assume—as much of church tradition has assumed—that she chose sin because of its intrinsic attraction. Perhaps her identity as a sinner results from factors far beyond her reasonable control. For example, sociologists find that deviance increases among persons who are socially marginalized, that is, those with relatively few attachments to other persons who accept the dominant norms.[32] I am told that deviant behavior also concentrates among survivors of trauma, who act out their victimization in other settings. Powerful as it is, the sinner label tells us little specifically about the character and history of the persons to which it applies.

When we encounter this woman as a sinner, then, her label raises more questions than it provides answers.

- Does she habitually participate in immoral behavior? What would it be?
- To what degree does her label reflect the social agenda of powerful groups in her day?
- If she does behave in immoral ways, what conditions and experiences brought her to this place?

Luke's story, of course, denies us the sort of background information we might desire concerning the woman. That is probably a good thing. It moves us away from evaluating her to considering the power of her presence in the story. Her entrance fills the room with tension: here is a sinner among professedly righteous men. And a woman to boot!

One more thing about the woman in Luke 7—and Jesus' interaction with her. Jesus pronounces her sins forgiven, but he never calls on her to repent. Indeed, the story demonstrates no interest in whether she changes her behavior or not. This, we shall see, is a common trait of Jesus' ministry. Not only does he allow sinners into his company, he joins them. Yet he never calls ordinary sinners to repentance.[33]

We have lots to learn from this story—not just about righteousness and forgiveness and not just about Jesus' compassion for the lost. Deep engagement with this scene teaches us about ourselves and our assumptions. So easily we evaluate others' worth with no real appreciation for their stories, their histories, and their struggles. So easily we encounter people whom society has pushed to the margins, and we assume they lack power or agency. What does our perception of weakness, vulnerability, and stigma hide from our vision? What do we fail to see in other people, and in ourselves, as a result of such categories?

Chapter 2

JESUS, FRIEND OF SINNERS

Mark's Gospel tells it this way: at the outset of his ministry Jesus collects some disciples. Finding Simon and Andrew casting their net into the sea, Jesus commands, "Follow after me, and I will make you anglers of people" (1:17).[1] Likewise for James and John, who abandon their father Zebedee in the boat to follow Jesus.

A little later in the story Jesus calls another disciple with the same directive, but this invitation leads to controversy. Jesus finds Levi sitting at the tax booth, says to him, "Follow me," and Levi leaves his career behind. The next thing you know, Jesus and his disciples are reclining at Levi's table with a host of tax collectors and sinners. Mark explains that many such disreputable folk followed Jesus and then describes the complaint weighed against Jesus by the scribes:

For what reason does he eat with tax collectors and sinners (2:16)?

For what reason indeed? What do we make of Jesus' companionship with sinners? Why does Jesus choose such company, and what did this practice mean for the believers who told and retold these stories in their small gatherings?

17

DINING AND FRIENDSHIP IN JESUS' DAY

Few human activities so reveal the truth about our social lives as our dining company.[2] From the late 1960s movie, Guess Who's Coming to Dinner, which depicts a white middle class family's stress when they learn that their daughter is marrying a black man, to the current decade's Mean Girls, in which high school students draw a map that indicates which kind of students sit where in the cafeteria, our dining practices reflect our social realities. (Before I had ever seen Mean Girls, I used to invite youth to draw up a social map of their cafeterias; they can do it every time.) This is why many churches have taken on dining as a path to racial reconciliation. Many white households have never welcomed visitors of color, so some churches have begun swapping dinner invitations across congregations and across racial lines.

Dining played just as significant a role in Jesus' day.[3] We see its importance in two major categories of gospel stories, scenes involving Jesus' presence in other people's homes, particularly at meals, and Jesus' own stories (or parables) that revolve around meals and feasts.

The social customs of Jesus' day differed in some important respects from our own conventions. Still, modern readers can also relate to many of the dynamics at play. What people eat, how they issue invitations and to whom, where they sit, what they do before, during, and after eating—all these dynamics shape the social experience of a meal. Though these conventions vary from culture to culture, they all reveal the important role meals play in society. Meals reflect basic social realities. Social scientists would say that societies *encode* their values in their dining practices.

> If food is treated as a code, messages it encodes will be found in the pattern of social relations being expressed. The message is about different degrees of hierarchy, inclusion and exclusion, boundaries and transactions across the boundaries.[4]

One example of how meals reflect social values—and social stresses—is the participation of women in ancient meals. Kathleen E. Corley has shown that from the second century B.C.E. through the second century C.E., Greek women increasingly participated in public meals.[5] Prior to this period women seldom dined with men, even in private. A dining room was "male" space, in which women only served or entertained. It was often assumed that entertainment by women, often slaves or prostitutes, included sexual service. Roman wives often accompanied their husbands to dinner, but while the men reclined at table, the women usually sat nearby. Because women did play leadership roles in some social organizations, they must have participated in meals, though perhaps they sat separately from the men. Not surprisingly, as women's participation in public meals increased, their presence remained a controversial matter. The depiction of women at meals as slaves or prostitutes continued well beyond the time of Jesus.

People in Jesus' world knew their place—or were kept in it—at the table. The typical seating arrangement at a banquet was U-shaped, three sides of a rectangle. The closer one sat to the host, the higher one's own status. To be the "right-hand man" showed that one was the guest of honor. Modern people maintain a similar practice in formal meals, reserving head tables for program members or honored guests, but we normally refrain from assigning seats according to status in our homes. At home we seek to maintain an air of egalitarianism. Not so in the ancient world, where a person's status constituted public knowledge.

Jesus' own teaching reflects these realities, according to the Gospels. He scolds the scribes and Pharisees for seeking the best seats at feasts, just as they do in the synagogues (Matt 23:5-7). In Luke 14 Jesus attends a banquet in a prominent religious leader's home. Jesus notices the invited guests vying for the best seats, and he offers his famous teaching.

> When you are called by someone to a wedding banquet, do not recline into the best seat, lest a person of higher status than you has been invited by him; and then the one who called you both might come and say to you, "Give the place to this other person." Then, in shame, you would begin to recline at the last place. (14:8-9)

Sage advice, this, and it reveals the conditions of the day. Seating at meals provided a measure of people's status. Even more shocking to modern sensibilities, these distinctions often carried beyond seating to the amount and quality of food themselves. Although not everyone approved, some hosts reserved the best quantities and qualities of food for their "better" guests. Consider this account of a meal by the Roman Pliny the Younger.

> I supped lately with a person, who in his own opinion lives in splen-
> dour combined with economy; but according to mine, in a sordid but
> expensive manner. Some very elegant dishes were served up to him-
> self and few more of the company; while those which were placed
> before the rest were cheap and paltry.[6]

After eating, the host was responsible for guests' entertainment. In the Greco-Roman world, that usually meant musicians and dancers. Often sex workers entertained the guests more directly. More phil-osophical gatherings might skip the bawdier forms of entertainment for high level conversation, as in Plato's *Symposium*. We assume the latter model applied in Jewish meals in the Galilee of Jesus' day. We might imagine the meal conversations in which Jesus participates as serious after-dinner talk.

If we have any doubts concerning the significance of table fellowship in Jesus' day, we may recall that table practices posed the single greatest challenge in first- and second-generation Christianity. The first controversy involved whether Gentiles could join the Jesus movement, which was exclusively Jewish or nearly so. Paul's letters and the Book of Acts reflect the stakes. Jews were prohibited from eating many items that Gentiles relished. As a result, Jewish and Gentile Christians could not share table company unless some resolution was achieved. According to Acts 10, the pathway to this resolution came to Peter in a vision — a vision of food. Confronted by a cloth covered with prohibited meats, Peter hears a heavenly voice, "Rise, Peter, kill and eat." When Peter refuses to defile himself, the voice insists, "What God has purified, you shall not declare impure." Finally, after three occurrences of the vision, Peter is prepared to accept the first Gentile convert. And when church leaders gather in Jerusalem to assess Paul's mission to the Gentiles, their compromise resolution requires Gentiles to respect Jewish dietary customs (Acts 15:20). Paul relates this agreement differently in Galatians 2, but division surfaces over the same issue. Peter, Paul relates, abandons the table he shares with Gentiles on the arrival of Jewish church leaders from Jerusalem (2:11-14).

The second controversy, less familiar among modern Christians, involved food tainted by idolatry. We shall discuss this in more detail in chapter 7, but in the ancient world much of the meat available in the public markets had already passed through the local temples. Some Christians regarded all meat as "idol-food," tainted by pagan worship, whereas others ate it with hardly a second thought. We ought not underestimate the seriousness of this debate. Its divisiveness surfaces three times in the New Testament, receiving significant attention in Romans, 1 Corinthians, and Revelation. What one ate, and with whom one dined, mattered greatly in Jesus' day.

JESUS' TABLE COMPANY

Meals figure prominently in the gospel narratives. Jesus' opponents recognize his frequent party attendance, calling him "a glutton and a drunkard" (Matt 11:19; Luke 7:34). Jesus also receives criticism for feasting but not fasting (Mark 2:18; Matt 9:14-17; Luke 5:33-38). We find Jesus at table, feeding crowds, and including meals in his parables. When Jesus imagines the rule of heaven, he describes a banquet to which many will come from east and west (Matt 8:11).[7] His parables depict wedding banquets, rich people feasting in splendor, and celebratory parties. According to three Gospels, the woman who anoints Jesus for his burial does so while he is at table (Matt 26:6-13; Mark 14:3-9; John 12:1-7).[8] Luke's Gospel particularly emphasizes meals, featuring both Jesus' participation in banquets and his parables about them.[9] As Robert J. Karris observes, "In Luke's Gospel Jesus is either going to a meal, at a meal, or coming from a meal."[10]

One striking aspect of the traditions about Jesus' behavior at meals is how Jesus, who has no residence, sometimes plays the role of host.[11] This primarily happens not in ordinary settings but in those stories that reveal Jesus' messianic identity. When Jesus feeds the crowds, he *takes* the food, *gives thanks* for it, *breaks* it, and *gives* it (Mark 6:41; 8:6; Matt 14:19; Luke 9:16). This same pattern occurs at his final meal (Mark

14:22; Matt 26:26; Luke 22:19). It repeats itself when Luke relates how the risen Jesus made himself known to two disciples at Emmaus.

> And when he was reclined at the table with them, having taken bread, he blessed it, and having broken it, he gave it to them. Then their eyes were opened, and they recognized him. (24:30-31)

The image of Jesus as a banquet host came to mind naturally when early Christians remembered Jesus.

Yet Jesus' table activities provoke controversy. We have noted the complaints of Jesus' opponents: Jesus overindulges, and neglects fasting. But the gravest accusation concerning Jesus' table practices involves the company he keeps. "Why is he eating with tax collectors and sinners?" his opponents demand (Mark 2:16; see Matt 9:11; Luke 5:30). Luke particularly underscores this theme, linking Jesus' company with sinners and meals—and the controversy that attends it—four times (5:30-32; 7:36-50; 15:1-2; 19:1-10).

Jesus ate with sinners. The Gospels do not relate what transpires during these meals. What are the conversations like? Are they religious at all, or perhaps the sort of conversations "real" sinners enjoy? Is Jesus some sort of wild party animal, as one scholar described him?[12] Or does Jesus try to convert these wicked people? Nathan Baxter, now bishop of the Episcopal Diocese of Central Pennsylvania, once delivered the funniest line I have ever heard in a sermon: "Whoever said, 'I'd rather be a doorkeeper in the house of the Lord than dwell in the tents of sinners,' has never dwelt in the tents of sinners." Maybe Jesus is just having fun?

Two classic cases demonstrate how early Christians remembered Jesus and applied what his example meant for their own sense of identity. The first, Jesus' call of Levi, is the one that motivates the complaints from Jesus' opponents, to which Jesus replies that he has come to call sinners (Mark 2:13-17; Matt 9:9-13; Luke 5:27-32). Matthew, Mark, and Luke each tell the story differently, but the basic line holds true. Jesus had already called two pairs of brothers: Simon Peter and Andrew and James and John. The simple command, "Follow me and I will make you anglers of people," drew the first pair (Mark 1:16-20; Matt 4:18-22). Matthew and Mark provide no hint that Jesus already knew these new disciples when he called them, though Luke tells the story differently (see Luke 4:38-39; 5:1-11). In Matthew and Mark, we later find Jesus visiting Simon and Andrew's house, where he restores Simon's mother-in-law to health. It is likely that her response, "serving" Jesus and his companions, creates a meal setting.

LEVI, TAX COLLECTOR

Through the ages people have wondered what was so objectionable about tax collectors (also known as publicans, or tax collectors) like Levi. Our ancient sources do not tell us directly why these people were so despised. Not surprisingly, professional interpreters have supplied various answers to the question.

The Roman Empire extracted tribute from all of its territories. The local authorities needed people to collect these funds, so they hired or contracted tax collectors. The Romans couldn't have cared less how those funds were raised, so long as the methods didn't lead to sedition. Nor did the local authorities. All that mattered was getting the money flowing into the system.

I am only guessing, but this system suggests three reasons that people likely resented Levi and his ilk. First of all, the tax collectors diverted resources from an already impoverished population and sent those resources to an exploitative empire. Second, a system like the Roman one left lots of room for corruption. Levi and his colleagues likely kept all the personal profit they could, so long as they delivered on their required quotas. Third, if most tax collectors were corrupt or exploitative, they likely enjoyed limited social options. Perhaps other "sinners" made their best company.

Jesus' famous parable of the Pharisee and the Tax Collector expresses his own attitude concerning sinners (Luke 18:9-14). The Pharisee praises God for his own righteousness—here I am reminded of the Heisman Trophy winner who said, "I want to thank

God for making me the outstanding person that I am." But the Tax Collector, without promising to repent or reform, humbly and emotionally begs mercy. Jesus never questions the Pharisee's integrity, and he implicitly affirms the Tax Collector's identity as a sinner. Still, he does commend the Tax Collector, who goes home justified rather than (or more than) the Pharisee.

Likewise, Jesus sees Levi at the tax booth and commands, "Follow me." Levi directly gets up and follows Jesus and then has Jesus over for dinner. So far, Levi's story seems just like those of Simon, Andrew, James, and John. The difference comes with the people Levi invites—a host of other sinners and tax collectors. This is what provokes Jesus' opponents to complain.

I am making a fine point here, but I believe it bears attention. No one complains that Jesus called Levi or that he ate with Levi. When these things happen, one might assume that Jesus is bringing a sinner to repentance. Now that he is in Jesus' company, perhaps Levi will change both his behavior and his company. But that is not what happens. Instead, Levi throws a party—with his same old crowd! Just as scandalous, Jesus and his disciples blend in—apparently without batting an eye. This is what elicits the accusations from Jesus' righteous opponents. Jesus and his disciples eat with sinners without bringing them to repentance.

This is how the Gospels remember Jesus: as one who welcomes sinners without reservations. To appreciate why this poses such a scandal, we might consider the tension between the image of Jesus the rigorous moral teacher and the immoral company he kept. Not all the Gospels depict Jesus as a strict moralist—this is primarily Matthew's contribution—yet we find his rigorous teaching regarding marriage, divorce, sexuality, possessions, and violence scattered throughout Matthew, Mark, and Luke. No wonder the Gospels testify that Jesus' contemporaries object to an apparent contradiction between Jesus' reputation as a moral teacher and his open embrace of sinners.[13]

In this light, the second case, that of Zacchaeus, just leaps off the page (Luke 19:1-10). Zacchaeus, not only a tax collector but a "chief tax collector" and a rich man, so wants to see Jesus that he climbs a tree to gain an unobstructed view. Jesus sees Zacchaeus and calls out to him, "Zacchaeus, come down in a hurry, for today I must stay in your house." One might think that, because Jesus knows Zacchaeus' name, the two have already met. However, Luke tells us that Zacchaeus climbs the tree "to see who Jesus is," revealing that this is their first encounter. In welcoming Jesus, Zacchaeus surely provides a meal.

The Zacchaeus story gets really interesting when people complain that Jesus is joining a sinner. Once again, we notice that Jesus says nothing critical of Zacchaeus; rather, he seeks out Zacchaeus' hospitality. By inviting himself over, Jesus enhances Zacchaeus' public status. At no point does Jesus call Zacchaeus to repent.

In the eyes of most readers, Zacchaeus does repent.[14] When people grumble about him, he says to Jesus,

> Look, half of my possessions, Lord, I give [*present tense*] to the poor, and if I have extorted anything from anyone, I repay [*present tense*] it fourfold. (19:8)

It seems that Zacchaeus, recognizing his own contribution to the corrupt revenue system, offers to rectify his own behavior. Jesus uses his encounter with Zacchaeus to point out that "The Son of Man has come to seek out and to save the lost" (19:10). Yet if Zacchaeus is repenting, he does so without Jesus telling him to. In other words, this story may bear out the pattern from Luke 5:32. Jesus brings sinners to repentance, but not through his words. Instead, sinners come to repentance simply by being part of Jesus' circle.

I agree that the Zacchaeus story involves his repentance. Yet another dimension of the story merits our attention. What if Zacchaeus' speech involves not only repentance but also a defense of his own dignity? Luke describes Zacchaeus as "standing and speaking to the Lord" over against (the Greek particle is *de*) the hostile crowd. In modern language, we might say he stands up for himself. His audience is not public opinion but Jesus, whom he addresses directly. And Jesus celebrates Zacchaeus' reply. Zacchaeus' corruption does not erase his humanity or his participation in Israel. He remains a child of Abraham. Jesus, without criticizing his old behavior or requiring his new resolution, names him so. I suspect that the first generations of Jesus' followers treasured stories such as those of Levi and Zacchaeus because they could identify with these characters.

One of Jesus' own stories, the parable of the great dinner, further bears out Jesus' attitude toward company. Early Christians circulated at least three versions of that dinner in Luke 14:15-24, Matthew 22:1-10, and a version in the *Gospel of Thomas* 64. These three versions differ greatly, with the one in Matthew being the most distinctive. Yet all share some basic elements: a man invites guests to a banquet, the invited guests decline to come (making excuses in Luke and Thomas), and the host then invites the rabble from the streets. Matthew describes the banquet as full of guests, both good and bad, whereas Luke names them as "the poor, the crippled, the blind, and the lame."

Whatever the differences among the versions, the story of the great dinner depicts invitations to the usual suspects. These people have businesses and respectable family affairs. For them, the invitation means little, and they disrespect it. The host, shamed by their behavior, insists on having a full company. The new dinner guests are persons of lower status, who cannot repay this invitation. As Jesus says previously in Luke 14,

> When you give a luncheon or a dinner, do not invite your friends, your brothers, your relatives, or your rich neighbors, lest they invite you in return and you would be repaid. But when you give a reception, invite the poor, the crippled, the lame, and the blind (14:12-13).

Conventional wisdom says, "Birds of a feather flock together." Ancient Mediterranean persons were keenly aware of one another's relative status and so monitored the company they kept. By associating with sinners, Jesus identifies himself with them. This is why one scholar concludes that "deviant, inclusive, status-leveling, honor-reversing meal practices were indeed characteristic of the behavior and teaching of the historical Jesus."[15] This memory persisted among the first few generations of his followers. Along with the parable of the great dinner, the stories of Levi and Zacchaeus confirm this verdict.

JESUS AND SINNERS' REPENTANCE

When Mark and Matthew introduce Jesus they feature repentance as a basic part of his message: "The time is fulfilled. The kingdom of God is near. Repent, and believe in the good news!" (Mark 1:15; cf. Matt 3:2). Oddly though, Jesus speaks precious little about repentance in the gospel stories themselves. Instead, he accompanies sinners without condemning them or criticizing their behavior. As a result many scholars believe that Jesus welcomed sinners, inviting them to participate in his ministry without calling them to repent.[16]

It seems obvious that a righteous teacher like Jesus would call for moral rectitude—or at least for a general effort—but it seems Jesus did not call individual sinners to repent. This marks perhaps the most remarkable thing about Jesus' fellowship with sinners: he enjoys their company but does not scold them.

One might not be shocked that Jesus kept company with sinners, especially if he aimed to reform them. If one assumes this conventional view—that Jesus befriended sinners in order to bring them to repentance—a passage like Luke 5:32 makes sense: "I have not come to call the righteous but sinners toward repentance."[17]

Matthew 9:12-13*	Mark 2:17*	Luke 5:31-32*
But when he heard this, he said, "Those who are well have no need of a physician, but those who are sick. Go and learn what this means, 'I desire mercy, not sacrifice.' For I have come to call not the righteous but sinners."	When Jesus heard this, he said to them, "Those who are well have no need of a physician, but those who are sick; I have come to call not the righteous but sinners."	Jesus answered, "Those who are well have no need of a physician, but those who are sick; I have come to call not the righteous but sinners to repentance."

*Taken from the New Revised Standard Version (NRSV).

Challenged regarding the company he keeps, Jesus likens himself to a physician: "The healthy do not need a healer, but the sick do" (Mark 2:17; see Matt 9:12-13; Luke 5:31-32). Likewise, Jesus describes the heavenly joy that accompanies the repentance of an individual sinner (Luke 15:7). According to Matthew, Jesus sought out the "lost sheep of the house of Israel" (15:24; see 10:6). Indeed, Mark's first summary of Jesus' proclamation features repentance:

> The time is fulfilled, and the rule of God has drawn near. Repent, and believe the good news! (1:15; cf. Mark 6:2; Matt 3:2; 4:17)

In short, the Gospels depict Jesus as a preacher of repentance, and some passages might confirm the assumption that he sought out sinners to encourage them to repent.

But do the Gospels really portray Jesus as befriending sinners to bring them to repentance? A closer look at these passages reveals that the conventional view rests on a shaky foundation. For one thing, the passages in which Jesus celebrates sinners coming to repentance all derive from Luke—and repentance reflects one of Luke's key emphases. For example, Matthew commands the church to forgive their brothers and sisters who do them wrong (18:21-22). Yet in the same context Luke's Jesus adds, "if that one returns to you seven times, saying, 'I repent,' you must forgive (17:3-4). For Luke the fundamental gospel proclamation after the resurrection promises "repentance and forgiveness of sins" (Luke 24:47; see Acts 2:38; 17:30). Because this pattern is not found in Matthew or Mark, many interpreters suspect that it derives not from Jesus' ministry but from Luke's theological and literary imagination.[18]

Even more telling, Jesus' celebration of repentance does not involve a call for individual sinners to repent—and that, I will argue, is the key point. Whatever our suspicions, this book does not use the Gospels to identify the "real Jesus" and what he said about repentance. Instead, our question involves how early Christians remembered Jesus in their stories and how those stories shaped their imaginations and their identities. Did Jesus desire for people to live morally and religiously faithful lives? I would imagine so, but that is not the question. The question is: Does the Jesus of early Christian memory admonish individual sinners to repent?

In my view, the Gospels present Jesus as encouraging repentance in general, but not singling out individual sinners for repentance. The Gospels do not explain why this is so, leaving us to our best guesses as to what to make of this pattern. For one thing, it is an easy thing to pick out individual sinners and tell them to repent. Doing so confirms the conventional wisdom that divides the righteous from the deficient. That same conventional wisdom allows "righteous" people to excuse themselves from the call to repentance because they can always compare themselves to the wicked. By refusing to challenge individual sinners to repent, Jesus honors their common humanity—"this one too is a son of Abraham" (Luke 19:9)—and refuses to endorse the shame they bear.

Another consideration involves the "sins" that attract Jesus' attention. Jesus routinely engages in conflict with persons of relatively high status. He has no qualms calling his enemies hypocrites, as he does in Matthew, Mark, and Luke. He condemns contemporary religious practices that impoverish the elderly (Mark 7:11; 12:20; Luke 20:47). He warns that the rich will struggle to enter the reign of heaven (Matt 19:23-24; Mark 10:25; Luke 6:24; 18:25). Clearly, Jesus is willing to condemn certain kinds of behavior. But he does not single out common "sinners." I am inclined to believe that the Gospels present Jesus as the enemy of people who abuse their status and the friend of those who are vulnerable. To those who consider themselves righteous, Jesus warns that even the tax collectors and prostitutes will enter the rule of heaven before them (Matt 21:31-32).

Many biblically literate readers will immediately object, recalling the famous story of the Woman Caught in Adultery (John 7:53–8:11). While Jesus is teaching in the temple precincts, a group of scribes and Pharisees bring the woman before him. Claiming that she was caught during an adulterous act, they remind Jesus that Moses' law prescribes stoning for such an offense. (Leviticus 20:10 and Deuteronomy 22:22 require the execution of *both* parties in adultery, though notoriously they have not brought the man.) Will Jesus affirm Moses' judgment, endorsing her stoning? Jesus defends the woman from the crowd about to stone her with the famous challenge: "Whoever among you is without sin, may throw a stone at her first" (John 8:7). When the crowd disperses, however, he admonishes her: "Go, and from now on sin no more" (8:11). Is this not a clear case in which Jesus tells a sinner to stop sinning?

It would be, but the story of the Woman Caught in Adultery is one of the most prominent object lessons for what scholars call "text criticism." Quite simply, *all* of our earliest and best manuscripts of John's Gospel lack this story. In some later manuscripts the story occurs in different places: after John 7:36, after Luke 21:38, even at the end of John or at the end of Luke. If you are among those readers who find this information surprising, you will find it summarized in a footnote to the passage in any reliable modern translation such as the *New Revised Standard Version* (NRSV), the *New International Version* (NIV), or the *New American Standard Bible* (NASB), among others. All this evidence suggests that the story originated independently of John's Gospel but found its way into the gospel traditions through a variety of paths. In short, it is a wonderful story, one I would not hesitate to preach in church, but it is not an original part of John's Gospel. Instead, it reflects more the imaginative sensitivities of third-generation Christian piety than early Jesus traditions or the Fourth Gospel. The story of the Woman Caught in Adultery does not disconfirm the portrait of Jesus befriending sinners regardless of their repentance.

SINNERS IN THE JESUS STORY, SINNERS IN JESUS' STORIES

This chapter has emphasized Christian memories regarding Jesus and his practice of dining with sinners. The Gospels depict Jesus as freely associating with sinners, without condemning them or their behavior. They further describe this practice as scandalous. Does Jesus, by his association with sinners, condone them and their practices? Is Jesus himself tainted by such associations?

Before moving along, I might briefly note the prominent role sinners play in both the stories of Jesus (the Gospels) and Jesus' own stories (the parables). Jesus' birth and death both presented potential scandals for early Christians. Our only traditions concerning Jesus' birth describe him as the son of Mary, sometimes naming Joseph as his father. (Consider Luke's genealogy, which names Jesus as "the son, as it was supposed, of Joseph" [3:23].) Matthew and Luke portray Jesus as Mary's biological son, miraculously begotten by the Holy Spirit. To outsiders, those who do not buy into the miraculous conception theory, Mary's pregnancy poses a potential scandal. Likewise, Jesus' execution results from his sentence as "King of the Jews" and places him on a cross between two criminals. Paul twice calls the cross an "embarrassment" or a "scandal" (1 Cor 1:23; Gal 5:11). (We will devote more attention to the circumstances and significance of Jesus' death in chapters 5 and 6.) Both traditions created possible obstacles for early Christian preachers.

The circumstances of Jesus' birth quickly raised a problem for defenders of Christianity. During the second century, the Christian apologist Justin Martyr (died c. 165) takes on an extensive debate with Jews who deny Mary's virginity (*Dialogue with Trypho* 43.8; 66.2; 71.2–73.6; 77–78; 84:1). Claudia Setzer judges that, "Justin devotes so much space to his proofs of the virgin birth that it must have been a live point of debate between Jews and Christians."[19] Later Jewish authors offered various hypotheses concerning Jesus' birth, including the notion that Jesus' true father was a Roman soldier.[20]

Or consider the obscure early Christian apocalypse the *Ascension of Isaiah*, probably composed in the early second century C.E., which is profoundly concerned with accounting for the general rejection of Jesus by Jews. According to this text, not only does Mary conceive as a virgin, but also her pregnancy lasts only 2 months. No wonder she is surprised when a small infant simply appears before her eyes! After the delivery, Mary's womb is restored to its former condition. When the news circulates around Bethlehem, some marvel, whereas others are "blinded" concerning Jesus, saying, "She did not give birth, the midwife did not go up (to her), and we did not hear (any) cries of pain" (*Ascension of Isaiah* 11.1-16).[21] Within decades of the composition of the Gospels, the *Ascension of Isaiah* testifies to creative debates between Christians and Jews concerning Jesus' birth.

Luke's Gospel simply narrates Mary's pious acceptance of her mission as the Savior's mother. But Matthew takes another approach. Careful readers know that Matthew self-consciously responds to Jewish polemic concerning Jesus. In particular, only Matthew relates the charge that Jesus' disciples stole his body from the tomb—"and this story has been circulating among the Jews, even to this day"

(28:15). Likewise, Matthew responds to concerns about the propriety of Jesus' conception.

Matthew does this in a fascinating way. Before narrating Mary's miraculous conception, Matthew provides a genealogy of Jesus. This genealogy, remarkable for its day, includes four women. Even more striking are the women Matthew includes: Tamar, Rahab, Ruth, and Bathsheba. Tamar *acted* like a prostitute to bear offspring for her deceased husband (Genesis 38). Rahab, who *was* a prostitute, welcomed the Israelite spies into Jericho, winning a place for herself and her family in Israel (Joshua 2; 6:17-25). (Rahab, by the way, enters the list of faithful witnesses in Hebrews 11:31.) Ruth, widow to a man from Judah, seduces his wealthy relative to secure her own fortune and that of her mother-in-law. And Bathsheba, once confiscated into David's harem at the hands of armed men, becomes a powerful force in palace intrigue and secures the throne for her son Solomon (2 Samuel 11–12; 1 Kings 1–2).

Why would Matthew include such unexpected women in Jesus' genealogy? In my view their stories prepare the way for Mary's story. Each of the four women finds herself in dire circumstances. Each expresses her sexuality in ways that transgress social norms, though Bathsheba does so unwillingly. Each finds her own way to secure her future. And each plays a critical role in the sacred story of Israel. To potential objections regarding Mary's status, Matthew counters that her story participates in a familiar, and blessed, pattern. These women, sinners according to conventional measures, are heroes in Israel's sacred story.[22]

Jesus' crucifixion also places him, literally, among sinners. The Gospels insist that Jesus' cross stood between two other criminals (Matt 27:38; Mark 15:27; Luke 23:32-33; John 19:18). Remarkably, although Mark and Matthew describe the two as *lēstai*, or bandits, and Luke calls them *kakourgoi* (criminals), John simply calls them "two others."[23] In Luke's telling, one of the two criminals insults Jesus from his cross, whereas the other defends his innocence. Here Luke's emphasis on Jesus' favor toward sinners shines through. To the criminal who speaks up for him, Jesus promises, "Truly I say to you, today you will be with me in Paradise" (23:42).

The narratives of Jesus' trial further suggest that the Jerusalem crowd regards Jesus as even worse than the rebel Barabbas. After all, when Pilate gives them a choice between Jesus and Barabbas, the crowd prefers that Pilate release Barabbas and crucify Jesus (Mark 15:7-15; Matt 27:16-26; Luke 23:18-24; John 18:39-40). Thus, even in his death Jesus identifies with sinners.

Not only do stories *about* Jesus associate him with sinners, but Jesus' *own* stories sometimes employ sinners as their protagonists. One might expect a "moral teacher" like Jesus to cast sinners only in losing roles. But that is not how it works out. I have noted the Tax Collector who pleads for mercy in Luke 18:9-14. The single most striking sinner-hero in Jesus' parables is the Dishonest Manager of Luke 16:1-13. This parable has confounded interpreters through the ages. Arland Hultgren describes it as "the most puzzling of all" the parables.[24] Apparently, Luke, too, is baffled, for verses 9-13 append multiple, mutually conflicting, "lessons" to the parable.

The point of all the confusion? The hero in this story is really a villain. He finds himself charged with squandering his rich employer's wealth. One might wonder if these charges are accurate, but Jesus himself tells us the Manager is dishonest at the end of the story. At any rate, the Manager finds himself out of a job and looking for a place to live. He is hardly an admirable character. Too weak to dig, ashamed to beg—at least he is honest with himself—he begins slashing debts for those who owe his master in hopes that they will welcome him into their homes when he is out on the street. Jesus does not tell us how things work out for the Manager. But he does pronounce a verdict: "[T]he master praised the Dishonest Manager because he had done shrewdly" (Luke 16:8). Why would Jesus feature such a scoundrel as an object of praise?

The answer may reside in the Manager's gravest fault. Dan O. Via, perhaps the most perceptive interpreter of this parable, offers this judgment: "A degree of sympathy is won for the steward [i.e., manager] by his trait of at least being candid about his desire for an easy life."[25] The Manager's sagacity resides in his honest self-appraisal and the decisive response he offers to his crisis.

Such practical wisdom distinguishes another of Jesus' characters, the Man who finds treasure hidden in a field (Matt 13:44; see Thomas 109). Matthew's version compares the realm of heaven to a Man who finds the treasure hidden in a field that does not belong to him. He then covers up the treasure, goes off, and sells all his property to purchase the field and its hidden contents. Once again, the parable baffles interpreters. They cannot agree whether the man's behavior is illegal, immoral, or neither. Bernard Brandon Scott aptly describes the problem: "Interpreters and interpretations divide into two camps: those who think what the man did was right and those who think what he did was wrong."[26]

I agree with the second group. This parable is not a simple object lesson on the joy of finding the realm of heaven. One interpreter sees this parable as indicative of the "realism" of Jesus' parables,[27] but I cannot agree. How many peasants stumble across hidden treasure? More to the point, consider Matthew 13, which includes several unrealistic parables. Do birds of the air *really* nest in a mustard plant? What would happen to the kitchen if a woman *hid* (the text says "hid") yeast in fifty pounds of flour? If someone found a pearl of great value, would they sell *all* their property in order to purchase it? (Would that not leave them with nothing to eat and nowhere to live?) I doubt realism is the point.

I have two other reasons for seeing the Man who finds the treasure as a scoundrel. For one thing, he *hides* the treasure after he finds it. That is, he goes to great lengths to conceal his find and his plan from the treasure's rightful owner. That action hardly recommends him as a person of conscience. For another thing, the *Gospel of Thomas* cleans up the moral problem raised by the parable.[28] In its version, the one who winds up with the treasure buys the field without knowing its hidden contents. Thomas' innocent spin suggests that the parable likely aroused moral reservations among its early hearers.

So where does this leave us? Jesus tells two parables about wise characters who do immoral things. In the parable of the Dishonest Manager, the hero receives praise for his wisdom. The parable of the treasure compares the realm of heaven to the hidden treasure stolen by its hero. Moral rectitude constrains neither the storytelling imagination of Jesus nor those of his followers.[29]

CONCLUSION

Early Christians repeated the stories of how Jesus invited sinners into his company and invited himself into sinners' homes. Friends and enemies alike knew Jesus as a friend of sinners. Though his opponents' charge that he was a glutton and a drunkard may represent just standard polemic, that charge probably reflects the company Jesus kept more than how much he ate and drank. He proclaimed sinners as closer to the reign of God than the supposedly righteous. His companionship with sinners had no strings attached. He did not scold them for their behavior. Though the Gospels explicitly associate Jesus with prostitutes and tax collectors, he never addressed their sexual sins or personal corruption. He may have desired their repentance, but the Gospels include no stories in which he calls an individual sinner to repent.

It would be entertaining to speculate concerning the motives for Jesus' friendship with sinners. I am on firmer ground by describing its significance. In a culture of honor and shame, one could raise or lower one's status by the company one kept. Jesus' companionship with sinners opened the path for people to challenge his uprightness. Some people, perhaps many people, believed that a respectable religious leader like Jesus had no business cavorting with sinners. Yet Jesus identified himself with sinners. And some sinners joined his movement. That is how the Gospels tell it, perhaps because early generations of Christians identified with the sinners in the stories.

EPILOGUE: THE POWER OF BLESSING

Brian was only twelve years old when he arrived at the youth home. Throughout his childhood he had observed his parents' fights, and he had fought with his own siblings. Often his parents' disputes ended this way: the father would walk over to the gun cabinet, pull out a pistol and place the barrel right under Brian's mother's chin. "If you say another word, I'll blow your fucking head off!" Brian had seen this many times.

One day Brian and his sister fought over the last bowl of cereal in the house. She sat down at the table with the cereal, and Brian's protests achieved no effect. When she poured milk on the cereal, Brian headed for the gun cabinet. He put the gun to the back of his sister's head, saying, "If you take one bite of that cereal, I'll blow your head off." No way his sister would give in to this, so she took the bite.

Now Brian was in the youth home. The staff determined not to mention *why* Brian was there until he brought up the subject himself. A couple of months passed, and the staff grew increasingly concerned. Brian was quiet; he was compliant—to the degree that the staff noticed that Brian never showed any emotion. He was turning in on himself, not a good thing for a preadolescent murderer. Maybe, the staff wondered, we need to take the initiative and address Brian's grisly crime directly. That decision remained open.

One day a staff member took Brian over to a nearby pond to fish. While they were fishing, this staff member said, "Brian, you're a neat kid. I really enjoy being with you." Brian replied, "You wouldn't say that if you knew why I'm here." His guard down, the staff member blurted, "I know why you're here." Startled, Brian replied, "You do?"

"Of course I do. We all know why you're here."

Confronted with such unconditional acceptance and blessing, Brian began to sob, letting his emotion come through for the first time in months. That moment proved a turning point in Brian's life.

When I heard Brian's story I immediately considered the power of unconditional blessing. Brian had committed the unimaginable. He was—not just in his self-perception, but objectively—a sinner of the worst sort. He had murdered his sister over a bowl of cereal. No wonder he had turned in on himself. His salvation came not through the condemnation of his behavior. Brian could do that well enough on his own. It came through blessing, the acceptance of his presence regardless of his history.

Chapter 3

JESUS AND IMPURITY

It has been a staple of Christian preaching that Jesus transgressed the law of Israel, or Torah. He healed on the Sabbath. He violated the purity laws by touching lepers and menstruating women and transgressing dietary regulations. He ate and drank without washing his hands. His behavior aroused the ire of the religious establishment, setting them against them to such a degree that they colluded in—if not brought about—his death. Such preaching is historically inaccurate—and it is ethically dangerous.

Let us be honest. This kind of preaching means to present Jesus as compassionate and inclusive, but it also carries the strong odor of anti-Jewish polemic. If people were bound by all these purity laws, where did they come from? From Judaism, of course. Because the early church grew gradually less and less Jewish, that is, more and more Gentile, Jesus' transgression of the purity laws anticipates the inclusion of Gentiles—the most impure people in the world. Thus, Jesus has stepped beyond the "rigid boundaries" of Jewish "particularism," opening the path for a new, inclusive, universalist Christianity. Preachers and scholars have resorted to this argument for centuries.[1]

Did Jesus observe the law of Israel, the Torah? In several controversy scenes people *accuse* Jesus of violating the Torah. Usually
the accusation involves purity issues. All of these stories include Jesus'
retort, which quiets his critics. Yet the question remains. Did Jesus
disregard the law?

Before we answer this question, we should think through its implications. If Jesus actually violated the Torah, then most of his Jewish
contemporaries would have seen him as a sinner. But the question is not
so simple. For one thing, the gospel stories in which Jesus is accused of
transgressing the law always include his response. That is, other people
may have *accused* Jesus of breaking the law, but he may not have seen
things that way. This leads to a second consideration: perhaps Jesus
was not alone in his opinions. Perhaps his accusers were in the minority
of public opinion, participating in common debates concerning proper
observance. Finally, the Gospels themselves assess this question differently. Mark, it seems, describes Jesus as violating the law willfully,
whereas Matthew insists that Jesus observes it in minute detail. What
is at stake in the controversies involving Jesus and the law, especially
the laws concerning purity?

CLARIFYING PURITY

On encountering examples of impurity in the Bible, many readers con-
fuse impurity with sin or with dirt. After all, we live in a culture that
contests "sexual purity" and distills "pure" water. In most cases, however, impurity implied neither morals nor hygiene in the Judaism of
Jesus' day. How can we can get a handle on purity and impurity, if they
do not mean what we often taken them to mean?

Perhaps we might begin by considering that many acts could make
a person impure without involving them in sin.[2] For example, contact
with a corpse rendered a person impure, but treatment and burial of the
dead was a necessarily obligation in ancient Israel. Likewise, menstrua-
tion and childbirth rendered a woman ritually impure until she went
through a ritual of cleansing. Of course, Jews did not regard menstrua-
tion as sinful. At the same time, sexual relations with a menstruating

woman did constitute sin (Lev 18:19). The point is, impurity often had nothing directly to do with sin; instead, it pertained to holiness. Purity and impurity specified what was appropriate or inappropriate for sacred persons, places, times, and actions.

AN IMPRECISE ANALOGY

In a system of purity and impurity everything has its appropriate place and season. When I teach this concept in the classroom, I use beach sand as an example. People go to the beach for lots of reasons, one of which is to enjoy the sand. We sunbathe in it, build castles with it, and play volleyball in it. The fittest among us jog on it, whereas many of us (reaching for classroom giggles here) fantasize about other activities in the sand. Beach sand is great.

However, most of us eventually leave the beach. And when we do, beach sand is a nuisance. It is hard to get out of our hair and off our bodies. It shows up in the car, in the laundry, and in the beach house or hotel room. When we return from vacation, we can even count on some of the beach sand making it into our homes. Beach sand is remarkably persistent.

The point is, beach sand is great in certain places, at certain times, and for certain functions. Outside those specified times and places, beach sand is—well, dirt.

The law defined certain categories of persons, notably lepers and men with physical defects, as impure. This implied a stigma; it did not constitute a moral judgment. Leprosy was neither a sin nor necessarily a punishment for sinful behavior. It consisted of various skin blemishes. These could heal, and the former leper could undergo a ritual purification. The blemishes could get so bad that the entire skin would transform to the same color. Remarkably, this circumstance would actually end the impurity because all the skin would again be consistent. "If the leprosy has covered all his skin, [the priest] shall declare the blemish clean. It has all turned white. He is clean" (Lev 13:13).[3] And although castration was occasionally practiced in the ancient Near East, birth defects and accidents could also render a man unfit for priestly service. Regardless of the causes, men with defective, injured, or incomplete genitalia were regarded as unclean (Deut 23:1).

Purity, then, had to do with holiness, what Bruce J. Malina helpfully calls "set-apartness."[4] It involved setting apart persons, times, places, and activities as holy, dedicated to God in a special way.

Why be pure? Most purity laws involved eligibility to enter the temple or to deal with holy things.[5] Some purity laws applied to all Jews at all times and places, and people paid careful attention to these. The primary examples involved food and sex; most Jews were keenly aware of these regulations. To violate them constituted sin, an offense against God. Otherwise, Israel's purity laws had little bearing on daily life but rather with preparation for worship in the temple. As Paula Fredrikson observes, "Most people, under normal circumstances, would be in this state of impurity most of the time."[6]

Some Jews, however, valued purity for its own sake. They created ways in which to honor the biblical purity laws apart from the temple, especially in domestic settings. Philo of Alexandra, for example, advocated ritual washing after mourning. This practice restored persons to purity in every respect short of entering the temple.[7] That Philo lived in Egypt, outside the land of Israel, is telling. Scattered throughout the Mediterranean world, Jews attended carefully to maintaining their distinctive identity and practices.[8]

This is where the Pharisees come in. When the Gospels depict Jesus in controversies involving purity, his opponents are always the Pharisees.[9] This is important because the Pharisees had their own distinctive take on purity and impurity, a view that probably put them in a small minority among the larger Jewish populations. The Pharisees extended the purity regulations that applied to priests and temple, interpreting them so that all Jews could participate in a holy nation. Although we cannot know all the details—for example, did the Pharisees bury their own dead?—their vision was dramatically liberal. It envisioned a renewal of Judaism, to which every person could contribute.[10] Perhaps the Pharisees' extension of purity laws to ordinary people and ordinary times reflects an implicit compensation for a perceived impurity that affected Israel as a whole as a result of corruption and oppression by Gentiles.[11] In any case, these innovations democratized religion by bringing ordinary persons and daily life into contact with the sacred.[12] When Jesus is accused of violating Israel's purity codes, it always involves a conflict with the Pharisees and their allies.

JESUS AND THE PHARISEES ON PURITY

In the conventional view, Jesus' mortal enemies are the Pharisees and their allies, the scribes. The Gospels link the scribes with the Pharisees as highly skilled interpreters of the Torah who engage in conflict with Jesus. Mark calls all or some of them "the scribes of the Pharisees" (2:16). This depiction is likely historically inaccurate, as we lack independent evidence that the scribes formed an identifiable ideological, religious, or political group within the Judaism of Jesus' day.[13] Jesus argues with them constantly, usually at their provocation. According to this view their disagreements generally involve the Torah: the Pharisees and their allies criticize Jesus for violating the law. In this view, the Pharisees represent a narrowly legalistic Judaism, whereas Jesus embodies a more human-centered vision of grace and blessing. Although Luke records that Jesus occasionally enjoys positive relationships with the Pharisees and the scribes, (Luke 7:36; 11:37; 13:31; 14:1; possibly 5:17), this conflict plays a major role in his eventual arrest and execution.

This conventional view indeed grounds itself in some of the gospel traditions. A lengthy section in Mark involves Jesus in a series of disputes with Pharisees and the scribes (2:1–3:6). Jesus heals on the Sabbath, enjoys a feast with sinners, his disciples do not fast (a conflict not initiated by the scribes or the Pharisees), his disciples pluck grain on the Sabbath. When Jesus wins all these arguments, the Pharisees begin plotting his death immediately (3:6; parallel passages Matt 12:14; cf. Luke 6:11). This conflict shapes the rest of Mark's story.

Though popular tradition blames the Pharisees for Jesus' death, and though Mark describes them as conspiring to kill him (3:6; 12:13), it seems highly unlikely that the Pharisees had much to do with Jesus' arrest at all. However much Mark may vilify them, the Pharisees do not appear in the narratives of Jesus' arrest, trial, and crucifixion. John alone has the Pharisees recruit Judas to betray Jesus (18:3). In Mark, they disappear after we learn that they are trying to entrap Jesus; in Matthew, they only reappear to express concerns about his body (27:62); in Luke they leave the scene on Jesus' entry into Jerusalem. How, one wonders, does one blame the Pharisees for a crime they were not present to commit?

The Pharisees did not cause Jesus' death, but Jesus' interactions with them and the scribes reveal a great deal about his relationship to the law, and to purity in particular. As we have seen, the Gospels describe this relationship in diverse ways. Mark and John have nothing good to say about the Pharisees. In Luke, the Pharisees often clash with Jesus, yet they also interact socially. Once some Pharisees even warn Jesus of impending danger (13:31).[14] Matthew, however, offers a unique portrayal of the Pharisees—one that suggests a complex relationship between Jesus and the Pharisees.

Like Mark, Matthew never portrays the Pharisees—or the scribes or the Sadducees—in a flattering light. They always carry malicious intent; their speech indicates not only their hostility toward Jesus, but also their duplicity.[15] This is why Matthew's Jesus so often castigates the Pharisees as hypocrites (15:7; 22:18; 23:13, 15, 23, 25, 27, 29; and possibly 6:2, 5, 16). So Matthew, like Mark, characterizes the Pharisees only in negative ways. Unlike Mark, however, Matthew also attributes two sayings to Jesus that indicate some degree of respect for the scribes and the Pharisees.

Matthew 5:20	Matthew 23:2-3
For I say to you that unless your righteousness exceeds that of the scribes and the Pharisees, by no means you will enter the kingdom of heaven.	Upon the seat of Moses sit the scribes and the Pharisees. Do and observe everything they tell you, but do not do according to their deeds. For they talk, but they do not do what they say.

Both sayings use the scribes and the Pharisees as negative examples. On the other hand, they betray a grudging acknowledgment that both groups (a) attain a recognized level of righteousness and (b) teach the law more or less accurately. This accords with Josephus' report that the masses admired the Pharisees (*Antiquities* 13.288-89) and with the testimony of Acts (22:3; 26:5) and Josephus that the Pharisees interpreted the law accurately (*War* 1.110; 2.162; *Antiquities* 17.41; *Life* 38). When Paul recalls his "former" life in Judaism, he claims to have been a Pharisee, "blameless" according to the law (Gal 1:13-14; Phil 3:5-6).[16] Jesus likely entered conflict with the Pharisees, but Matthew suggests that their understandings of the law were more similar than different. In fact, Jesus seems to have agreed with the Pharisees on two of the controversial issues of the day. He acknowledged the Law and the Prophets as authoritative writings (some Jews revered only the Torah), and he expected the resurrection of the just. Matthew's Jesus may criticize them, but he shares many of their preoccupations and opinions. Perhaps, then, Jesus' conflict with the Pharisees resulted not from a vast area of disagreement but from their close proximity to one another.

One story in particular captures Jesus' conflict with the Pharisees on purity issues—even though it proves how difficult it is to assess Jesus' relationship to the law. Matthew and Mark share an episode in which some Pharisees and scribes query Jesus because his disciples do not wash their hands before they eat (Matt 15:1-20; Mark 7:1-23). Jesus' opponents appeal to "the tradition of the elders," that is, the traditional interpretations of the law to which Pharisees appealed. In both Gospels, Jesus' first reply involves a criticism of the Pharisees and scribes. They abandon the (literal) commandments for human tradition. Even worse, they interpret the law to suit their own selfish interests. The second charge is a simple *ad hominem* attack. There is no reason to suppose that Pharisees and scribes were especially hypocritical. But the first accusation reflects a likely tension between Jesus and his Pharisaic opponents. The Pharisees believe Jesus' disciples are violating the Torah, but Jesus rejects this claim. The disciples *are* breaking the law—but only according to the Pharisees' interpretation. They are *not* violating the letter of the law. This is important. It is not that the Pharisees observe the Law and Jesus does not; rather, Jesus does not share the Pharisees' *interpretation* of the law.

Now things get more complicated. Though they word it differently, both Matthew and Mark relate Jesus' declaration that it is not what goes into a person that makes one impure, but what comes forth from a person that matters. Taken literally, this saying would go against the law, which describes precisely which foods render one unclean. One need not take the saying literally, however. Matthew does not. Matthew interprets it as a moral maxim, a wisdom saying that conveys an essential point about the relative value of one's moral disposition in comparison to ritual observance. This point would have been familiar to some of Israel's prophets, who raised ethical behavior above sacrifice.[17]

Mark's Gospel, however, takes Jesus' words literally, going so far as to explain them to its audience. Jesus had "made all foods clean" (7:19). If Jesus indeed declared all foods clean, then he had violated the clear sense of the Torah. The author of Matthew, who used Mark as a source, famously deletes this line from the story.

How do we account for this serious discrepancy? Most scholars believe Matthew addressed an audience composed largely of Jewish followers of Jesus who observed the Torah, whereas Mark's audience consisted mainly of Gentiles. This would explain why Mark occasionally explains Jewish customs to its audience, as is the case in our story. Indeed, Mark overstates the case by saying that "the Pharisees *and all the Jews*" wash their hands before eating and perform other ritual washings (7:3-4). Mark, then, is concerned with a Gentile audience that is unfamiliar with such customs.

In contrast, Matthew is concerned with the inclusion of Gentiles but writes for a Jewish audience that has no intention of disregarding the Torah. Matthew's Jesus insists on this point.

Don't even think that I have come to abolish the Law and the Prophets. I have come not to abolish them but to fulfill them. For

truly I tell you, until heaven and earth pass away, not one letter or
a stroke of a letter will pass away from the Law until all things are
accomplished. (5:17-18)

This thesis, stated early in the Sermon on the Mount (chapters 5–7
of Matthew), carries through in Jesus' famous antitheses (5:21-48).
Six times Jesus says something like, "You have heard that it was said,"
then quotes the Torah. Each time he follows the Torah quotation with,
"but I say to you. . . ." Although the "you have heard/but I say" formula
may hint that Jesus is weakening or contradicting the law, in fact he
intensifies its demands in each case. Not only is murder condemned, one
must master one's anger. Not only must one avoid adultery, one must
eliminate illicit desire. Not only must one provide one's wife with legal
verification of a divorce, one may not divorce a wife at all. Not only
must one keep one's vows, one must not declare vows at all, eliminating
the remotest possibility of breaking a vow. Not only must one restrict
one's response to evil to a proportionate retaliation, one may not retali-
ate at all. Not only must one love one's neighbor, one must love one's
enemy as well. (Matthew 5:43 is fascinating in that the law does not
enjoin hatred of one's enemy. In this case Jesus apparently comments
on the common understanding of the law and not the literal wording.)
In short, Matthew's Jesus does not compromise the Torah; he makes it
even more demanding.

With respect to the Torah and its purity codes in particular, what
may we learn from Jesus' conflicts with the Pharisees and their allies?
The Gospels disagree with one another. Jesus *may* have disregarded the
purity codes, especially with respect to food, but that is far from obvious. Indeed, I believe there are strong reasons for believing that Jesus
did not willfully violate the Torah. If we are to believe the book of Acts
and Paul's letters, Jesus' first followers continued to observe the Torah
for years after his death. If Jesus disregarded the law, apparently they
missed the message. Chances are, Jesus observed the law to his best
understanding.[18]

Jesus' observance of the Torah is one thing, but people's perceptions of him is entirely another. The Pharisees and their allies charac-

terized Jesus as a person who willfully disregarded the Torah. He also associated with sinners. Lepers and other unclean persons found him attractive, and he may have performed ministry among Gentiles. These patterns identified Jesus among the unclean, lending credence to other accusations. Whether the charges that Jesus disregarded the law and its purity codes swayed popular opinion, we may never know.

DOES JESUS GET TOO MUCH CREDIT?

Jesus receives credit for crossing purity boundaries in several notable gospel stories.[19] He touches and heals a leper, a bleeding woman, and an apparently dead girl. He also offers healing to Gentiles. In these ways Jesus is credited for violating the oppressive boundaries set by the law.

Let us look at particulars. Matthew, Mark, and Luke all credit Jesus with healing lepers. In one story, Jesus cleanses an individual leper by means of *touch* (Mark 1:40-45; Matt 8:1-4; Luke 5:12-16). In this case Jesus takes the leper's impurity on himself, crossing the boundary that separates clean from unclean persons.

Before giving Jesus so much credit, let us look more closely at Mark's version of the story. It is the most explicit, and it provides the framework for Matthew's version. First, we note that Jesus does not approach the leper; the leper kneels down before Jesus. This action impedes Jesus' movement and commands his attention. Although Jesus does put forth his hand and touch the leper, he does not initiate the interaction. Second, Mark's Gospel features a notorious text critical problem; that is, our earliest Greek manuscripts do not agree in their wording. Here is the traditional reading of Mark 1:41, according to the NRSV.

Moved with pity, Jesus stretched out his hand and touched him. . . .

However, one ancient text family, technically known as the Western tradition, reads differently.

Angered, Jesus stretched out his hand and touched him. . . .

The passage reads more easily when we imagine Jesus as feeling compassion rather than anger, and that is how most translators and commentators understand it. But there are reasons to suspect that Mark may originally have written that Jesus was angered by his encounter with the leper. For one thing, Matthew and Luke do not mention Jesus' motives. It is hard to explain why they would omit Jesus' compassion, a virtue for which Matthew and Luke credit Jesus elsewhere (e.g., Matt 9:36; 14:14; 15:32; 20:34; Luke 7:13; see Matt 18:27; Luke 10:33; 15:20). Conversely, it is easy to understand why Matthew and Luke would strike out a reference to Jesus' anger at a needy leper. Likewise, one readily understands why copyists of Mark might change Jesus' anger into compassion, whereas one struggles to imagine what would motivate a copyist to work in the opposite direction. One more thing: although Jesus heals the leper, his treatment falls far short of kindness. Immediately Jesus admonishes (one could translate it, "grumbles at") the leper and "casts him out" (which is how we normally translate the Greek word *ekballō*).[20] Perhaps the man has angered Jesus by making a demand on his time or slowing him down. Or perhaps he offends Jesus by doubting Jesus' willingness to heal, "If you choose. . ." (1:40).[21] And perhaps—we cannot know for certain—Mark actually wrote that Jesus felt compassion. This text critical problem undermines a simple path that affirms Jesus' willingness to violate the law here.

One further consideration settles the issue. Jesus does not violate the Torah here. On the contrary, he affirms it by sending the leper to the priest for ritual acknowledgment of his healing. In this story, Jesus may *cross* the boundary between clean and unclean, but in doing so he does *not* violate the Torah. Jesus himself could have undergone a cleansing process after this contact (Lev 22).

The other famous instance involves the woman with a flow of blood and the apparently dead girl (Mark 5:21-43; Matt 9:18-26; Luke 8:40-56). Mark "sandwiches" the story of the bleeding woman within the framework of the healing of the girl, a technique Mark apparently enjoyed. Here Jesus gets credit on two accounts. He touches the "menstruating" woman, and he touches the "dead" girl. In addition to the literary "sandwich" technique, interpreters link these stories in two ways. The number 12 identifies both the girl's age and the duration of the woman's hemorrhage. Also, the woman's flow of blood and the girl's death supposedly render both unclean. Again, Jesus receives credit for crossing purity boundaries with his touch.

As in the story of the leper, Jesus often receives more credit than he deserves, at least when it comes to purity issues. First, Jesus does not seek out the bleeding woman or the child. Not only does the child's father approach Jesus, but it also is the *woman* who touches him and not the reverse! (From reading commentaries and hearing sermons, you would get the opposite impression.) Though the woman is unclean on account of her hemorrhage, Jesus violates no purity boundaries here because she is the one doing the touching. As for the twelve-year-old girl, she is not actually dead — if we believe what Jesus says: "She is not dead but sleeping" (Mark 5:39; Matt 8:24; Luke 8:52). In neither case does Jesus violate any purity code at all.

Again, even if Jesus does contract impurity from the woman's touch, and even if the little girl were dead, Judaism had mechanisms for cleansing a person from such impurity. Jesus, even if he deserved credit for touching a bleeding woman and a corpse, still would have violated no purity codes. We might observe that nowhere in these stories does anyone express shock or amazement concerning Jesus' conduct. If the Gospel authors wanted to emphasize purity matters here, they easily could have done so. But they did not.[22]

Beyond lepers, bleeding women, and corpses, Jesus is also credited for reaching out to Gentiles. Although the law does not suggest that contact with Gentiles requires purification, the boundary between Gentile and Jew clearly posed a major obstacle. For example, Paul censures Peter for refusing to eat at a common table with Gentiles (Gal 2:11-14).

In two stories, one shared by Matthew and Mark and one from the Q tradition (Matthew and Luke), Jesus brings healing to Gentiles. Matthew (8:5-13) and Luke (7:1-10) describe a centurion who requests healing for his "boy." Most translations understand this "boy" (the Greek is *pais*) as a servant, though much can be said for understanding this as an erotic relationship between the centurion and his slave.[23] The other story involves a Gentile woman—a Syrophoenician in Mark (7:24-30) and a Canaanite in Matthew (15:21-28), who begs Jesus to cast out a unclean demon from her daughter. Interpreters frequently appeal to both stories as signs that Jesus' blessing includes Gentiles.

The two stories indeed feature Jesus blessing Gentiles, something that portends the gospels' later progress in Gentile communities. Yet both stories share something rare in the gospel traditions: in neither case does Jesus actually visit the afflicted person. In the case of the centurion's boy Jesus expresses his willingness to do so, but the centurion's faith in his power cuts Jesus off. As for the woman's daughter, Jesus simply pronounces her free of the demon. If Jesus wants to demonstrate his solidarity with Gentiles, he fails to seize an opportunity in these cases.

This is not to say that in the Gospels Jesus demonstrates hostility to Gentiles. His dealings among Samaritans are noteworthy (Luke 9:52-53; 17:11-19; John 4:4-42), as is a Samaritan's contribution as hero in one of Jesus' parables (Luke 10:25-37). Moreover, Mark repeatedly describes him traveling in largely Gentile territory (4:25; 5:20; 7:24-31). On the other hand, Matthew has Jesus forbid his disciples to travel among the Gentiles (10:5), though the Gospel clearly envisions their evangelization after the resurrection (24:14; 28:18-20). In the Gospels Jesus focuses on Jews, but he occasionally includes Gentiles.

DIFFERENT EVANGELISTS, DIFFERENT ANSWERS

In this book I have largely avoided speculation concerning what Jesus actually did and said and how authentically the canonical Gospels present his actual words and deeds. Throughout, my interest lies in how early Christians remembered Jesus, and I have treated the Gospels as examples of early Christian values and as sources of more or less reliable historical data about Jesus. Sometimes, however, the individual tendencies of the evangelist must be taken into account. This is certainly the case with respect to purity concerns, as we see in a few instances.

1. In Mark Jesus declares all foods clean (7:19). Matthew relates the same story (15:1-20) but omits this notorious saying. Luke omits the story altogether.
2. All three Synoptic Gospels describe Jesus traveling in areas with large Gentile populations, but Mark emphasizes these locations more intensely (3:8; 5:1-20; 7:24, 31).
3. Only in Matthew does Jesus forbid his disciples to visit Gentiles (10:5).
4. Matthew and Mark relate the story of Jesus and the Gentile woman, whereas Luke omits it. Perhaps Luke judges Jesus' demeaning treatment of the woman unsuitable?
5. Jesus visits Samaritans only in Luke and John.

These considerations encourage us to consider the likelihood that when it comes to Jesus and Gentiles, the four Gospels have diverse agendas. Matthew allows Gentiles to come to Jesus, but Jesus does not go directly to them during his career. Mark includes Gentiles early on. Indeed, if Mark was written with a Gentile audience in mind, that would explain Jesus' declaration that all foods are clean. Luke and John, less interested with Gentiles during Jesus' career, display some interest in his relations with Samaritans.

As in the cases of the leper, the woman, and the daughter, Jesus does not initiate his interaction with Gentiles. In the case of the centurion's boy, Jesus responds immediately. With the Syrophoenician/Canaanite woman, however, Jesus comes off much less favorably. Like the leper, she encroaches upon Jesus' space. In Mark he initially declines her request, calling her a dog. In Matthew he does these things after pointedly ignoring her. I have heard many Christians suggest that

Jesus is simply "testing her faith," but nothing in either Gospel suggests such a facile resolution. The woman prevails on Jesus, provoking his admiration. If anything, Jesus deserves credit for responding to these Gentiles with blessings, even reluctantly and from a distance, but not for reaching out to them.

The leper, the bleeding woman, the presumably dead girl, and the Gentiles all involve Jesus coming into contact with impurity in one form or another. In every case Jesus brings blessing, even taking on a measure of ritual impurity in the process. Clearly, the Gospels depict Jesus as one who brings blessing to all persons, in all states, even across conventional social boundaries. Yet in none of these stories does Jesus actually break Israel's purity laws. Moreover, in every case the supplicants approach Jesus and beg his action; he does not reach out to them. The stories may depict Jesus as one willing to bring cleansing to persons in a state of impurity, even willing to become unclean himself in the process, but by no means does Jesus eliminate the purity system.

Thus, I cannot agree with those who see Jesus violating or challenging the purity laws, as does David Rhoads in his study of Mark. On the other hand, Rhoads points to something profoundly powerful about Mark's testimony to Jesus, something shared among all four Gospels. Some people in the world regard purity (or holiness) as something to be protected. In this view, purity is easily contaminated by impurity. But others—and this is how Jesus appears in the Gospels—treat purity (or holiness) as more powerful than impurity. They bring holiness to bear on uncleanness. In Rhoads' words, in this view "people are to overcome uncleanness by spreading wholeness."[24]

All the same, let us spread the credit around: as the Gospels tell it, Jesus spreads holiness as much as a follower as a leader. Sometimes provoked, sometimes reluctant, usually at the instigation of others, Jesus brings holiness where impurity had been before. The Gospels depict Jesus traveling to bring blessing and healing, but some of his most remarkable encounters begin at the initiative of others.

CONCLUSION

A popular view has it that Jesus disregarded Judaism's purity laws. He restored lepers, healed bleeding women, and touched dead bodies. He even ministered among Gentiles. In doing so, he angered the authorities, particularly the Pharisees, who eventually saw to his death. According to this conventional view, Jesus died because of his progressive and inclusive vision that placed blessing individuals above observing purity laws.

We have observed several problems with this conventional view. First, it seems Jesus did not willfully violate the Torah in any respect. Among the Gospels, only Mark suggests that he did. His opponents may have disagreed with his interpretation of the Torah, but that does not mean that he accepted their verdict. This includes the purity laws. Second, most of the purity laws did not impinge directly on the daily life of ordinary people. If Jesus contracted impurity, so what? He would simply undergo a purification process before entering the temple precincts. Third, the gospel controversies involving purity routinely feature the Pharisees and their allies. Those figures play no role in Jesus' arrest, trial, and execution. Thus, it makes no sense to attribute Jesus' death to his supposed transgression of the Torah.

What if we turned the question around? What if, instead of looking for ways in which Jesus seeks out those who are unclean and blesses them, we took seriously how the Gospels actually describe his interaction with lepers, bleeding women, near-dead people, and Gentiles? In every case, we find that Jesus does not so much reach out to these people as he responds to their initiative.

For his modern-day admirers Jesus does provide an example, though perhaps not as we are accustomed to thinking. Indeed, the Gospels testify that holiness is more powerful than impurity. Jesus does not fear the touch of lepers, nor does he flee the presence of Gentiles. However, if Jesus is the hero of the gospel purity stories, it is because he responds to the initiative of those labeled impure by his own society. If contemporary Christians took seriously the possibility that those outside the boundaries of the church might hold the promise of renewal, if we ceased regarding ourselves as the source of salvation and the secular world as a potential threat, and if we emulated Jesus' example in accepting the faith and the courage of those who live beyond conventional standards of purity, well, I can hardly imagine how things would look.

Chapter 4

WE WERE DEADBEATS, ME AND PAUL

Most people, maybe even most scholars, have not noticed it, but quite a few biblical scholars are exploring the topic of masculinity these days. Not long ago, *gender* meant *women*. That is, we have (correctly) assumed that the Bible was largely produced by, and for, males, but we have further (and problematically) assumed that biblical masculinity was obvious. The interesting stuff, we thought, lay in what the Bible has to say about or what the Bible reveals about women in the ancient world. Thankfully, scholars have begun to appreciate that masculinity is not quite so obvious, that attention to gender is appropriate for men and for women, and that attention to masculinity may enlighten our understanding of biblical texts and the people who produced and read them.[1]

Some recent masculinity studies have the playful flair that one might find in a literary journal, whereas others are oriented toward more traditional historical research. Although I enjoy both kinds of scholarship, for the purposes of this chapter I am interested in the more

This title is derived from Willie Nelson's lyrics for "Me and Paul."

historical approach. What did ancient people value in a man? What values determined how ancient men experienced their social roles *as men*? And what behaviors did society reward? More specifically, how does the conduct of Jesus and his earliest followers—as described in early Christian literature—relate to conventional expectations of men in that world?[2]

This chapter assesses Jesus and his (male) followers, particularly Paul, in the light of ancient understandings of masculinity. In what ways do or do they not conform to conventional expectations? When they do not conform, what significance would their neighbors assign to such deviance? How did early Christians—men and women, so far as we can tell—address the question of masculinity, and how did these decisions contribute to their sense of identity?

Although Jesus, his disciples, and Paul affirmed, sometimes exceeded, conventional masculinity norms in some respects, they deviated from those norms in important ways. In particular, I will suggest that early Christians remembered Jesus for his powerful public presence, his self-control, his endurance, and his oratorical skills; traits highly valued among men in that cultural context. At the same time, the Gospels characterize Jesus as a "deadbeat," a man who fails to build a household or contribute to the public economic welfare, one who encourages peace above physical resistance, one who encourages his disciples to abandon household, family, and work "for my sake" (Matt 19:29; Mark 8:35; 10:29). Moreover, some of these same gender-deviant traits manifest themselves—with a twist—among early Christians like Paul, who often subverts conventional gender norms.

WHAT A MAN'S GOTTA DO

One day my younger daughter and I were driving home from the public library. She asked, innocently I thought, "Daddy, what do you do again?" When I told her that I am a seminary professor, she went on the offensive, "That's a woman's job." What I did not know is that I had been set up. Emily had checked out a new book, *101 Ways to Bug Your Parents*, that suggests telling your parents they have an opposite-gender job.[3] Girl colors and boy colors, girl movies and guy movies, girl jobs and boy jobs, that is the world in which our children grow up.

Yet in comparison with contemporary North America, early Christians lived in an even more gender-conscious society. Though the criteria for assessing masculinity vary among our sources, and though our sources scarcely allow us access to how most ancient persons experienced their world, they do betray a prevalent concern for defining what a man should do and should be.[4] Popular wisdom assigned appropriate places, roles, relationships, activities, traits, and biological factors to men and women on the basis of gender. Early Christian descriptions of Jesus conform to these conventions in some important ways, and we will consider those. In other respects, they deviate from conventional notions of masculinity, and those factors also prove interesting.

Ancient conceptions of gender differed significantly from those popular today. People thought of male and female as two extremes along a continuum, rather than as mutually exclusive options. Women and men were considered to be made of the same biological "stuff," with the exception that women develop differently—in fact, deficiently—in the womb. One ancient writer, for example, describes the "low-spirited man" in effeminate terms: a wrinkled face, weak eyes, and a stooping posture accompany "softness" and "effeminacy." Charitable men are delicate, pale, bright-eyed, and prone to tears.[5] Thus, a man was relatively more or less masculine than other men. His identity as a man was precarious, in that his masculinity might decline (or enhance) over time.[6] As a result, men carefully monitored their appearance and deportment, even their urges. Masculinity was essentially competitive, in that it was only measured in comparison to the relative masculinity of others. One quality defined masculinity above all others: power. One was a man to the degree that one controlled other persons, public affairs, one's household, and oneself.[7]

Jesus, then, lived in an agonistic culture. That is, one man's status—and his masculinity—always stood in competition with that of others. The keyword here is *honor*, that is, one's relative standing in society.[8] A man could acquire honor by being born into the right family, by demonstrating excellence in public affairs, by performing acts of charity or public service, by being recognized by persons of higher status, and by besting others in competitive contexts. Because honor is always relative, when one man acquires honor, he does so at the expense of others. (One could also lose honor, a fate men would go great lengths to avoid!) As we shall see, the Gospels demonstrate agonistic contests for honor especially clearly in the controversy stories, that is, those stories that pit Jesus in verbal exchanges against his opponents.

Masculinity related to status and honor in Jesus' world was in a way quite different from contemporary North American values. For the most part, our sources reflect elite sensibilities, so that we can say little about how ordinary people evaluated one another. Our modern notion that "real" men perform labor with their bodies, that (for example) there is something masculine about cowboys or construction workers, does not conform to ancient sensibilities. Masculinity did require a man to demonstrate physical ability, primarily in military affairs and also in athletics, but ordinary labor was considered demeaning. In this context, we recall that hard labor did not lead to physical fitness for ancient men; on the contrary, it accompanied inadequate nutrition and brutal living circumstances. Manual labor actually shortened one's life expectancy rather than extended it.[9] Status and honor indeed required that a man attain self-sufficiency, particularly material prosperity without resorting to manual labor. When we consider the Gospels' portrayal of Jesus, we find a tension. By birth and occupation, Jesus is a person of relatively low status, yet he competes on the public stage with persons of fairly high status. Presumably, this is because Jesus has acquired notoriety and a public following.

Men typically demonstrated their competence outdoors and in public settings. This reflects the typical indoor/outdoor division of labor and space assigned to men and women in many cultures. Whereas women managed domestic space, men competed for goods, wealth, and status in the open marketplace. Surely, women and men worked together in common space within and around the home, and in Roman times women were also active in a variety of outdoor and public settings.[10]

However, Jerome H. Neyrey has compiled various ancient sources that not only assign genders to appropriate spaces but also articulate the social, biological, and philosophical reasons these divisions make sense. Xenophon observes that people need shelter for some activities but most conduct other activities outdoors, then maintains that a man's nature is better suited to the outdoor activities and women to indoor tasks (*Oeconomicus* 7.19-22). Aristotle asserts that providence has given men greater strength than women, so that men defend the home whereas women keep watch over it (*Oeconomica* 1.3.4). Philo, the Jewish philosopher and scholar, puts forth that men are better suited than are women to engage the hustle and bustle of public affairs, as women are more timid than are men (*De specialibus legibus* 3.169). And Hierocles assigns spaces and activities to the sexes in "the usual manner" (*On Duties* 4.28.21).[11] In short, public spaces provided the site in which elite men competed for status and other social goods.

In such a competitive society, speech provided a basic index of a man's competence. Speech represented a form of power. It moved people to action, promoting one's own interests and status above others. Skill in public speaking proved essential for male property owners; thus, education beyond the level of reading, writing, and arithmetic focused on rhetoric, the art of public persuasion. In Cato's famous phrase, education in rhetoric aimed to produce "a good man, skilled in speaking" (Quintilian, *Institutio Oratoria* 12.1). Decrying a decline in both rhetoric and masculinity, Seneca plays on the word *man*, maintaining that education in declamation might cure some of the (in his view) rampant effeminacy of his day (*Controversiae* 1.8-9).[12] Indeed, audiences routinely evaluated speakers according to the masculinity demonstrated by their speech making. Posture, gesture, diction, tone of voice, clothing, and personal grooming—all these figured into public evaluation.[13]

Further, patronage provided a crucial index of a person's honor in the ancient world. We know that women and men provided support for individuals and institutions, including the ministries of Jesus and Paul.[14] For men and women, material contributions to local institutions demonstrated both prosperity and beneficence. Acquisition and distribution of wealth further reflected a man's success in the public sphere.

Jesus and his earliest followers also faced expectations concerning men, marriage, and family. Such expectations vary from one cultural context to another, from one time period to another. They also reflect the material culture in which they develop. In Jesus' day, for example, the overall population of the Roman Empire was not growing. In fact it held steady at about 60 million—or even declined—over a period of centuries, despite the influx of persons from beyond the Empire's boundaries. With high infant mortality, the threat of epidemics, and popular recourse to both infanticide and abortion, life was simply difficult to sustain. Indeed, some have found a severe shortage of women in the Greco-Roman world, with perhaps 140 males for every 100 females.[15] Under conditions such as these, a woman would need to complete five pregnancies on average just to sustain the population level. As a result, several Roman emperors enacted laws designed to promote marriage and procreation. Although Cicero's proposed ban on celibacy did not win the day, other actions did—with little effect. In 9 C.E. Augustus Caesar exacted penalties from childless couples and unmarried adults. Subsequent emperors sustained similar policies.[16] In short, a man who did not marry and father children was not holding up his end of the social bargain, as it were.

Finally, we turn to self-control (in Greek, *enkrateia*) and domestic control. Because men functioned as heads of households, their ability to manage household affairs—including the behavior of women and children—provided an index of masculinity.[17] Domestic control expressed the most basic masculine trait, power, over the affairs within a man's most immediate sphere of influence. Self-control, however, reflected an even more fundamental form of power, the ultimate test of manhood. In its most basic form, self-control required moderation: too much food, too much drink, too much sex, and too much greed all have their danger. Some, particularly in the elite philosophical traditions, went beyond elementary moderation toward a more athletic form of self-control, asceticism, or self-renunciation. We most commonly associate asceticism with sexual discipline, though it includes diet, exercise, and luxury as well. Asceticism allowed the individual man to exert power, even to the point of asserting independence against prevailing social and political forces.[18]

We have surveyed here only a few of the many factors that contributed to ancient conceptions of masculinity. Our selection largely reflects the topics that will inform our understanding of how Jesus and his earliest followers negotiated masculinity. We have given scant attention to factors such as appearance and grooming because the earliest Christian texts reflect little interest in these matters. Yet this brief survey reveals why masculinity may help us understand how early Christians remembered Jesus and how they developed their own ways of living in the world.

REMEMBERING JESUS

How do the Gospels portray Jesus' masculinity? Given the importance ancient persons assigned to the indices of masculinity, one could scarcely object that this question is irrelevant. In some important respects, Jesus meets and exceeds conventional expectations. In others, Jesus not only fails to meet those standards, he seems to transgress them with a purpose. Weighing this diverse evidence will prove tricky.

The Gospels insist that Jesus was a public man, skilled in speaking. The vast majority of his activities are located in public space. Once he is an adult, it is unclear whether Jesus establishes his own household, rarely even in his hometown or among his own family. Instead, we encounter Jesus in synagogues, out in the open air, and in private homes. In Jerusalem, Jesus takes up the most public spaces imaginable, a road into the city and the temple precincts. (We do note, however, that even during this last week he characteristically retreats from the city.)

Jesus occasionally withdraws by himself or takes his disciples aside, yet even this private time speaks to his public influence. The Gospels often remark that Jesus seeks refuge from the crowds, who follow him wherever he goes and who intrude on him in private contexts. Matthew's Gospel mentions the "crowds" (*ochloi*) over forty times *before* Jesus' last week; every chapter of Mark 2–12 mentions them more than once; a similar picture emerges in Luke; and the crowds figure prominently in John 5–7 and 11–12. This overlooks the many references to the "people" (*laoi*) who populate the Gospel accounts. The crowds follow Jesus, they wonder at his teaching, they press in on him, and they acclaim his entry into Jerusalem. Eventually they call for his crucifixion. The crowds testify to Jesus' significance, even to the degree that they intimidate his enemies (Mark 12:12; 11:18, 32; see Matt 21:26, 46; Luke 22:6; John 7:32).

Effectiveness as a speaker provides one explanation of Jesus' crowd appeal and affirms his masculinity. The Gospels provide only the tiniest details about Jesus' technique. Sometimes he sits (e.g., Matt 5:1; Mark 4:1; 12:41; 13:3; Luke 5:3), and sometimes he stands (e.g., Luke 4:16; 6:17; John 7:37). In John he sometimes raises his voice (John 7:28, 37; 11:43; 12:44). We get precious little beyond this, certainly nothing helpful about grooming, clothing, or other aspects of his appearance. Yet the Gospels insist on the power and authority of Jesus' speech. If we read Matthew, for example, from beginning to end, we see that Jesus can best Satan in a verbal exchange (4:1-11), and his calls to potential disciples immediately effects their obedience (4:18-22). In particular, two kinds of stories demonstrate Jesus' power in speaking: amazement stories and controversy stories.

Matthew spends four chapters introducing Jesus and his ministry, noting teaching and preaching among his characteristic activities and the "great crowds" that follow him (4:23-25). To introduce the content of Jesus' speech, Matthew inserts the Sermon on the Mount early in the narrative, chapters 5–7. Though Jesus primarily speaks to his disciples (5:1-2), the gathered crowd responds with amazement.

> And it happened when Jesus had completed these discourses, the crowds were amazed at his teaching, for he was teaching them as one having authority [or power, *exousia*], and not as the scribes. (Matt 7:28-29)

When Jesus returns to his home synagogue, people voice their amazement at his "wisdom and mighty acts" (13:54). All four Gospels pick up on this reaction to Jesus' teaching (see Mark 1:22; 6:2; 11:18; Luke 2:47; 4:32; 7:16; John 7:46).

We find perhaps the most important testimonial to the power of Jesus' words in his deeds of power. When Jesus calms the storm and when he curses the fig tree, his disciples get the point. Amazed, they exclaim, "What sort of person is this, for even the wind and the sea obey him?" (Matt 8:27; see 14:33; 21:20). Jesus' exorcisms and healings elicit essentially the same response (Matt 9:8; 9:33; 12:23; 15:31). We might also include Jesus' claim that he has the authority to forgive sins as a sign of his power (Matt 9:6-8; see Mark 2:10-12; Luke 5:24-26; 7:48).

Apart from the crowds' amazement, Jesus' verbal jousts with opponents communicate essentially the same message: Jesus is a man of power, whose speech confirms his authority. Time after time, Jesus' opponents challenge him verbally. In an agonistic culture these exchanges are not mere academic debates; they represent attacks on Jesus' public stature. Jesus wins all of these exchanges (with one exception, discussed later). Often Matthew simply gives Jesus the last word, without evaluating its effect (e.g., Matt 9:13, 17; 12:1-8; 12:22-32; 12:38-42; 15:1-20; 16:1-4; 17:24-27; 19:1-12; 22:34-40). One of the questions involves Jesus' authority; refusing to accept his opponents' challenge, Jesus declines a direct reply (21:23-27). As conflict escalates during Jesus' final week, however, Matthew begins to report the demoralization of his opponents. When Jesus handles their question about paying tribute to Caesar, even his opponents show their amazement and wander away (22:15-22). Matthew records the crowd's amazement at his response to the challenge concerning the resurrection (22:23-33). Matthew concludes the process by which Jesus' speech overpowers his opponents with the debate concerning David's son (22:41-46). After Jesus' reply, "No one was able to reply with an answer, nor from that day did anyone dare ask him anything." Enough said.

A couple of counterexamples potentially undermine the image of Jesus as the powerful speaker, however. Only one character in the Gospels bests Jesus in a verbal exchange. Significantly, she is a woman. This is the story of the Syrophoenecian (Mark 7:24-30) or Canaanite (Matt 15:21-28) woman, whose tenacity and clever response win over Jesus to heal her daughter. One popular interpretation has it that Jesus is merely challenging the woman to demonstrate faith, but nothing in either Gospel suggests such an interpretation. One can only speculate, but perhaps Jesus' masculinity is less threatened by his "loss" to a woman than it would be should he "lose" to another man. Or perhaps Jesus still demonstrates his authority through his ability to provide healing.

The other questionable case involves Jesus' trial, where he remains relatively silent. In each Gospel account, however, Jesus provides a brief statement that suggests his authority, or at least his self-control (Matt 26:64; 27:11; Mark 14:62; Luke 15:2; 22:67-70; 23:3, 9; John 18:20-23, 34-37). Demonstration of self-control in the face of death provides one index of supreme masculine power.[19]

Both Jewish tradition and Roman imperial policy promoted marriage and child rearing. In this context Jesus and his earliest followers definitely stand out. The Gospels depict Jesus and his immediate circle as persons on the move, many having abandoned household and family. There are indications that Simon Peter was married. Jesus heals Peter's mother-in-law, for example (Mark 1:30), and Paul mentions that Peter and others among Jesus' associates travel with their wives (1 Cor 9:5). However, the gospel portrait has Jesus on the road, along with men and women, and never mentions spouses or children. Not a shred of family life survives in the Gospel accounts.

Some have protested that Jesus could not have been single, let alone celibate, because any respectable rabbi would marry, and if possible, father children. That argument does not hold water: Jesus was not a rabbi in any technical sense, and our sources concerning rabbis date from long after Jesus' career. Moreover, we possess lots of evidence that some men, even religious devotees, pursued celibacy. These would include some who lived at Qumran and produced the Dead Sea Scrolls and some Greco-Roman philosophical traditions. One wonders as well why Paul would encourage celibacy in 1 Corinthians 7, if that practice had no connection with Jesus himself. Simply, the Gospels portray a Jesus whose ministry is defined by travel and not by household, who associates with women but does not marry.[20]

More striking than Jesus' apparent celibacy is his attitude toward the family. Sometimes Jesus comes across as indifferent to the conventional household of his day, in other cases, he is outright dismissive. For one thing, Jesus calls his disciples to abandon home and family to follow him. Simon and Andrew may abandon their nets, but who can forget the image of Zebedee abandoned in the boat by his sons James and John (Matt 4:22; Mark 1:20)?[21] More striking is Jesus' rebuff to a would-be disciple who asks to bury his father: "Leave the dead to bury their own dead" (Luke 9:59; Matt 8:22). Though some interpreters seek to clean the passage of its offense—"the buriers of the dead are those who have rejected Jesus and his proclamation" who "love father and mother more than Jesus and have chosen death instead of the life of the kingdom"—one cannot escape that Jesus here dismisses traditional family values as a hindrance to following him.[22]

Jesus condemns those who cite religious principles to avoid their obligations to their parents (Mark 7:9-13; Matt 15:4-8), and he inveighs against both adultery and divorce (Mark 7:22; 10:2-12; Matt 5:27-32; 15:19; 19:1-9; Luke 16:18). In these sayings some perceive an attempt to hold families together, particularly at a time when the traditional household shuddered under pressure from economic and cultural factors.[23] Both the teaching concerning parents and that regarding adultery and divorce protect vulnerable persons—the elderly, women, and possibly children—against exploitation and neglect. At the same time, Jesus insists that following him will lead persons away from their families. We might arrange such sayings in order from their milder forms to their most provocative.

Mild: Jesus warns that those who love parents and children more than himself are not worthy of him (Matt 10:37). Luke's version of this passage is far more inflammatory: "Whoever does not hate father and mother, wife and children, brothers and sisters, and even life itself, cannot be my disciple" (14:26).

Attention-grabbing (A): Jesus promises that those who leave households, including brothers, sisters, mothers, fathers, children, and fields "for my sake and the sake of the gospel," will receive a hundredfold more in return. The catalogue of "new" items includes everything one has abandoned with the exception of fathers (Mark 10:29-30). Is Jesus indicating a fundamental criticism of patriarchy, in that his movement does not provide "fathers"?[24] Matthew and Luke provide much milder versions in which the list of things gained does not appear (Matt 19:29; Luke 18:29-30).

Attention-grabbing (B): While Jesus is teaching, his mother and brothers send word that they are standing outside looking for him. Jesus asks, "Who are my mother and brothers?" and then says to the assembled crowd, "Here are my mother and brothers, for whoever does God's will is my brother and sister and mother" (Mark 3:31-35; see Matt 12:46-50; Luke 8:19-21).

Inflammatory: Jesus claims that he has come to bring not peace but division (a sword, according to Matthew), setting children against their parents (Matt 10:34-36; Luke 12:51-53). Notably, Matthew connects this saying with the milder teaching concerning leaving family (10:37-39), whereas Luke separates the two (see Luke 14:26-27).

Clearly, some degree of tension tugs the Jesus tradition away from conventional household values.[25] Scholars conventionally describe people of Jesus' day as rooted in household and village, largely taking on the identities assigned to them by their places in life. We might call this a group-embedded personality.[26] Jesus' invitation calls people to adopt values that likely conflict with their roots. This may fall short of calling people to act as autonomous individuals. At a minimum, it invites them into an alternative community, one that removes them from their households of origin.

How do we evaluate these gospel family traditions? As with our Gospel passages, a survey of three interpreters covers a spectrum from mildly countercultural to inflammatory assessments.

> **Mild**: F. Scott Spencer surveys the traditions concerning Jesus and family and concludes, "In place of a bland, one-dimensional portrait of Jesus' enacted family values, the Gospels offer a more textured, multifaceted presentation." According to this view, the Gospels sometimes depict tension between Jesus and conventional family values, but their major emphasis lies in Jesus' invitation to all who would pursue God's will.[27]

> **Attention-Grabbing**: According to John P. Meier, Jesus' invitation to abandon family so countered conventional sensibilities as to invite hostility and persecution. "By the word 'follow' Jesus meant literally, physically accompanying him on his preaching tours and therefore leaving behind one's home, parents, and livelihood—with no indication of a geographical or temporal limit on the commitment. . . . Such an open-ended commitment that demanded abandonment of home and livelihood could entail not just risk but also hostility and suffering, even at the hands of one's own family, as Jesus knew from his own experience."[28]

> **Inflammatory**: What if the Jesus traditions fundamentally subvert the family values of the day? Halvor Moxnes argues that Jesus and his male disciples fundamentally abandon their assigned masculine roles. They abandon not only the household places, but also the village places of life and work. "To leave and to follow Jesus' call was to forsake a definite masculine space," Moxnes writes. They are creating "alternative forms of masculinity" entailing "a new set of values" over against prevailing norms.[29]

The social status of Jesus, his male disciples, and the first Christian communities adds some texture to this more inflammatory assessment. Very few people in the ancient world enjoyed material or social security. Jesus and his disciples emerged from Galilee, where ordinary people

resisted extraordinary pressure in order to hold on to their land and
to keep their families intact. Jesus' parables, with their tenant workers, absentee landlords, and resident managers, reflect this reality.[30]
For Jesus and his disciples, Moxnes suggests, traditional means of
demonstrating masculinity were moving beyond their grasp.

Jesus' travelling lifestyle ruled out building a household, establishing a trade, accumulating wealth, or patronizing local institutions. The
Gospels depict Jesus and his followers abandoning home and trade,
forging new communities in which people beg and share.[31] After all,
"foxes have holes, and the birds of the air have nests, but the Son of Man
has nowhere to recline his head" (Matt 8:20; Luke 9:58). In doing so
they abandoned traditional standards of masculinity. More precisely, the
Gospels depict Jesus and his disciples as imperfect or alternative men.

With respect to specifically sexual masculinity in the Jesus traditions, one passage just jumps off the page. Having just provided his
teaching on divorce, Jesus says,

> There are eunuchs who were born such from their mother's womb;
> and there are eunuchs who were made eunuchs [or, *castrated*] by
> men; and there are eunuchs who have made themselves eunuchs [or,
> *castrated* themselves] for the sake of the reign of God. Whoever is able
> to accept this, let him accept it. (Matt 19:12)

This passage stands alone: nothing like it occurs elsewhere in Matthew
or beyond it in the other Gospels. The closest thing we might find is
Jesus' saying that it is better to cut off a hand or pluck out an eye if it
causes one to fall, also in Matthew (5:29-30); but everyone "knows" that
is just hyperbole. The passage mentions three kinds of eunuchs—those
born as eunuchs, those (presumably) forced to be eunuchs by others,
and those who choose to be eunuchs for religious reasons. The first
group includes all persons with predominantly masculine features but
who are physiologically unfit for marriage.[32] The second group includes
men who have been castrated, usually under coercion, as a precondi-
tion of their service in royal court and elite households. (One recalls
the Ethiopian eunuch of Acts 8:26-39.) According to Scripture, all such

men were excluded from the priesthood and from areas of the temple (Lev 21:20; 22:24; Deut 23:1). However, the book of Isaiah promises restoration for eunuchs in the house of YHWH (56:3b-5).[33]

But what of the third case, the voluntary eunuchs? Modern interpreters generally assume that Jesus is speaking metaphorically of men who renounce marriage in order to pursue the gospel. I tend to agree, yet two factors give reason for hesitation. Not only do we hear of voluntary castration in other ancient religious movements, we know that some early Christians took Matthew 19:12 literally and performed the deed themselves. This group includes the great and influential theologian Origen.[34] The Jewish writers Josephus and Philo both express scorn for such persons: Josephus on the grounds that such persons have forfeited their masculinity and Philo because they belong neither among men nor among women (Josephus, *Antiquities* 4.290-91; Philo, *De somniis* 2.184).[35] Pagan writers likewise record scandalous reactions.[36] We may not simply rule out then, that Matthew 19:12 implies actual voluntary castration, though that is not my point. What is lacking in the conventional interpretation is not the possibility that Jesus promoted literal self-mutilation. What is lacking is the recognition that in Jesus' context to abandon marriage, procreation, and household was to compromise one's masculinity, which was a choice that would invite scorn from at least some of one's neighbors. Though some men clearly took on voluntary celibacy, the choice had its consequences.

Beyond household and sex, self-sufficiency and productivity provide another index of masculinity. Several gospel stories depict Jesus and his companions carrying no provisions for themselves. For example, when Jesus sends forth the Twelve to teach among the villages, he instructs them to carry no bread, no bag, and no money. Instead, they are to rely on local hospitality for their needs (Mark 6:6b-13; Matt 10:1-15; Luke 9:1-6), presumably offering healing and spiritual blessing in return. We do hear that some of Jesus' traveling companions — *women!* — support his ministry out of their wealth (Mark 15:41; compare Matt 27:55; Luke 8:2-3).

Attention to the material dimensions of the gospel stories reveals what deadbeats Jesus and his disciples were. In addition to begging for lodging and food, Jesus sometimes dines with persons of relative means. He seems to have built a network of allies, so that, for example, he can call on someone to provide a donkey for his entry into Jerusalem (Mark 11:2-3; Matt 21:2-3; Luke 19:30-31).[37] For at least one meal someone provides a room for him and his disciples during their stay in Jerusalem.

We encounter several stories in which Jesus has no food or no money. Though Jesus miraculously provides food for 5,000, his disciples have with them only five loaves and two fish (Mark 6:38; Matt 14:17; Luke 9:13; John 6:9). Likewise, they have but seven loaves when they feed 4,000 (Mark 8:5; Matt 15:34 adds a few fish). Even after these miraculous feedings, we hear how the disciples forget to bring bread on a sea journey, so that only one loaf is with them on the boat (Mark 8:14; Matt 16:5). Likewise, when the question of taxation confronts Jesus, he never has funds to cover the tax. Instead, suggesting that his disciples are free from the obligation to pay imperial taxes (Matt 17:26), Jesus instructs Peter to go fishing. The first fish he catches will have a coin in its mouth (17:27).[38] Again, when his enemies confront Jesus with the tax question, he demands that they show him the coin with Caesar's image and inscription (Mark 12:13-17; Matt 22:15-22; Luke 20:20-26). In doing so, Jesus suggests two things. Neither does he pay the tax, nor does he carry money.

Occasional passages in John's Gospel suggest that Jesus and his disciples carry money (4:8; 12:6; 13:29).[39] And we have observed how a group of women seems to have underwritten their ministry. Otherwise, one looks in vain to find money in Jesus' hands. On its own this may not seem odd. Taken together with his instructions that his disciples carry no money, and these two instances in which he requires money from others, it suggests that Jesus lives beyond the ordinary system of commerce and trade. In this light, his instructions to consider the birds and the lilies, who receive their needs without labor or anxiety (Matt 6:25-34; Luke 12:22-31), along with his command to seek heavenly rather than common wealth (Matt 6:19-21; Luke 12:33-34), hardly resemble sentimental piety. Not to mention the Lord's Prayer: "Our daily bread, give us day by day" (Luke 11:3; cf. Matt 6:11).

What, then, do we make of the itinerant, mobile life attributed to Jesus and his disciples? Both itinerancy and sexual asceticism created space for persons to experiment with individual and group freedom. Alternative lifestyles, including ascetic practices, allow individuals and groups to express control over something, if only their own bodies. They also set people free from attachment to status, finances, and relations of dependence. Ancient Stoics practiced renunciation for set periods as a way to prepare themselves to confront deprivation with virtue. Cynics traveled light and renounced household so that they might be beholden to no one. In every case, these behaviors demonstrated the chief quality of ancient masculinity—self-control—even as they abandoned other traditional measures of masculine achievement, such as power, wealth, and progeny. The Gospels describe Jesus and his disciples forging a complicated, even aberrant, masculinity. By abandoning home and the struggles for masculine accomplishment, but still demonstrating strength in the public realm, Jesus and his disciples set themselves free to pursue the reign of God.

PAUL: LIVIN' THE LIFE

Apparently Jesus and his disciples spent most of their lives in the rural and village settings of Galilee. These stories would have played out somewhat differently in the more urban contexts of the Roman Empire, where our Gospels took shape, as did the rest of early Christian literature. There, the first Christian communities grew among persons from diverse rungs of the socioeconomic ladder. Those churches included persons whose relative wealth may or may not have corresponded to their public status—precisely the kinds of people who pursued philosophy, new religious movements, and other forms of personal meaning-making.[40] Although such audiences may not have imagined themselves traveling from village to village, they, too, may have been interested in alternative ways of defining identity and freedom.

Early generations of Christians continued to explore alternative ways of engaging the world. Social experimentation, including experimentation with gender roles, populates the early Christian literature, as does adverse reaction to these experiments. Although we lack space here for a thorough investigation of masculinity in the early churches, a brief survey reveals that Jesus' countercultural memory lived on in the early churches.

The apostle Paul provides a fascinating case.[41] Deserved or otherwise, Paul carries a reputation as a chauvinist. He expresses scorn for "soft" men (*malakoi*) in 1 Corinthians 6:9, probably a slight against men who act out the receptive role in homoerotic sex.[42] This view suggests Paul's acute sensitivity to gender matters. It may even explain, at least in part, his aversion to same-gender sex among men. Furthermore, Paul sometimes uses father language to characterize his ministry, along with child language to describe the believers among whom he ministers. Even if some interpreters insist that Paul is a gentle, benevolent "father," he employs such language to bolster his authority. Because Paul also refers to God as "Father," there is no denying that he comes across as both paternalistic and authoritarian.[43] Consider these passages.

> For though you may have myriad tutors in Christ, you do not have many fathers. For in Christ Jesus through the gospel I became your father. I appeal to you, therefore, become imitators of me. . . . What do you desire? Shall I come to you with a rod, or with love and a gentle spirit? (1 Cor 4:15-16, 21)

> You are witnesses, and God as well, how devoutly, justly, and blamelessly we were among you believers, even as you know how, with each one of you, we appealed to you and consoled you like a father with his children. (1 Thess 2:10-11)

This combination of gentleness and authoritarianism, here balanced between Paul's meek "parenting style" among the Thessalonians and his threat to bring a stick for the Corinthians, marks Paul's letters.

Although many have noted Paul's father language, Beverly Roberts Gaventa offers two profound observations. First, Paul employs paternal metaphors for his own ministry less frequently than he does feminine imagery. Second, these metaphors reflect different experiences of parenting, marked by the cultural context in which Paul wrote. When Paul appeals to his identity as a father, he is talking about the initial stage in founding a church or converting individuals. In contrast, his maternal imagery applies to the relational process between Paul and his churches. These metaphors connote processes that develop over time: pregnancy, labor, and nursing (1 Thess 2:7; 1 Cor 3:1-2; Gal 4:19). According to convention in Paul's context, this makes sense: at least in Paul's metaphorical universe fathers beget, but mothers nurture.[44] Gaventa may overstate the case because Paul uses father imagery to foster discipline in the churches or to remind believers of their ongoing obligations. However, his maternal imagery is striking in its portrayal of ongoing care and nurture. In this context we recall Jesus, who likens himself to a hen protecting her chicks (Matt 23:37; Luke 13:34).

Sandra Hack Polaski intimates that perhaps Paul's outlook is not always determined by "the strict rules of gender-appropriate behavior and attitudes that . . . characterize his social setting."[45] Indeed, as Galatians 3:28 suggests, in Christ there is neither male and female, and perhaps Paul is not interested in maintaining conventional gender distinctions at all. Some say Paul occasionally defers to convention as a pragmatic measure for living in the present age, as he does with respect to divorce (1 Cor 7) and the veiling of women (1 Cor 11:2-16). In my view, however, his larger purposes are more subversive.[46] Paul's gospel proclamation that Christ delivers humankind from the present evil age (Gal 1:4) implies a fundamental resistance to hierarchical convention.

If speech provides a basic index of ancient Mediterranean masculinity, then Paul provides a fascinating study. Paul employs undeniable rhetorical skill, both in his letters and (presumably) in person. Interpreters disagree on the details, as we always do, yet attempts to interpret his letters according to the conventions of ancient rhetoric have proven remarkably fruitful. For his own part, Paul reminds the Thessalonians and the Corinthians how he brought the word of God to them with power (e.g., 1 Thess 1:5; 1 Cor 2:4; 5:4; 2 Cor 6:7).

Yet Paul gives away the perception that some regard his speech as a liability. "'His letters,' some say, 'are weighty and mighty, but his bodily presence is weak and his speech contemptible" (2 Cor 10:10). We recall that ancient people considered physical appearance in their evaluations of oratorical skill; Paul expresses gratitude that the Galatians did not reject him on account of an unknown physical infirmity (4:13-14). Contrasting himself against competing "super-apostles," Paul confesses that he may be "unlearned in speech, but not in knowledge" (2 Cor 11:5-6). Instead, he repeatedly celebrates how God's power manifests itself not in conventional measures of strength but in Paul's weaknesses. This applies to his physical vulnerabilities (e.g., 2 Cor 12:7-10), the hardships he endures for the gospel (notably 2 Cor 4:7-12 and 6:4-10), and his apparent deficiencies in wisdom and speech (1 Cor 1:17–2:5).

As a public figure, Paul further complicates masculinity in his disposition toward income and labor. Ancient persons did not value manual labor, but they did honor self-sufficiency. For his part, Paul insisted on maintaining as much independence as possible in some contexts, while he happily drew support from others. In 1 Corinthians Paul actually boasts that he provides the gospel free of charge (9:1-18), as he reminds the Thessalonians how hard he worked so as not to burden them (1 Thess 2:9). In fact, it seems that some among the Corinthians complained because Paul rejected their support, relying on help from other cities instead (2 Cor 11:7-11). Paul's opponents may have objected that his manual labor brought shame on the congregation, that "real" teachers should receive compensation, or that he had shown favoritism by accepting gifts from others.[47] On the other hand, he writes to the Romans to solicit their support for a mission to Spain (15:24), while he thanks the Philippians for the support they have provided for his ministry and during his imprisonment (1:25; 4:16-18). Self-sufficient in some cases but not in others, supporting himself through the work of his hands, Paul hardly qualifies as the ideal of masculinity.

Finally, we come to the question of sexual asceticism, or celibacy. As in the Jesus traditions, sexual discipline stood in a complicated relationship to the gender standards of the day. Celibacy demonstrated self-control, yet it also precluded the possibility of establishing a household with progeny. All the available evidence suggests that Paul was celibate, that he encouraged others to become "as I am myself" (1 Cor 7:7), and that he fully recognized that celibacy was not for most people. In this respect Paul carries on one of the interesting practices we find in the Jesus tradition.

Even more interesting is how later Christian traditions, particularly those associated with Paul, continue the struggle over gender roles and family values. Written in Paul's name, 1 Timothy spins the tradition to affirm marriage against those who prohibit it (4:3). A similar dynamic may be in play in Colossians (2:16-23), though that remains unclear. However, along with 1 Timothy, Colossians (3:18–4:1) and Ephesians (5:21–6:9) adapt Paul's voice to defend the patriarchal household. The book of Revelation, which shows some familiarity with the Pauline tradition (1:4), praises "those who have not defiled themselves with women" (14:4), though one cannot attribute this view to an interpretation of Paul. In all these cases, it seems that Paul's preference for celibacy has provided a source of controversy. Some have taken celibacy as an absolute value, whereas others resist it, even to the point of reinforcing the patriarchal household.

One ancient Christian story, the Acts of Paul and Thecla, describes a young woman captivated by Paul's message. While she sits entranced by Paul's message of virginity, her mother perceives the apparent danger and calls Thamyris, to whom Thecla is betrothed. Intimidated by Thecla's new passion, Thamyris researches Paul's message. He learns that Paul indeed deprives men of wives and virgins of their husbands and has Paul put in prison. Because Thecla visits Paul in prison, she is brought to Paul's trial. Amazingly, Paul is scourged and sent out of the city, whereas Thecla—at her mother's insistence—is condemned to be burned. Saved by divine intervention in this case, saved again from the wild beasts after she resists the sexual assault of a young man in Antioch, Thecla finds Paul, who commissions her to teach the word of God.

Thecla's story reveals a couple of things about Paul's celibacy message. First, Paul's message remained a disputed topic in early Christian circles, perhaps more than a century after his death. Christians debated the merits of marriage and celibacy for centuries.[48] The Acts of Paul and Thecla confirm that some boiled down Paul's legacy to a primary essential, sexual asceticism. We see this as well in the pseudepigraphal Epistle of Titus (not to be confused with the canonical Epistle to Titus). Though the story became controversial for other reasons as well, primarily the tradition of a woman who preaches, it drew sharp criticism from such a prominent theologian as Tertullian, who disputed its authenticity. Second, the story proposes a social reality we should take seriously. Although Thecla is probably a historical figure, most of the Acts of Paul and Thecla almost certainly consists of fiction. Nevertheless, the story indicates how celibacy threatened the entrenched patriarchal framework of the day. By following Paul, Thecla makes her own path. She also brings shame on her own household and on Thamyris, such that in their eyes her call to celibacy represents a capital offense. That Thecla's legacy continued to inspire other Christians, particularly women, suggests the countercultural power of her story.

Pauline tradition, like the Jesus traditions, demonstrates an ambivalent relationship to ancient gender conventions, particularly with respect to masculinity. Paul is a man of the public sphere, who possesses rhetorical power, provides for his own needs, and manages community affairs. He insists on his authority as father to the churches among whom he ministers. And his sexual asceticism demonstrates his self-control, an essential masculine trait. Yet Paul is complicated. He recognizes that others perceive his bodily presence as weak. He sometimes requires physical help and financial support. Despite his father language, he more often describes his ongoing work among the churches in feminine imagery. His fundamental disposition toward conventional gender roles remains a debated topic, even as early Christians appropriated his legacy to foster everything from patriarchal households to independence through celibacy.

PICKING UP AFTER JESUS: MASCULINITY
IN PAULINE TRADITIONS

This chapter has almost exclusively focused on masculinity. I do not mean to deny or diminish the contribution and presence of women in the Jesus movement or the early churches, thereby reinforcing the traditional privilege assigned to men and their activities. On the contrary, I am suggesting that according to the standards of their day, Jesus and his earliest followers, including Paul, made for imperfect men, problematic men. As Halvor Moxnes sagely suggests, one might hope that the peculiarities of early Christian masculinity may have created space for new ways for men to relate to women and children as well.[49]

I find it keenly ironic that today the most prominent defenders of patriarchal family values, complete with an odd hypermasculinity, emerge from among the so-called Bible believers. One can read through the Bible from one cover to another in a vain attempt to find those elusive "biblical family values." I know, because that is exactly what I did as an adolescent new convert. Those values simply are not there.[50] How does one account for this among those Christian traditions that appeal to Jesus and Paul as particular sources of authority, two men who neither married nor promoted marriage and who marched out of step with the masculine cadences of their time?

Most remarkable, in my view, are the points of consistency between the Gospel accounts of Jesus and the Pauline traditions. Neither Jesus nor Paul establishes a household. Neither marries. Both travel, build networks, and communicate in public. Both accept support from others, including women, though Paul often insists on working to support himself. Both movements apparently attract women, who find a measure of freedom and influence through their participation. I suspect these commonalities are more than coincidence. Memories of Jesus and his disciples carried on into the ministries of Paul and other early Christians. In diverse cultural contexts, and among diverse audiences, these movements shared a critique of conventional masculinity. They did not forge a new manhood, but they did create space for men to consider themselves—and the other women, children, and men around them—differently.

Chapter 5

JESUS, THE CONVICTED SEDITIONIST

Jesus was executed by the legitimate authorities of his day for acts he actually committed.

This claim, to which many Christians would take offense, demands clarification. For one thing, I am not passing judgment on Jesus' morality. I am not saying Jesus was crucified because he did bad things. I am not even saying Jesus committed a crime in the technical sense of breaking a law. That question is unclear. Nor am I defending the actions of those who determined Jesus' fate. They may have been performing their duties, but their motives are lost to us.

What am I saying? The Gospels remember Jesus as a person who staged a procession into Jerusalem for the Passover feast, who created a public disturbance at the temple, who proclaimed the destruction of that sacred site, and who undermined Rome's right to exact tribute from its provinces. An objective observer watching Jesus during the last week of his life could have predicted his death. All these behaviors were provocative, and as the Gospels tell it, they led inexorably to the cross.

THE "INNOCENT" JESUS?

Each of the Gospels has its own way of presenting Jesus as an innocent victim. Yet each of the Gospels also lays out the basic activities that provoked authorities to execute him. And each agrees on the basic charge levied against Jesus: he was "king of the Jews."

I will begin with Mark's Gospel, though in many respects the same basic pattern applies to all four canonical Gospels. Early in the narrative Mark reports a conspiracy against Jesus on the part of Pharisees and Herodians (3:6). As in Matthew and Luke, but not John, Jesus travels only once to Jerusalem, his fateful observance of the Passover festival. Soon after his arrival, the chief priests and scribes likewise plot against Jesus. Mark attributes this to their fear of Jesus, for the whole Passover crowd was astonished at his teaching (11:18).

In other contexts Mark relates how the "chief priests, scribes, and elders" attempt to entice Jesus to say something that will get him in trouble. Will he alienate Jewish audiences by claiming inappropriate authority (11:27-33)? After Jesus' reply, these enemies want to arrest him. Out of fear for the crowd that approves of Jesus, they bide their time (12:12). In reply to a question from the Pharisees and Herodians — "Is it lawful to pay taxes to the emperor or not?" — will he commit treason or align himself with the Roman imperial oppressors (12:13-17)? Pressed by the Sadducees, will he earn opprobrium by advocating silly notions regarding the resurrection (12:18-27)?

Mark carefully discriminates among Jesus' enemies in Jerusalem. The Pharisees and Sadducees are fairly minor players here, but persons associated with the temple establishment — chief priests, scribes, and elders — play a major role. Ultimately they are the ones who see to Jesus' arrest and his transfer to Roman authority. Mark places the temple authorities and their allies at the center of Jesus' final conflict.

The plot against Jesus intensifies during this final week. Although Jesus' enemies continually seek to kill him, they withdraw due to his popularity with the crowds. All four Gospels basically agree that Judas Iscariot, one of Jesus' chosen twelve, seeks out the chief priests and arranges Jesus' betrayal. Free from the risk of causing a riot by confronting Jesus directly, the chief priests send an armed mob to arrest Jesus at night. Jesus protests their rough treatment, "Do you come out with swords and clubs to capture me as if I were a bandit?" (Mark 14:48; Matt 26:55; Luke 22:52). This objection, common to the first three Gospels, emphasizes Jesus' innocence. He is not a violent person. He does not deserve this sort of arrest.

The Gospel accounts intensify the authorities' duplicity. They have arrested Jesus, yet they still have not found the testimony they need to execute him. As a result they bring in false witnesses who contradict one another's testimony (Mark 14:55; Matt 26:57-75). Luke's version of Jesus' Jewish trial (22:66-71) lacks the scene in which the authorities cook up testimony against Jesus, though Pilate finds no reason to believe their charges (23:1-5). Any accusation will do.

For the purpose of getting Jesus killed, the best charge would involve sedition. That way, the authorities can pass Jesus along to the Romans without incurring the wrath of the Passover crowd. That is how Luke tells the story: the temple authorities cite Jesus for misleading the people, forbidding the payment of taxes to Caesar, and claiming to be a messiah, or king (23:2).[1] Matthew and Mark do not specify the temple authorities' accusations, though Pilate's first question to Jesus involves sedition: "Are you the king of the Jews?" (Mark 15:2; Matt 27:11). John's Gospel tells it slightly differently: the temple authorities do not weigh a specific charge against Jesus. Pressed by Pilate, they reply, "If this man were not a criminal, we would not have handed him over to you" (18:30). Yet all three Gospels agree on Pilate's first question: "Are you the king of the Jews?" (Luke 23:3; John 18:33).

Pilate's question creates a luscious irony. Is Jesus king of the Jews? In all four Gospels he goes to some lengths to avoid that appellation. No single person could read all the scholarly pages devoted to this riddle. Jesus' followers may so recognize him, yet even then he does not go about pronouncing his messianic identity. Even John's Gospel, notorious for how much Jesus has to say about himself, has Jesus avoiding the crowds who desire to install him as king (6:15). The classic story concerning Jesus' identity, Peter's confession at Caesarea Philippi, has Peter recognizing Jesus as the Messiah. But Peter cannot grasp what

Jesus' messianic identity means, for he cannot comprehend how the Messiah could endure suffering, humiliation, and death (Mark 8:27-33; Matt 16:13-23; though Luke 9:18-22 differs). As a result, Jesus commands the disciples not to spread the news.

So, is Jesus the king? According to all four of the Gospels, the charge against Jesus is nailed to the cross along with him, "This is Jesus, the king of the Jews" (Matt 27:37; Mark 15:26; Luke 23:38; John 19:19). Yet a poll of the Gospels does not clear up anything. Upon Jesus' lips, the Gospels place ambiguous responses to Pilate's question.

Matthew 27:11; Mark 15:2; Luke 23:3	John 18:33-37
Pilate: "Are you the king of the Jews?" **Jesus:** *"You say."* [Is this an affirmation or an evasion?]	**Pilate:** "Are you the king of the Jews?" **Jesus:** *"Do you say this on your own, or did others speak to you concerning me?"* **Pilate:** "Am I a Jew? Your own people and the chief priests have handed you over to me. What have you done?" **Jesus:** *"My dominion is not of this world. If my dominion were of this world, my subordinates would be fighting to keep me from being handed over to the Jews. But now, my dominion is not from here."* **Pilate:** "So then, you are a king?" **Jesus:** *"You say that I am a king. . . ."*

So is Jesus a king, or not? John's Gospel insists that Jesus is a king, but his rule apparently poses no direct threat to Pilate's. The Synoptic

Gospels—Matthew, Mark, and Luke—settle for a more opaque reply. Pilate says Jesus is a king, but Jesus neither confirms nor denies that assessment.[2] Thus, the charge affixed to Jesus' cross makes a lot of sense. From Pilate's point of view Jesus is a convicted seditionist, the would-be king of the Jews.[3] The Gospels, however, maintain Jesus' innocence throughout. Whatever it means to him, he never owns his royal identity.

Famously, the Gospels focalize Jesus' innocence through the waffling tyrant Pilate. Precious few historians imagine that Pilate actually agonized over sending Jesus to the cross, but the Gospels depict this process in order to dramatize Jesus as a righteous victim. In all four Gospels Pilate demonstrates reservations concerning Jesus' guilt. Pilate recognizes that the temple authorities have handed Jesus over out of jealousy (Mark 15:10; Matt 27:18). When the crowd demands Jesus' crucifixion, he demands, "Why, what evil has he done?" (Mark 15:14; Matt 27:23; Luke 23:22). In John, Pilate even challenges the people to "Take him yourselves and crucify him"—a patently illegal action—"I find no case against him" (19:6). Luke reminds us that Pilate questions Jesus' guilt three times (23:22). Most dramatically in Matthew, Pilate washes his hands of responsibility for Jesus' death—though of course one cannot wash off guilt for a killing one fully intends to execute (27:24).

In several ways, then, the Gospels present Jesus as a righteous victim. The temple authorities conspire against him. They hire Judas to betray him, capture him in the middle of the night, round up false witnesses against him, and manipulate Pilate into seeing to Jesus' execution. The charge against Jesus, that he would be "king of the Jews," either is categorically false or misrepresents the nature of Jesus' ministry. As the Gospels tell it, Jesus is handed over by jealous religious authorities and then crucified on a misleading charge. He is an innocent victim.

Yet we will see how that charge against Jesus, "king of the Jews," opens a window into another dimension of the gospel stories. Jesus may be morally righteous and he may be guilty of no formal crime, but, deserving or not, he was executed for good reason—and early Christians knew why. The Gospel accounts reveal this, too.

RESPONSIBILITY FOR JESUS' DEATH

The Gospels depict the temple authorities pressing on Pilate, forcing him to pronounce Jesus' doom. As the gospel traditions develop, the blame for this shifts from the temple authorities (Mark) to the Jewish "people" as a whole (Matthew, Luke, and John). John has the crowd questioning Pilate's loyalty to Caesar: "If you release this man, you are no friend of Caesar. Whoever makes himself king opposes Caesar" (19:12). This threat forces Pilate's hand. Even more chilling, Matthew places the following words in the mouths of the crowd: "His blood be upon us and upon our children" (27:25). As a result, many Christians through the centuries—and even today—believe "the Jews" were responsible for Jesus' death. The suffering of countless Jews may be attributed to this belief. In response to this tragedy, many churches and scholars have condemned anti-Semitism and inaccurate interpretations of the role of Jews in Jesus' death. I recommend one particular collection of resources on this topic from the Roman Catholic tradition, *The Bible, the Jews, and the Death of Jesus: A Collection of Catholic Documents.*[1]

One brutal fact disproves the notion that the Jews killed Jesus. Scholars debate whether Jewish authorities in the Judea of Jesus' day held the authority to execute capital punishment, but only Roman authorities held the right to perform a crucifixion for a charge of sedition. In other words, some Jewish authorities may have played an important role in seizing Jesus and handing him over to Pilate, but only Pilate had the legal right to authorize Jesus' crucifixion.[2]

---

[1] *The Bible, the Jews, and the Death of Jesus: A Collection of Catholic Documents* (Washington: United States Conference of Catholic Bishops, 2004).

[2] See, for example, John T. Carroll and Joel B. Green, *The Death of Jesus in Early Christianity* (Peabody, Mass.: Hendrickson, 1995), 203; François Bovon, *The Last Days of Jesus* (Louisville: Westminster John Knox, 2006), 44–50; Raymond E. Brown, *The Death of the Messiah* (ABRL; New York: Doubleday, 1994),1:363–72; Gerard S. Sloyan, *Why Jesus Died* (Minneapolis: Fortress, 2004), 27.

HOW JESUS GOT HIMSELF KILLED

"How Jesus got himself killed." This is not the most delicate way to frame the discussion, but it does help us understand the issue in a historical way. So long as our primary way of understanding Jesus' death involves assuming his innocence, we cannot understand one basic issue: Why would the temple authorities and the Roman governor see Jesus as worthy of the cross?

We will say more about the social significance of crucifixion in chapter 6, but we should explore one thing about this gruesome punishment right away.[4] The mode of Jesus' execution gives away a great deal about how the authorities perceived him. The Romans used crucifixion primarily as a political form of execution. It was public.[5] It largely applied to petty criminals and especially to enemies of the state. In Jesus' case, all signs indicate that Jesus died as he did because the authorities saw him as an enemy of the state. The Gospels indicate the things Jesus did that provoked this conclusion. We hardly have to read between the lines.

One essential element of Jesus' execution is its timing: Jesus meets his fate during the Passover celebration. Among contemporary historians E. P. Sanders stands out for sketching the circumstances that attended Passover. Drawing heavily on the works of Josephus, Sanders describes Jerusalem during Passover week as intensely overcrowded and politically tense. One of three annual pilgrimage festivals in Judaism, Passover may have drawn literally hundreds of thousands of pilgrims from around the Jewish world into a city with a residential population of less than 30,000.[6] If we imagine a situation like Auburn (Alabama) on a football Saturday, multiply its intensity several times, and consider that the visitors are staying for days on end with no hotels, we might get the idea. No wonder the gospel Passion Narratives themselves frequently mention the crowds or mobs. During Passover week, Jerusalem was acutely overcrowded, a situation that would concern any responsible administrator.

Beyond the crowding, Passover created a political hotbox.[7] Modern Christians, especially in North America, may struggle to understand how a religious holiday can carry heavy political significance, but ancient people did not so discriminate between the political and the religious realms. Passover commemorates the deliverance of Israel from bondage to an ancient imperial power, Egypt. Passover, then, was a freedom holiday, a sort of Independence Day. But in Jesus' day Israel was hardly free. Jews did not struggle to make the connection between bondage to an ancient empire and the occupation they faced in their own day. As a result, trouble occasionally attended the Passover season.

Josephus observes that seditions typically break out during the festivals (*War* 1.88), then relates at least four such occurrences. As Sanders notes, "this despite the fact that both Jewish and Roman rulers were prepared for trouble and had forces near by."[8] One example will serve our purposes. Not long before the death of Herod the Great, ruler of Roman Palestine, some Jews cut down the golden eagle—a symbol of Roman imperialism—affixed to the gate of the temple. Having rounded up the offenders and those who instigated them, Herod had them burned alive (*War* 1.648-55; *Antiquities* 17.149-67).[9] On Herod's death in 4 B.C.E., while the memory of this massacre remained fresh, pressure mounted against Herod's son Archelaus, who was expecting to inherit the southern region of Herod's dominion, including Judea. Things boiled over on Passover, with a "countless" throng of pilgrims in the city. With a seditious party gathered in the temple, Archelaus responded by sending an armed regiment. When chaos followed, Archelaus sent an even greater force on the crowd. Three thousand Jews died at Archelaus' hand (*War* 2.10-13; *Antiquities* 17.213-18). Soon, Varus, the Roman legate in Syria, brought three legions into Judea to put down the disorder.[10] Ultimately Archelaus lost his fledgling dominion, as the Romans desired a more reliable administrator. That is how a Roman administrator, Pontius Pilate in Jesus' day, came to govern Judea.

Archelaus' case reveals the touchy relationships between Roman imperialism, Judean religion, and Jewish political hope. Roman imperialism manifests itself in the image of the eagle, a prominent symbol especially among the Roman military, and in Rome's power to appoint rulers for the various regions of Palestine. The original conflict involved the placement of this imperial symbol at the temple, the primary site of Judean religion. The conflict became a bloodbath precisely when local political aspirations ran high, that is, in the power vacuum following Herod's death. Fueled by the hot Passover climate, the winds of imperial domination, indigenous religion, and anti-imperial resistance created the perfect storm.

Pilate no doubt was keenly aware of Archelaus' misfortune and the broader risks that attended the festival seasons. For most of the year he lived not in Jerusalem but in the seaside resort of Caesarea Maritima. He ventured to Jerusalem primarily to keep order during the major festivals. At those times, due to the fear of sedition, he brought additional troops to support the small Roman garrison in the city. Then Roman soldiers patrolled the temple, using elevated lookout posts.[11]

The tense Passover context frames the provocative actions of Jesus' last week. Historians debate the veracity of the Gospel accounts. Did Jesus really ride into Jerusalem to popular, even messianic, acclaim? Did he storm around the temple precincts, overturning the exchange tables? Did he speak out against the temple and its administrators? Did he discourage payment of taxes to Caesar? Moreover, if some of these events occurred, what was their significance to Jesus and his contemporaries?

One cannot prove that the Gospel accounts are historically reliable on all these points, but there is something to be said for them. They do explain how Jesus met his grisly end. If Jesus roused public anticipation, disrupted the goings-on in the temple, and spoke out against Jewish and Roman authorities—all during Passover week—it requires no great imagination to understand his execution. Jesus was no innocent victim. He died on account of the things he did.

For simplicity's sake, I will follow the story as Mark tells it.[12] The first sign of trouble is called the triumphal entry, a tradition that occurs in all four canonical Gospels (Mark 11:1-11; Matt 21:1-11; Luke 19:28-40; John 12:12-19). In Mark's telling, the scene that breaks out is no accident. Jesus orchestrates it by sending ahead for a colt that has not yet been ridden.[13] As Jesus rides—processes, really—into Jerusalem, the crowds cover his path with their cloaks and with branches. What does

Jesus' procession mean to them? They see Jesus as the heir to David's throne, the Messiah who will deliver Israel from its oppressors.

> Hosanna! Blessed is the one who comes in the name of the Lord! Blessed is the coming reign of our ancestor David! Hosanna in the highest! (Matt 11:9-10)

WHAT IS A MESSIAH?

Many contemporary readers find themselves confused by the titles *Messiah* and *Christ*. In some respects they have every reason to be confused, as scholars still debate precisely what such terms connoted in Jesus' time. Moreover, whether Jesus actually promoted himself as a messiah or accepted that title from others remains a point of contention. It seems to me that most historians do not believe that Jesus promoted himself as a messiah, though some do. I am inclined to agree that he did, but I am not entirely confident myself.

However, it stands beyond doubt that Jesus' first-generation devotees regarded him as the Messiah/Christ. What would those terms have meant in that historical context? First, messiah and christ mean the same thing. Messiah derives from Hebrew and Aramaic, whereas christ is a Greek term. They both mean "anointed one." Although our primary sources for Jewish messianic interpretation hardly offer a single consistent picture, we might recall that Israel's kings were anointed for their sacred purpose. Consider Psalm 2:

> The kings of the earth set themselves,
> and the rulers take counsel together,
> against the LORD and his *anointed*. . . .
> I will tell you of the decree of the LORD:
> He said to me, "*You are my son;*
> today I have begotten you." (Psalm 2:2, 7 NRSV, emphasis mine)

We cannot know how many Jews in Jesus' day were anticipating a messiah or what they expected one to do. We do know that several popular messianic movements emerged during the decades

surrounding Jesus' career, some of which gained serious historical momentum. In each case of which we are aware, the messianic
claimant sought to deliver Israel from the hands of the Romans,
establishing a new age of independence and righteousness.[1] When
the Romans affixed the charge, "King of the Jews," to Jesus' cross,
they almost certainly had that sort of thing in mind. They saw Jesus
as a rebel, a would-be messiah who would reign over a restored
Israel.[2]

[1] See Richard A. Horsley, *Jesus and the Spiral of Violence: Popular Jewish Resistance in Roman Palestine* (Minneapolis: Fortress, 1993), 52–54.
[2] For a concise survey of contemporary scholarship on messianic expectation in Jesus' world, see James D. G. Dunn, *Jesus Remembered* (Grand Rapids: Eerdmans, 2003), 617–27.

How one escapes the conclusion that Jesus' entry feeds revolutionary expectations escapes me. Besides the crowd's reaction, consider
the donkey on which Jesus sits. In case we miss the point, Matthew,
who often explains Mark's subtle allusions to Scripture, spells it out
for us. The donkey evokes Zechariah 9:9, which announces the arrival
of Israel's king.[14] As Absalom, Mephibosheth, and Solomon attest, a
donkey procession amounts to a royal claim (2 Sam 18:9; 19:27; 1 Kgs
1:32-40).[15] Though triumphant and victorious, this king demonstrates
humility and accomplishes peace. "Rejoice greatly! Shout! Look!" the
prophet commands. Here comes the king!

Marcus J. Borg and John Dominic Crossan imagine Jesus' procession as one of two that occur on this same day. The other involves
Pontius Pilate's imperial procession, accompanied by thousands of troops
to keep order during the holiday. While Jesus enters from the east with
his unimpressive band of followers, Pilate leads imperial cavalry and
soldiers. The reign of God, versus the power of empire, that's how Borg
and Crossan see it. The "central conflict" that led to Jesus' execution.[16]

Jesus' entry into Jerusalem, as the Gospels portray it, is a counter-
imperial demonstration. It pits the peaceable reign of Jesus against the

unassailable power of Rome. Jesus, of course, cannot confront Rome's power directly. As the Book of Revelation asks, "Who is like the Beast, and who can fight against it?" (13:4). Nevertheless, he signals his intentions on this first day by marching into the city, invading its temple, scouting it out, and then leaving both temple and city for one evening (Mark 11:11).

Jesus' second Jerusalem initiative directly confronts the temple authorities (11:15-19). Mark's version of the story creates the impression that Jesus totally stops business in the temple for a time. He drives out everyone doing commerce in the temple, overturns the money changers' tables, and disrupts the selling of doves. Now the temple was an enormous complex, so that it is highly unlikely that Jesus' actions actually put a stop to temple commerce during Passover week. They amount not quite to a takeover of the temple, but to a public demonstration. Scholars have long understood that this action reveals a great deal about Jesus' mission and explains why the Romans and the temple authorities would want him dead.[17]

What did this dramatic demonstration mean? Mark has Jesus allude to Jeremiah 7:1-11. Among other things, that passage insists that people may not worship in the temple legitimately until they repent and treat one another justly. God's house, perverted to serve injustice, amounts to a "den of robbers." In short, Jesus' action condemns the temple as a site of exploitation. As Richard A. Horsley observes, "It is difficult to imagine how Mark could have presented a stronger portrayal of Jesus' opposition to and condemnation of the temple and high priests."[18]

Now the temple authorities surely would not have embraced Jesus' assessment of their institution. After all, it was their job to keep the temple system running smoothly, especially during a season such as Passover. It was necessary to provide currency exchange services. After all, the money available to many pilgrims had idolatrous images or mottoes. People could not reasonably carry doves over hundreds of miles. So the temple provided space for the purchase of sacrificial animals. Jesus has not only spoken out against the authorities. He has disrupted the legitimate, even necessary, functioning of the temple—and during Passover week! Worse, Mark says, Jesus has incited a crowd.

As we continue to read, we learn that Jesus is not simply calling for temple reform. He fundamentally opposes the temple. He looks forward to its destruction.[19] Jesus did not stand alone in his condemnation of the temple. Many Jews (we cannot know how many) regarded the temple authorities as fully corrupt. Their opinions varied. Some, like the members of the community that produced the Dead Sea Scrolls, thought the wrong people were in charge as priests and that they were performing their ritual obligations in the wrong way. Others resented the wealth that flowed into and through the temple, all of which had been drained from ordinary people. Still others saw the temple authorities as Roman lackeys, corrupted by pagan idolatry and imperial bloodlust.[20] To stand over against the temple would not have made Jesus unique. To stand over against the temple in Jerusalem at Passover time, however, would soon make him dead.

Several of Jesus' sayings confirm his condemnation of the temple and those who administered it. Mark describes the unfortunate fig tree that withers on Jesus' curse. The interesting thing about this story is how Mark weaves it into the narrative of Jesus in Jerusalem. This is one of Mark's standard compositional techniques, splitting one story so that it surrounds a related story. When he encounters the tree, Jesus is on his way to his temple demonstration (11:12-14). Hungry, but seeing no figs on the tree, he curses it: "May no one ever eat fruit from you again!" In case we are reading this story as merely involving a hungry Jesus, Mark astutely notes that, "it was not the season for figs." Jesus then abandons the tree for his temple action, returning later to find that the fig tree has withered (11:20-25).

Jesus' reaction is famous. If a person of faith says to "this mountain," "Be removed and cast into the sea," it will be done for him or her. Mark, like countless Christian preachers down the ages, applies this saying to the work of prayer. But it also features a deeper, directly political angle. "This mountain," in the context of Passover week, is not just a random conceptual mountain. One mountain dominates the terrain at the moment: the Temple Mount. Jesus is calling for the destruction of the temple.[21]

Mark has so crafted the story as to emphasize Jesus' opposition to the temple. The barren tree recalls the prophetic denunciation of Israel as a fruitless fig tree—an image too familiar for ancient audiences to miss (Isa 28:3-4; Jer 8:13; 24:1-10; 29:17; Hos 9:10, 16-17; Joel 1:7, 12; Mic 4:4; 7:1).[22] By inserting Jesus' temple action within the flow of the fig tree episode, Mark allows the one story to interpret the other. In cursing the fig tree, Jesus implicitly denounces the temple. Jesus further appeals to agricultural imagery in his parable of the vineyard tenants, in which the distant landowner destroys the tenants (Mark 12:1-12). The temple authorities immediately perceive "that against them he spoke the parable," and so desire to arrest Jesus. "Whoever says to this mountain. . . ."

Jesus' polemic against the temple authorities intensifies. We have already discussed the several controversy stories—concerning Jesus' authority, taxation (more later), the resurrection, the greatest command-ment, and David's son (Mark 11:27–12:37)—concluding with Jesus' warning concerning the authorities: "Watch out for the scribes!" (Mark 12:38-40). The culmination of this pattern is Jesus' notorious prediction of the temple's destruction (Mark 13:1-37). When his disciples mar-vel at the temple's stones and buildings, and they were by all accounts marvelous, he pronounces the institution's doom. "There will not be left here stone upon stone, which will not be thrown down" (Mark 13:2). This is the saying that resounds when the authorities accuse Jesus: "We heard him saying, 'I will destroy this temple made with hands. I will build another, not made with hands'" (Mark 14:58; see 15:29). When Jesus continues his denunciation, he positions his body to express his political position. He sits on the Mount of Olives, "opposite the temple" (Mark 13:3).

When we fully appreciate Jesus' conflict with, and condemnation of, the temple authorities, two particular passages leap off the page in a fresh light. Each has routinely been misinterpreted in popular Christian conversation, including countless sermons. The first involves paying taxes to Caesar (Mark 12:13-17). "They," meaning the temple author-ities, seek to trap Jesus by sending Pharisees and Herodians to ask whether it is legal to pay taxes to Caesar. This is no empty question.

For one thing, Mark tells us the authorities are trying to trap Jesus. For another, taxation posed a notorious hot topic in Jesus' day. Not long after his birth, in fact, a revolt had broken out—and been subsequently crushed—in response to a census conducted for taxation purposes (Josephus, *War* 2.118; *Antiquities* 18.23).[23] Moreover, Roman coins violated Jewish monotheistic sensibilities. They featured images of the emperor or the imperial gods, along with religious slogans. Jesus' opponents are trying to force him to take sides. Either he could affirm Roman taxation, effectively renouncing the spirit of the Passover celebration and losing all credibility with his followers, or he could denounce taxation, marking himself as a seditionist.

Interpreters who use Jesus' reply to legitimate a division between the political realm and the spiritual—"render to Caesar"—entirely pervert his point. First, Jesus calls his enemies to produce a coin. Doing so, he points out their hypocrisy. Why would they ask such a question, since their possession of the coin demonstrates they have already made their own answer? Moreover, their possession of the coin embarrasses them as purported leaders of the people, particularly at Passover time. As for Jesus himself, he carries no such coin.

Second, Jesus demands that his enemies acknowledge what is on the coin: Caesar's image and inscription. This action reveals the question's fundamental nature. It is a matter of loyalty. Like all coins, Roman coins amounted to propaganda. They advanced claims regarding who is really in charge.

Finally, there is Jesus' pronouncement: "The things that are Caesar's, repay to Caesar; and the things that are God's, to God." The context of this pronouncement shows its power. Jesus cannot say that one should not pay taxes to Rome. Doing so would sign his death warrant. Like countless persons confronted by the weight of imperial power, he finds another path. He turns the legal question into a theological question. What belongs to Caesar, and what belongs to God? Caesar, in Roman imperial propaganda, demands everything. Thus, the claims of Caesar conflict directly with the claims of God. When one truly accounts for what belongs to Caesar and what is due to God, what would be left over for Caesar?

Jesus has rejected Roman imperial taxation, but without saying something that amounts to treason. In fact, Luke places this accusation on the lips of the temple authorities. They tell Pilate, "We found this one perverting our people, forbidding people to pay taxes to Caesar, and proclaiming himself as king" (Luke 23:2).

One other story, usually misinterpreted, underscores Jesus' opposition to the temple. Mark relates the story of the poor widow, who places her final two copper coins into the temple treasury (12:41-44). Jesus, in the popular (mis)interpretation, praises her generosity in comparison to the rich people who have contributed larger amounts: "Truly I tell you, this poor widow has put in more than all those who are contributing to the treasury." By contributing all that she has, the interpretation goes, she demonstrates model generosity.

I wonder how we could imagine Jesus finding it a good thing for a vulnerable widow to empty her possessions for any religious purpose. Would we ever advise someone to do such a thing? Fortunately for those of us who admire Jesus, that is precisely *not* what Jesus does. Our major clue lies in how Mark situates this story. First, Mark squeaks the story between two passages distinctively hostile to the temple and those who run it. The first, Mark 12:38-40, is the "Watch out for the scribes!" admonition. But look what Jesus says about those nasty scoundrels: "They devour the households of widows and for a cover-up they make long public prayers!" The appeal to the oppression of widows links the two passages. The second, Mark 13:1-37, pronounces the temple's doom. How, one wonders, would Jesus praise giving to an institution that he condemns throughout the entire length of Mark 11–13? Mark's second way of situating the story involves where Jesus places himself. Just as Jesus sits "opposite the temple" when he pronounces its destruction, he sits down "opposite the treasury" when he observes people's contributions. His body positioning expresses his point of view.

We have been following Mark's story throughout because it provides one example of how early Christians remembered Jesus. In my view Mark reveals a little more clearly than the other Gospels how Jesus came to his horrific end. At the same time, the basic story is common to all the Gospels. Jesus did not die as an innocent victim. He did and said things at a particularly tense time and place that led the authorities to regard him as a threat to public order, if not a revolutionary. As Marcus Borg and John Dominic Crossan have it, "*Jesus went to the capital city of his people to confront Roman imperial power and religious collaboration with it*" (emphasis in the original).[24] He orchestrated a public demonstration and then disrupted temple proceedings with his dramatic temple action.[25] He continued his attacks against the temple and its authorities by means of his teaching, including his implicit criticism of paying tribute to Rome.

CONCLUSION

Why did Jesus die? What did he do to get himself killed?

The temple authorities' role makes some historical sense in the light of Jesus' actions. One might even say that in arresting and then executing Jesus they were just doing their job. The temple authorities had two major concerns. They had to administer Passover, and they had to keep the Romans at bay. If trouble broke out during the Passover season, then lots and lots of people could get hurt. It had happened before. This explains the famous statement attributed to Caiaphas in John's Gospel: "It is better for you for one man to die on behalf of the people than for the whole people to be destroyed" (11:49-50). Caiaphas probably never said any such thing, but the sentiment reflects the political reality.

For his part, Pilate also had two simple concerns: to keep order and thereby to collect revenue for Rome. Passover brought lots—and lots—of revenue into Jerusalem. Any disturbance, particularly one that might stir up a revolt, was bad business. I strongly doubt that Pilate agonized over Jesus' fate, as the Gospels suggest. But I do not doubt for a minute why he would send Jesus to the cross. "King of the Jews," that was Jesus' crime.

The Gospels relate Jesus' last week in two ways. First, Jesus died in the tradition of righteous victims. His enemies arrested him out of jealousy and fear, and in secrecy. They trumped up false charges, of which Pilate was suspicious. Jesus never directly threatened the local authorities or Roman imperial power. He was innocent.

Yet the traces of a second reality also animate the Gospel accounts. Jesus was crucified as a seditionist, under legitimate Roman authority, and for actions he actually committed. He created multiple public disturbances in Jerusalem at Passover time, and his teachings directly subverted loyalty to Israel's temple and Rome's imperial rule. Righteous though he was, the Gospels insist, he died on account of the things he did and said.

Taking the Gospels seriously requires us to rethink the image of Jesus as the innocent victim. The pietistic Jesus, the lamb led to the slaughter, the man who died because he loved "us" so much is largely alien to the passion accounts. Instead, Jesus stands in the line of martyrs and prophets, those killed on account of their faithful testimony. Early Christians remembered Jesus as a righteous victim, one crushed by imperial power for his resistance.

Interlude

THE SINLESS JESUS?

Hebrews 4:15 presents the classic statement of Jesus' sinlessness: "For we do not have a high priest who cannot sympathize with our weaknesses, but rather one who has been tempted in every respect just as we are—yet without sin." This confession hardly stands alone within the New Testament. Paul writes, "God made him who knew no sin to be sin on our behalf, in order that we might become the righteousness of God in him" (2 Cor 5:21). The First Epistle of Peter appeals to the example of Christ, "who did not sin, nor was deceit found in his mouth" (2:22). First John 3:5 confesses that Christ was revealed "so that he might take away sins, since there is no sin in him."

We might track all sorts of interpretive debates regarding these passages. Does Paul mean that Jesus never actually committed sin or simply that the incarnation required the heavenly Christ to enter into the sinful state of humankind? Is 1 Peter talking about Jesus' behavior during his arrest, trial, torture, and execution? Does 1 John imply not a claim that the flesh and blood, historical Jesus avoided sin entirely, but rather the confession that the heavenly Christ who became flesh and blood is free from sin? We could invest ourselves in these debates, but

I think the point will remain fairly clear: several New Testament documents presuppose Jesus' sinlessness.

Apparently Jesus' sinlessness did not pose a major issue for early Christian doctrine. Once the church had embraced Gentiles without requiring their conversion to Judaism, the question of Jesus Christ provoked the greatest controversies among early Christian groups. In particular, what does it mean to confess the divinity of the actual, flesh and blood human being? The raging debates related to this question did not produce a definitive statement of Jesus' sinlessness until the Council of Chalcedon in 451. Chalcedon draws on Hebrews 4:15 for its language: Jesus Christ is "coessential with us—the very same one—as to his humanity, being like us in every respect apart from sin."[1] Though Jesus' sinlessness enters the ecumenical creeds fairly late, there is strong evidence that many early Christians assumed it.[2]

What is at stake in this doctrine? The primary issues are the paired doctrines of soteriology and atonement, matters related to what qualifies Jesus Christ to bring salvation. Gregory of Nazianus (c. 329–389) put it in a nutshell: "What Christ did not assume, he cannot heal" (*Epistle* 101).[3] For Christ to bear divine salvation, orthodoxy reasons, he must be fully divine; for him to redeem humanity, he must also participate fully in the human condition. The doctrine of Jesus' sinlessness allows that, like all mortals, Jesus endured suffering, temptation, limitation; however, as God incarnate he did not (many would insist, he could not) commit sin or even desire sin. Should we concede even the tiniest crumb of sin in the person of Jesus, many say, we disqualify him as savior of humanity. His sinlessness is a theological necessity.

It is not my aim to refute the doctrine of Jesus' sinlessness. However, I will argue that this doctrine has some serious liabilities and that it perhaps exerts a harmful influence on contemporary communities of faith. My suggestion is this: let's ditch the language of Jesus' sinlessness and talk about his righteousness and faithfulness instead.[4]

Theoretical problems attend the doctrine of Jesus' sinlessness. First, perhaps it does not take sin seriously enough. We often think of sin in terms of wrong moral choices made by individuals. One imagines Elmer Fudd with an angel on one shoulder and a devil on the other.

But sin runs deeper than individual choices to basic patterns of human life, what theologians call "structural sin." I may not desire to harm someone else; nevertheless, I have been born into a position of relative privilege. My material comfort, my groceries, my transportation, all these things depend on patterns of global commerce and exploitation in which I hardly have a vote. Indeed, for the most part I am not even aware of them. Moreover, any measure of success I have enjoyed is in part a result of U.S. racism: throughout my life I have received all sorts of opportunities that my neighbors of color never touched. Again, I may not have chosen all of these privileges, yet I have participated in them. How could I not? In this sense, structural sin is endemic to human existence. One cannot eat, clothe oneself, or travel without implicating oneself in sin at this level. Even Jesus could not. The Gospels say Jesus traveled a great deal—on roads, I assume, built by slaves.

Insights into what Wolfhart Pannenberg calls "the anthropological radicality of sin" multiplied as the twentieth century witnessed one catastrophic war after another.[5] No one, not even a pacifist, can escape the sinfulness of war, and theologians have begun taking this into account. The notion of Jesus, a lone moral hero undefiled by the world around him, does not (I think) stand up to such a serious accounting of sin's pervasiveness. Yet we may find gospel even if, no matter how virtuous, Jesus could not have escaped sin in this radical sense. One might say that in Jesus Christ God has entered into the human condition, even to the point of enduring sin. As Karl Barth put it, Jesus "is identical with our nature under the conditions of the fall."[6] In this sense, Jesus participates in the fullness of human life—its bitterness and its sweetness. If Jesus overcomes sin, he does so not by avoiding it but by overcoming it through righteous, faithful obedience to God.

A second theoretical liability in the doctrine of Jesus' sinlessness involves the process of human development. Not only do children gain intellectual knowledge as they grow, but they also grow in moral understanding and personal psychological development. For example, we hold children accountable for disobeying their parents, yet some measure of defiance plays a necessary role in a person's journey toward self-differentiation and independence. Would not one expect a fully human Jesus to display a measure of moral growth from childhood into adulthood and even in adulthood?

One early Christian text, *The Infancy Gospel of Thomas*, dramatizes a process of moral growth in the child Jesus. No one takes this gospel seriously as a historical source for Jesus' childhood; it simply testifies that early along Christians were asking these kinds of questions. Capable of astonishing miracles, little Jesus forms live sparrows out of mud. But when he loses his temper he curses people who annoy him. He cripples one boy and kills another. Only as he matures does he restore some of the damage he's created. The remarkable thing? According to *Infancy Thomas* Jesus always possesses divine power and intellectual knowledge; it is moral development he needs. The *Infancy Gospel* builds on Luke 2:52, which notes that Jesus "increased in wisdom and in years." Fanciful as it is, *Infancy Gospel* calls our attention to the question of moral growth, even moral transgression, in the process of Jesus' maturation. Without the experience of moral growth, one cannot gain a complete appreciation for honesty, courage, or compassion. Again, if we want to suggest that Jesus experienced the fullness of the human condition, some moral growth would be part of the bargain.

Those two issues—the unavoidable character of structural sin and the problem of moral growth—represent topics for technical theologians. In my opinion, both considerations suggest that sinlessness may not represent the best way to describe Jesus. However, more pragmatic considerations also call us to explore other ways to conceive of Jesus' righteousness. If righteousness amounts to avoiding sin, what does righteousness mean in extreme human situations? Do not some situations call us beyond avoiding guilt to other levels of faithfulness?

In my first year of full time teaching, I was leading a class of first-year college students in a discussion of the Roman philosopher Seneca. We had a standing rule: on good weather days, we would meet outdoors in the college amphitheater. Our discussion had come to Seneca's famous maxim, "No evil can befall a good man." First-year students, all of them bright and most of them from backgrounds of privilege, were debating the merits of Seneca's argument. Is it true that, no matter what happens, virtuous persons will turn it into an opportunity for moral growth?

As we talked, I noticed a middle aged man walking back and forth around the amphitheater. This was a small college, and outsiders did not normally just walk around the campus. I discerned that this man was a visitor and that he was walking around so that he could eavesdrop on our discussion. At the end of class he approached me.

The man shared his story. He was a sniper for a law enforcement agency. After years of training, he had—just weeks before—fired his first shot in the line of duty. He watched his target die on the spot. This incident disturbed the man greatly, so naturally his colleagues sought to comfort him. After all, snipers only fire when their target poses an imminent threat; he had probably saved innocent lives. He had followed procedures. He had done his job perfectly.

Yet none of this had resolved the man's dilemma. It is bad for your soul to kill another person. A weekend off, counseling, a month off, nothing had brought peace to this man yet. And while his wife was doing business on campus, this man had happened by our discussion of Seneca. Was it possible to turn this horrific incident into a good thing? "No evil can befall a good man." Really?

I am sure others could supply more fitting stories than my story of this sniper, but it illustrates the point I want to make. Sometimes our circumstances force us between impossible choices. The man who visited my class faced a stark choice. He could simply perform his job by killing someone, or he could abandon his job while allowing that person the opportunity to harm others.

The German pastor, theologian, and martyr Dietrich Bonhoeffer reflected seriously on those times of crisis. Writing during the Nazi era, Bonhoeffer regarded the avoidance of sin an irresponsible passivity. In his *Ethics*, Bonhoeffer evaluated his age as one of stark moral choices, "the black storm-cloud and the brilliant lightning-flash." Nevertheless, evil had draped itself in the garments of virtue—order, patriotism, law, legitimacy—confusing moral discernment. To resist evil required one to commit crimes such as treason. "The man with a *conscience* fights a lonely battle against the overwhelming forces of inescapable situations which demand decisions," he writes. To cling to private virtue is to deceive oneself. Without tracking Bonhoeffer's entire argument, it boils down to this: moral rules provide insufficient guidance. One turns, ultimately, toward "the simple love of God": "Not fettered by principles, but bound by love for God, [one] has been set free from the problems and conflicts of ethical decision."[7]

Bonhoeffer would live out this vision. His faithfulness had wavered from time to time, as when he declined to conduct the funeral of his Jewish brother-in-law's father as a result of fear. He once refused an invitation to join the German resistance and then left Germany to teach at Union Theological Seminary in New York. Under the circumstances, both decisions were defensible, yet Bonhoeffer recognized what they really signified. Staying in New York only a month, Bonhoeffer returned to Germany and to the resistance. While he collaborated in ecumenical efforts to undermine the Nazi regime, he continued teaching and preaching underground. It is uncertain how much Bonhoeffer was involved in assassination plots against Hitler, but in 1943 he was arrested for conspiring to rescue Jews. Having spent time in various Nazi prisons, Dietrich Bonhoeffer was hanged on April 9, 1945.

How did Dietrich Bonhoeffer move from the principled pacifism he confessed before the Nazi Era to participation in a resistance movement that attempted Hitler's assassination? When Bonhoeffer writes that "ethical fanaticism" and "moral principles" fall short in the actual struggle to follow Christ, it seems he is moving toward a more radical sense of human responsibility in the face of great moral crises. He took on this responsibility fully, committing acts that were, evaluated according to theoretical ethics, both treasonous and sinful. And he recognized them as sin, requiring genuine repentance.[8]

Eventually Bonhoeffer envisioned where this radical moral evolution would proceed: a "world come of age," humankind living in full awareness of its own responsibility, unable to use "God"—or Satan, for that matter—as an excuse.[9] God does not pass rules that determine human behavior in the face of evil; rather, persons must pursue God's will despite ambiguous situations. In a world come of age, people imitate Christ by throwing themselves fully into the world, not retreating into an other-worldly innocence. History presents people with impossible moral situations. In 1943 he writes,

> One may ask whether there have ever before in human history been people with so little ground under their feet—people to whom every available alternative seemed equally intolerable, repugnant, and futile. . . .[10]

As a result, Bonhoeffer realized that a responsible person cannot completely escape implication in sin and guilt.

> Here and there people flee from the public altercation into the sanctuary of private virtuousness. But anyone who does this must shut his mouth and his eyes to the injustice around him. Only at the cost of self-deception can he keep himself pure from the contamination arising from responsible action.[11]

One may not so flee from responsible engagement with evil. One must value the necessary deed above a spotless conscience and reputation, abandon "fruitless principle" in favor of "fruitful compromise," and even consent to what is bad to avoid what is even worse. Ultimately, "the man of duty will end by having to pay his obligation even to the devil."[12]

Bonhoeffer's appreciation for the inescapability of sin extended even to Jesus. For one thing, Jesus, out of his love for other persons, does not concern himself with "being good," instead, he enters "the fellowship of the guilt of men. . . ."[13] Rather than being the sole exception to human guilt, Jesus enters fully into it. "As one who acts responsibly in . . . historical existence . . . Jesus becomes guilty."[14]

Bonhoeffer is not quite saying that Jesus committed sin. He shies away from that conclusion, maintaining that Jesus demonstrates his sinlessness by entering human guilt and taking it on himself. This is a difficult concept, but it means that Jesus' participation in the human condition does not exempt him from sin's effects. One might say that Jesus' righteousness consists not in an avoidance of guilt but in loving humanity in and through its guilt.

> Through Jesus Christ it becomes an essential part of rational action that the [one] who is without sin loves selflessly and for that reason incurs guilt.[15]

Bonhoeffer, then, attributed guilt to Jesus—but not sin. He found in Jesus the model for disciples who find themselves thrown into a murderous world and who must find the way to love in impossible contexts. Moral purity, in that context, is meaningless. No one can avoid guilt. Bonhoeffer begins to extend this insight to Jesus, but he seems to stop just short. I propose we press just a little farther.

I suggest our problem lies in the language we use. *Sinlessness* and *innocence* indicate the lack of something. They define Jesus' worth in what he did not do, what he did not possess. The problem is, sinlessness might not be the best way of talking about Jesus. We need active, positive language for Jesus. As Graham Neville observes,

> The notion of sinlessness may in fact be misleading. It would be better to use an alternative vocabulary, which emphasizes the total self-giving love in Jesus which struggles with the intractable ambiguities of decision, recognizing that there are seldom perfect solutions to real dilemmas.[16]

In addition to these theoretical considerations, Neville suggests a more practical concern. Confession of Jesus' sinlessness directs our attention to what Jesus did *not* do, how he avoided sin—as if that were possible. Instead, confession of Jesus' righteousness and faithfulness points us to what Jesus *did* do: he companioned sinners, confronted authorities, and brought healing to persons with all sorts of disabilities. These acts of righteousness and faithfulness led to Jesus' death, something the portrayal of an innocent Jesus cannot explain.

Perhaps Bonhoeffer is correct. Perhaps it is the case that Jesus took on human guilt but avoided sin. I have sketched my reservations concerning this view. However, an "innocent" Jesus does not overpower sin. A righteous Jesus does. The world needs less innocence and more righteousness.

Jesus' friendship with sinners reveals what is at stake. We might believe sin is contagious. Believing this, we avoid sin and seek refuge from it. On the contrary, Jesus believed sin was far less contagious than love, mercy, and justice. Rather than avoid sin and sinners, he cast himself into the mix. In this Jesus manifests his righteousness, as one who pursues the ways of God in a world that does otherwise. Whatever we think of the doctrine of Jesus' sinlessness, it does not help us understand Jesus' life. Or his example.

Chapter 6

THE SCANDAL(S) OF THE CROSS

*The theological reasoning of our time shows very clearly that the parti-
cular form of the death of Jesus, the man and the messiah, represents a
scandal which people would like to blunt, remove, or domesticate in any
way possible. We shall have to guarantee the truth of our theological
thinking at this point. Reflection on the harsh reality of crucifixion in
antiquity may help us to overcome the acute loss of reality which is to be
found so often in present theology and preaching.*

—Martin Hengel[1]

My maternal grandparents attended a small Missionary Baptist church
way up on Ayers Hill. If you do not know where Ayers Hill is, it is in
a community called Poplar Creek. You will not find Poplar Creek on a
map. Leighton, Alabama, is the nearest town, six miles away.

Every church service at my grandparents' church followed the classic revival pattern. There would be a prayer, familiar hymns in the shape
note tradition, more prayer, an offering, more singing, and then—this
was the center of the worship service—reading from the Bible followed
by a sermon.

I did not like the sermons. I cannot recall the topic of any of them,
but they all wound up the same way. Preachers came and went, but

the pattern held true. The preacher would grow increasingly animated, his voice rising near an angry shout, every grammatical phrase ending in the syllable "-uh" ("David came to regret that deed-uh"). Often the preacher would loosen his tie and remove his suit coat. Finally, always, the preacher would plead with all the lost and wandering souls to come to Jesus. And there I would sit, determined not to subject myself to public scrutiny by walking up the church aisle during the gospel invitation, doubly determined never to "surrender" to anyone, even Jesus.

This was my Mom's family church, and I strongly preferred the more genteel environment of the country Presbyterian church my Dad had attended with my Aunt Modine and Uncle Norman Summers. I preferred the prettier building, cushions on the pews, and the more classical hymn tradition. Most of all, I preferred a church service that felt less anguished and less angry. I never could figure out how to join that church because the services lacked an invitation, but I was interested. If I could avoid going to hell, I would rather do it without being yelled at or having to surrender to Jesus.

Many of the hymns, prayers, and sermons at my mother's family church revolved around Jesus' blood. "Are you washed in the blood of the Lamb?" "Precious blood." And so forth. Blood everywhere. More respectable churches like the one Uncle Norman and Aunt Modine attended downplayed the blood language. Even more so in the city churches, attended—I will not say filled—by people in nicer suits and dresses. I wonder why.

My own church tradition, the United Church of Christ, has largely eliminated blood language from its hymnal and book of worship. Many would explain this choice in theological terms. We do not regard God as a violent despot who demands blood to appease his—I am using "his" intentionally here—wrath. We do not believe Jesus' death amounted to an accounting transaction between God and humanity, that in God's ledger Jesus' suffering somehow makes up for the suffering we deserve.

I suspect there is another reason we avoid blood language. It is messy. Blood language clashes harshly with the gilt crosses in our sanctuaries and the pretty crosses with which we adorn ourselves. Blood language comes too close to the grisly realities of Jesus' death. Blood language makes us uncomfortable.

This chapter is about how Jesus died. The Gospels themselves refuse to go into detail concerning Jesus' suffering. I will follow their lead. Glorifying Jesus' suffering, as an end in itself, often attends poor theology. This chapter will not rehearse the sequence of beating, scourging, procession, and crucifixion. We will not dwell on the mechanics of crucifixion, the physical trauma Jesus likely endured, or what happened to Jesus' body. All these things are relevant, but our focus rests elsewhere.

Our purpose involves not Jesus' pain but the social significance of his crucifixion.[2] What did it mean for early Christians to follow as Lord someone who had been, as Paul puts it, "clearly set forth as crucified" before their very eyes (Gal 3:1)? What does the Epistle to the Hebrews have in view when it says Jesus "endured the cross, despising the shame" (12:2)? How did Jesus' earliest followers come to terms with what one scholar calls "his shameful ending"?[3]

A HORRIFIC PUNISHMENT

Josephus, the ancient chronicler of Jewish history who survived the first great revolt against Rome, saw many crucifixions (Life, 76). He called crucifixion a "most pitiable of deaths." So horrific was it, that the Romans once compelled an entire Jewish garrison to surrender simply by erecting a cross and threatening to hang one of their captured comrades on it (War 7.202-3).[4]

Crucifixion's most obvious horror involved the pain inflicted on its victims. The Romans did not invent the punishment, but as in other matters they inflicted it on a grand scale and with technological creativity. Indeed, our words cross and crucify derive from the Latin verb cruciare, to torture.[5] Ancient records vary with respect to how persons were affixed to their stakes. The Roman philosopher Seneca portrays a variety of crosses, some with the victims head down, some impaling the victims' through their genitals, and others stretching out the victims' arms (Dialogue 6.20.3).[6] Josephus records an instance in which Roman troops made sport of one band of captives, crucifying them in various ways to suit their own tastes and in such numbers that the Romans ran out of room for their crosses and crosses for the bodies (*War* 5.451).

There was a basic pattern, however, for Roman crucifixion. The condemned first suffered flogging. If able, he ordinarily carried the beam of his cross to the place of execution. He then would be affixed to the cross, sometimes with rope but usually by having nails driven through the wrists and ankles.[7] Because the organs remained intact, death usually resulted from asphyxiation, often requiring days or even weeks. In short, and without going into detail, ancient crucifixion was extraordinarily painful.

Yet the horrors of crucifixion did not reside only in the prospect of a painful death. The Romans designed crucifixion as a public form of execution, hanging up their victims just outside city walls and along major highways. As the Gospels have it, they crucified Jesus along with two other criminals in quite a public place. Mark (15:29) and Matthew (27:39) mention "those who passed by" mocking Jesus, whereas Luke (23:35) mentions the people who stood by watching.[8] John (19:20) simply locates the crucifixion "near the city," noting that many persons could read the inscription on Jesus' cross. We also note that Jesus was stripped of his clothing. Although we cannot know the precise circumstances of Jesus' crucifixion, the Gospels' public settings accord with what we know of Roman practices. Crucifixion, in John Dominic Crossan's famous phrase, was a form of "state terrorism," intended to shame its victims and intimidate the populace. Philo describes the torture and crucifixion of Jews in Alexandria (38 C.E.) within the context of public entertainment, celebrated by dancers, clowns, musicians, and theater (*In Flaccum* 84–85).[9] Crucified bodies amounted to public billboards, advertising, "This will happen to you, if you defy the imperial order." For example, when the emperor Nero blamed Christians for the great fire that swept Rome in 64 C.E., he used them as public amusement. Some he fed to the beasts, and some he crucified, using their crucified bodies as torches to light the roads (Tacitus, *Annales* 15.44).[10] Thus we understand what the Epistle to the Hebrews has in view when it describes "the shame" of crucifixion (12:2).

Perhaps worst of all, victims normally hung on the cross beyond their deaths, leaving nothing for their relatives to bury. The satirist Juvenal depicts the vulture hurrying among dead cattle and dogs — and crosses (*Satires* 14.77–78), whereas Horace alludes to "feeding the crow" (*Epistles* 1.16.48) and Suetonius relates Augustus' threat to let the birds settle the matter of a captive's burial (*Augustus* 13.1-2). John Dominic Crossan and Jeffrey L. Reed make the point directly.

> Without minimizing the extended and excruciating pain, which was temporal, the shame of nonburial, which was eternal, was equally feared. In the ancient mind, the supreme horror of crucifixion was to lose public mourning, to forfeit proper burial, to lie separate from one's ancestors forever, and to have no place where bones remained, spirits hovered, and descendants came to eat with the dead.[11]

The Romans counted crucifixion, along with burning at the stake and dismemberment by wild beasts in the arena, among the three ultimate forms of capital punishment. All three punishments involved extraordinary pain, along with another common denominator: no remains left for burial.[12]

Ancient crucifixion, then, posed several and specific horrors. The word Crossan and Reed choose to describe the pain involved, *excruciating*, of course derives from the Latin, *crux*, or cross. That pain was accompanied by public humiliation, including a public procession, a prominent location, and exposure of one's naked body. And perhaps just as horrific, the prospect of death without proper burial brought both shame and eternal fear. No wonder Paul describes Jesus' death as "cursed" (Gal 3:13), appealing to Deuteronomy 21:23: "for the curse of God lies upon one who is hung up" on a tree.[13]

THE ROMAN PURPOSE OF CRUCIFIXION

The Romans crucified thousands upon thousands of victims, including many thousand Jews. Yet brutal as they were, even the Romans shuddered at the prospect of crucifixion.

One can scarcely improve on Martin Hengel's account of crucifixion in the ancient world, on which this discussion largely depends. Cicero described crucifixion as "the supreme penalty" (*In Verrem* 2.5.168), whereas others listed it above burning and death at the hands of wild beasts.[14] So hideous was the prospect that the word *crux* functioned as a curse, along with "Crossbar Boys" and "Food for Crows."[15] Hengel cites several Roman authors who attribute crucifixion to barbarism or criticize it as an undue cruelty, concluding that, "the Roman world was largely unanimous that crucifixion was a horrific, disgusting business."[16] So why did they do it?

A couple of features justify Crossan's assessment that crucifixion amounted to state-sponsored terrorism: the location of the deed and the persons subject to it. As we have seen, crucifixions were public affairs, located in prominent spots and drawn out over time. Unlike modern societies, historically most societies have inflicted punishment publicly in order to deter potential offenders.[17] In that sense the Romans differed little from everyone else. They used crucifixion for intimidation.

> Whenever we crucify the condemned, the most crowded roads are chosen, where the most people can see and be moved by this terror. For penalties relate not so much to retribution as to their exemplary effect. (Pseudo-Quintilian, *Declamations* 274)[18]

The persons subjected to crucifixion also inform us. Mark (15:27) and Matthew (27:38, 44) record Jesus' crucifixion between two bandits (*lēstai* in Greek). Luke calls the two "criminals" (*kakourgoi*, 23:32-33), whereas John simply names them as "two others" (19:18). Recent scholarship has challenged the conventional view that Jesus' two companions were common thugs, simple evildoers. Instead, the Romans typically categorized seditionists as *latrones*, or bandits. Likewise, Josephus calls Jewish rebels after the great revolt *lēstai*.[19] Drawing on sociological research, John Dominic Crossan portrays these two "thieves" as social bandits, the type of criminals who emerge when societies are under imperial oppression and extreme economic distress. Like ordinary criminals, social bandits are criminals in the eyes of the authorities, yet they maintain the high regard of their peasant neighbors. We need not think of the virtuous and generous Robin Hood, yet social bandits often become "heroes, champions, avengers, fighters for justice, perhaps even leaders of liberation" among their peers.[20] As Richard A. Horsley describes them, bandits are "'prepolitical' and are not revolutionaries, though they can become such," yet "they do resist the dominant oppression."[21] Horsley relates occasions when local villages rallied to protect their bandits or followed their leadership. In one instance the Romans crucified the local peasants who collaborated with a bandit group.

> Felix took prisoner Eleazar [ben Dinai], the brigand chief, who for twenty years had ravaged the country, with many of his associates. . . . Of the brigands whom he crucified, and of the common people who were convicted of complicity with them and punished by him, the number was incalculable. (Josephus, *War* 2.253)[22]

The two bandits beside Jesus place him among the political losers, the troublemakers of his day.

Extremely rarely were Roman citizens subject to this penalty. In one legal case Cicero maintained, "the very word 'cross' should be removed not only from the person of a Roman citizen but from his thoughts, his eyes and his ears" (*Pro Rabirio* 16).[23] By and large, crucifixion applied to slaves and members of the lower classes, soldiers, rebels, and traitors.[24] In short, crucifixion was applied only to the rabble, and primarily to those who threatened public order. When we consider both where crucifixions took place and against whom, we perceive the grim torture's purpose—to protect public order through intimidation and shame. This accounts for the mode of Jesus' death.

SCANDAL: CRUCIFIXION TALK

Jesus died a shameful death. His earliest followers could not dodge this reality. We observe how they dealt with this problem especially in the letters of Paul but also scattered throughout early Christian literature. The most remarkable thing about it is, that the early Christians did not dodge this reality. Instead, they found ways to embrace it.

The book of Revelation never mentions the cross directly, yet it provides one of the most creative examples in which Christians turned Jesus' shameful death into a religious resource. At first Revelation introduces the risen Jesus in terms both glorious and fearsome. He first

appears looking like a (or the?) Son of Man, dazzling because his head
and hair are white as snow, his eyes like a fire-flame, and his face shin-
ing with all the intensity of the sun. His voice sounds first like a trum-
pet, then like crashing waters. Upon this vision, John the Seer falls at
Jesus' feet as if dead (1:12-17). No wonder. We next encounter Jesus
introduced as the "Lion" of Judah (5:5). Yet immediately Revelation
transforms this image. We see no lion but a Lamb "standing as if it had
been slaughtered" (5:6). From now on, the Lamb provides Revelation's
dominant image for Jesus.

Revelation's Lamb imagery boggles the imagination. It is no ordinary lamb, with its seven horns and seven eyes. It executes judgment
and exacts wrath on the earth's inhabitants (e.g., 6:1, 16). It takes a
bride (19:7-9; 21:9-27). It conquers its enemies (17:14). It receives worship (5:9-14; 7:9-17; 15:3-4) and a throne (22:1).

Yet for all its power and glory, Revelation's Lamb imagery calls special attention to Jesus' death. We receive reminders of the Lamb's victimization (13:8). The Lamb merits worship *because* it was slaughtered,
setting people free through its blood (5:9). In one arresting image, the
saints wash their garments in the Lamb's blood (7:14; 12:11). Revelation
takes the grim facts of Jesus' bloody death and transforms his shameful
victimization into the means of victory. Jesus, who died as a "faithful
witness" (1:5; 3:14), wins the final battle with the sword of his mouth
(see 1:16; 2:12, 16; 19:15, 21). Although I cannot agree with those interpreters who see Revelation's Jesus as nonviolent, I do agree with David
Barr. Barr claims it is "absolutely fundamental to the Apocalypse that
the violence through which Jesus is said to conquer evil is the violence
done to him."[25] Through the image of the Lamb, Revelation takes, even
emphasizes, the shocking nature of Jesus' death and transforms it into
the power of God.

We find the classic example of counterintuitive cross talk in Paul's
discussion of the "scandal" of the cross in 1 Corinthians 1:17–2:5. I will
consider this passage again in chapter 7, but for now let us focus on how
the cross figures into Paul's argument. In his introduction to this epistle
Paul recognizes—first among all their gifts—the Corinthians' gifted-
ness in "all speech and all knowledge" (1:5). In the first few lines of all

his letters, Paul routinely hints toward the major themes that concern him. And in Corinth, knowledge was both a gift and a problem. A huge, controversial problem.

Looking beyond our passage, 1:17–2:5, we see how "knowledge" has divided the Corinthians. Sectarian divisions are popping up in Corinth (1:11-17), and that is why Paul preaches "the cross of Christ" rather than "cleverness [or wisdom] of speech." Knowledge problems resurface in chapter 8, and to some degree they dominate the rest of the letter. Some Corinthian believers "know" that eating meat that has already been offered to pagan deities does not corrupt believers, and Paul agrees. Yet, knowledge ranks beneath consideration on Paul's ladder of virtues. If other believers stumble when some exercise their freedom, then "those who know" should forego this prerogative. One person's knowledge can ruin another. After all, Paul insists, "Knowledge puffs up, but love builds up" (8:1 NRSV).

Another divisive issue among the Corinthians involved the use of spiritual gifts. It seems some believers enjoyed demonstrating their spectacular gifts, particularly the mystical ability to speak in heavenly languages during the worship assembly. Once again, knowledge figures prominently in this struggle. When Paul lists the spiritual gifts distributed among the Corinthians, he begins with "the word of wisdom" and "the word of knowledge" (12:8). Seeking common ground, he insists that knowledge, along with speaking in tongues, prophetic powers, and great faith, amount to nothing without the presence of love to guide their use (13:2). He further points to the limits of human knowledge, which is only temporary and cannot comprehend the greatest mysteries (13:8-12). Knowledge is essential for Christian communication (14:6), but it is not the ultimate criterion.

Before we return to Paul's message of the cross, we should briefly note how his treatment of knowledge is transformed in 2 Corinthians, presumably written at a later stage of his ministry with the Corinthians.[26] There, Paul wants to emphasize the knowledge of God (2:14; 4:6; 10:5), celebrating knowledge among the Corinthians' spiritual gifts (6:6; 8:7). It seems Paul achieved some success—or at least thought he had—in that first Epistle to Corinth.

In 1 Corinthians 1:17-2:5, however, Paul struggles against the knowledge that divides believer from believer. His approach is totally countercultural. Paul proclaims the word of Jesus' grisly crucifixion, an image he employs four times in just these few lines.

1. Paul speaks the gospel, but not with cleverness of speech, lest the cross of Christ be emptied of its power (1:17).
2. The message of the cross is foolishness to those who are perishing, but the power of God for those who are being saved (1:18).
3. Although Jews desire signs and Greeks demonstrations of wisdom, or so Paul says, Paul preaches "Christ crucified," which offends Jews and stands as foolishness in Gentile eyes (1:22-23).
4. Rather than practicing eloquence, Paul determines "to know nothing among you except Jesus Christ, and him crucified."[27]

Modern readers readily notice Paul's contrast between "worldly wisdom" and the foolishness of the cross, but we scarcely appreciate the effect it must have created among first-generation believers. How could we? It is not that the Corinthians would have been surprised by Paul's insistence on the cross. Instead, Paul is calling them to remember the shock that attended their first hearing of the message. Paul's cross gospel was foolishness because it announced that God's salvation had come through a man condemned by the legal authorities and displayed on a cross for all to see.[28]

This gospel was indeed offensive because it forced a gruesome image on the imaginations of Paul's audiences. Paul's single-minded insistence on the cross required believers to reject the dominant values of their culture, trusting that the "power of God," demonstrated first through Christ's vulnerability and then through the resurrection, revealed itself in that most repulsive of deaths.

As he does in 1 Corinthians, Paul will appeal to the cross to counter struggles for power within other churches. The cross reminds believers of the value inherent even in those with whom they disagree. These are those "for whom Christ died" (Rom 14:15; 1 Cor 8:11). Twice in his Epistle to the Philippians Paul appeals to the cross as a model for living. He censures the "many" competing preachers who (he says) are out to serve themselves. This ethos marks them as "enemies of the cross of Christ" (3:18). And when counseling the Philippians to share a common mind, a common spirit, and a common purpose, Paul instructs the Philippians to adopt the example of Christ, who "humbled himself, becoming obedient [even] to the point of death, indeed [one feels a heavy pause in the Greek here] death on a cross" (2:8). Calling people to imitate the crucifixion—what an astonishing innovation in early Christian discourse!

Paul's cross gospel is not simply a rhetorical resource for straightening out misbehaving Christians. On the contrary, the cross provides perhaps the most basic metaphor for Paul's Jesus talk. Paul believed that believers mystically participated in the being of Christ. He characteristically referred to persons being "in Christ." This mystical union implied a spiritual transformation that took its effect through Christians' participation in both Jesus' cross and his resurrection. Paul applies this image to himself in Galatians 2:19-20. Calling the Galatians to rely on faith rather than law observance for their justification, Paul claims he has "died to the law." How? "I have been crucified with Christ, yet it is no longer I who live, but Christ lives in me" (Gal 2:19-20).

Paul's visual image—crucified with Christ—was surely designed for a measure of shock effect. Yet in his letter to the Romans Paul presses even farther, challenging his audience to envision their own participation in the crucifixion. Once again the question concerns Paul's law-free gospel. In saying believers need not observe the law in order to be justified before God, has Paul abandoned morality altogether? More precisely, how can Paul call Christians to live well, if he has abandoned the law? Paul blends several images here.[29] He begins by blending baptism, burial, death, and resurrection all in one sentence.

> Therefore we have been buried with him through baptism into death,
> so that just as Christ was raised from the dead through the glory of the
> Father, even so we too might walk in newness of life. (Rom 6:4)

Paul's logic, expressed not so much in argument as in word pictures, calls the believer to imagine herself as dead to one mode of life but raised to a new life. But how does one participate in this death? Paul forges ahead, adding two more word pictures, crucifixion and slavery.

> [We know] that our former self was crucified with Christ, in order that the body of sin might be destroyed with the result that we are no longer enslaved to sin. (6:6)

This is the most graphic move. Paul encourages his audience to feel revulsion toward their former mode of life, so he invokes crucifixion and slavery, two of the most powerfully repulsive pictures available to him. Anything crucified, even crucified with Christ, is repulsive. Thus, Paul encourages believers to repudiate their former lives for union with the risen Jesus. His argument depends in part on the scandalous nature of the cross.

Paul, then, appeals to the cross in creative ways to shape Christian behavior and identity. Because it was familiar to him, however, Paul never loses sight of the cross's horror. In a sometimes pleading, sometimes scolding letter to the Galatians, Paul expresses his astonishment that some Gentile believers have submitted to circumcision. "You were running well. Who hindered you from obeying the truth?" (5:7). Then, in a cryptic statement, he raises the stakes by appealing to the crucifixion.

> If I am still preaching circumcision, why am I still being persecuted? Accordingly, the scandal of the cross would be exhausted. (5:11)

What does the offense of the cross have to do with circumcision? Not much, I would imagine. But it has a great deal to do with Paul's persecution, which results from his circumcision-free message. By enduring persecution, Paul participates in the cross, identifying with Jesus' scandalous end.[30] No matter how Paul invokes the image of the cross, or for what purposes, it remains ugly, no less than a scandal.

THE CROSS AS EMBARRASSMENT

Why would Paul name the cross a "scandal," or an "embarrassment," as he does in 1 Corinthians 1:23 and Galatians 5:11? So far, I have considered the cross in its social and political context. Crucifixion aimed not merely to make victims suffer, but to humiliate them and intimidate a restless populace. The mere mention of the cross carried shock value. Now I will turn to another problem the cross posed for early Christian preachers like Paul: How would one proclaim as Lord someone whom the authorities had publicly condemned as a criminal and then executed in the most severe fashion? What sort of people would worship a condemned criminal? Jews might perceive an even more particular scandal, the death of the alleged Messiah by crucifixion.[31] There is substantial evidence that Christians heard these objections from both Jewish and Gentile neighbors.

Among Jews, the scandal resided in the message of a crucified messiah. This is true for two reasons. First, the concept of a suffering messiah was entirely foreign to Jewish sensibilities. We know only a little about Jewish messianic expectation in the first century. Some Jews clearly expected a divinely anointed leader to rally the people, drive out their oppressors, and establish a new era of peace and righteousness. However, we have no realistic idea how many Jews held such hopes or how importantly messianic expectations figured into their imaginations. The one sure thing is that no ancient Jewish texts express the expectation that a messiah would suffer, particularly at Gentile hands. The Gospels themselves testify to this reality by describing — in a variety of ways — the difficulty the disciples experience in trying to rectify Jesus' passion with his messianic identity. "But we were hoping that he was the one who was about to set Israel free" (Luke 24:21; see Mark 8:31-32 par. Matt 16:21-22; Mark 10:35-45 par. Matt 20:20-28; John 6:15). A crucified messiah made no sense.

Second, proclamation of the crucified messiah was dangerous business. First century Jews were highly sensitive regarding "deceivers" who might lead the people astray into sedition. These fears were grounded in hard experience, as several resistance movements emerged in the decades surrounding Jesus' career. All of them, particularly the two great revolts of 66–70 and 132–135 C.E., ended in calamity. Not only did many rebels lose their lives, but many innocent persons also died alongside them. In some cases, the leaders of these movements either claimed messianic status or fed into widespread messianic hopes. In any event, Paul names it just so (1 Cor 1:23): proclamation of Israel's crucified messiah made no sense to Jewish ears.

Within a few generations of Jesus' death, Christians found themselves accused of a host of crimes, including impiety (many refused to honor local and imperial deities), sedition (many also refused to honor the emperor and his shrines), sexual perversion (what *were* they doing in those secret meetings?), cannibalism (associated with eating Christ's flesh and drinking his blood), magic (perhaps related to healing practices), and the promotion of secret associations (which were banned by law). Their neighbors regarded Christian religion as a superstition, a deception, and an innovation. Rome was extremely suspicious of cultural innovation, largely as a result of excesses associated with the rapid growth of "new" and foreign religious movements.[32]

Jesus' crucifixion does not play a direct role in these accusations, but Roman writers sometimes refer to it when they mention Christians. Tacitus, describing Nero's persecution of Christians, traces the movement to "Christus," who suffered "the extreme penalty" under Pontius Pilate (*Annales*, 15.44). Christians were not Lucian's primary object, yet he noted how they worshiped a man who was crucified in Palestine for bringing a new cult into the world (*Peregrinus*, 11).[33]

Christians themselves understood that the message of the cross exposed their movement to ridicule. Our access to many Roman charges against Christians comes not from their authors but as they are related by early Christian writers. Apparently Christians were aware that the cross presented a problem for their public image. Justin Martyr, acutely sensitive to public opinion, writes,

> They say that our madness consists in the fact that we put a crucified man in second place after the unchangeable and eternal God,

the Creator of the world. (*Apology* I, 13.4, as translated in Hengel, *Crucifixion*, 1)

In his refutation of Celsus' influential invective against Christianity, Origen acknowledges the cross as a problem. Celsus maintains that if Jesus were as great as Christians say, he should have displayed his divinity by escaping the cross (*Contra Celsum* 2.68).[34] He further scorns Christian logic.

> Everywhere they speak in their writings of the tree of life and the resurrection of the flesh by the tree—I imagine because their master was nailed to a cross and was a carpenter by trade. So that if he had happened to be thrown off a cliff, or pushed into a pit, or suffocated by strangling, or if he had been a cobbler or stonemason or blacksmith, there would have been a cliff of life above the heavens, or a pit of resurrection, or a rope of immortality, or a blessed stone, or an iron of love, or a holy hide of leather. (*Contra Celsum* 6.34)[35]

In this instance Celsus does not disparage Christianity on the basis of the cross alone, at least not directly, but others do. Minucius Felix relates how one Roman accused Christians of everything from secret marks on their bodies, to incest, to worshiping the head of an ass and revering their priests' genitalia. Because Christians revere a criminal crucified "on the fatal wood of the cross," this author concludes, they deserve a similar fate. "They worship what they deserve" (Minucius Felix, *Octavius* 9.4). According to Augustine, Porphyry relates an oracle of Apollo to the effect that Christians worship a deluded god, justly condemned by the authorities and executed by the worst of deaths (*Civitas Dei* 19.23).[36] Their neighbors saw the cross as an embarrassment, and Christians knew it. This sensitivity endured for centuries. As Hengel puts it, the message of the cross ran counter to the political, social, and religious values held by educated people in that day.[37]

I wonder how much the shame of the cross contributed to the rejection of Jesus' crucifixion among many gnosis-oriented Christians.[38] Gnosis-oriented Christianity valued knowledge (*gnōsis* in Greek) as the path to salvation, revering Jesus as one who reveals saving truth, not for his death and resurrection.[39] The *Gospel of Thomas*, for example, mentions neither Jesus' death nor his resurrection. In the *First Apocalypse of James*, Jesus denies ever suffering at all (31).[40] Some gnosis-oriented texts dramatize the process by which the true Savior rejoices while another suffers on the cross. These not only deny but even ridicule the notion that Jesus actually died on a cross.[41]

Scholars conventionally attribute the gnostic rejection of Jesus' crucifixion to metaphysics. Because gnosis-oriented Christians regarded materiality as perishable and therefore despicable, the notion of a material savior—one who could die, no less—proved abhorrent in their eyes. This judgment is confirmed by sources such as *The Testimony of Truth*, which insists that Christians who think they share in Christ's death fail to grasp "who Christ is."[42] Yet we ought not neglect the cross itself as an obstacle, or scandal, preventing some Christians from accepting Jesus' death. The *Gnostic Apocalypse of Peter* (one of two apocalypses attributed to Peter) depicts the "living Jesus" laughing while his fleshly double is "put to shame"—the text emphasizes shame twice—on the cross (81–82).[43]

CONCLUSION

In chapter 5 I reflected on how early Christians accounted for Jesus' crucifixion. That is, what did Jesus do that provoked his execution by Roman authorities? I concluded that Jesus was crucified for understandable reasons. His actions not only suggested disloyalty toward Rome and its authorities in Judea, but they also created a potentially dangerous public disturbance.

This chapter examines Jesus' death from a different angle, the crucifixion as a problem for the early Christian movement. In contrast to the pretty crosses that adorn sanctuaries and necks today, the message of the cross posed a major obstacle for early Christian self-definition. Designed to humiliate its victims, crucifixion branded Jesus as a loser in the most severe terms: a low-life criminal or seditionist whose body wound up serving as Roman imperial propaganda. Association with the cross painted his early devotees with the same brush. Early Christians like Paul, however, did not avoid the cross. Instead, they developed creative ways of acknowledging its offensiveness while claiming its saving power. Nevertheless, as Christians knew they would, their neighbors took offense in the cross, employing it to ridicule the new movement.

Chapter 7

FLIRTING WITH RESPECTABILITY

The church I knew in my childhood no longer exists. That church was white, Southern, Protestant, and—most of all—respectable. Everybody who was anybody was a member of some church or another. School teachers would ask a kid where he or she went to church. To say of someone, "He's a good Christian man," made a high compliment. So mainstream was that Christianity that two denominations—Baptists of all stripes and Churches of Christ—made up the majority of the population. Because those churches regarded consumption of alcohol as a sin, I grew up in a "dry" county. As a result, I knew genuine bootleggers in my youth. Today, however, Lauderdale County, Alabama, is no longer dry; that church I once knew is gone.

   To this day that "respectable" church still dominates media images. Presidents of both parties show up in church from time to time. Movies and television shows still set family scenes within the context of the respectable church. Particularly poignant scenes in one movie, *Normal*, revolve around the tension between a church's claim to respectability and its inability to accommodate its lone transgendered member. Sitting in the back row with her daughters, he is denied the offering plate and then quietly asked to leave.

The church remains a relatively privileged institution. But that respectable white Protestant church no longer dominates the religious scene. If respectable white churches once represented the majority, they will not hold that privilege for long and their particular representations of Christianity will not define the religion, even in the United States. Rapidly growing Pentecostal Christianity, with its informal worship and outbursts of spiritual enthusiasm, transcends racial and ethnic lines and clashes mightily with the staid formality of most Presbyterian and Baptist churches. The respectable white mainline Protestant church, with its manicured lawns and late model sedans in the parking lot, holds a declining share of the religious market.

In the United States, white Christianity has never rested so easily with its privilege. U.S. Christianity has long struggled with its relationship to culture. Some Christians have always claimed consistency between the values of the church and those of the larger culture, whereas others have emphasized the tension between gospel and society. Even today, many insist that the "United States is a Christian nation," and seek to conform the social agenda to the church's agenda. In its very name, D. James Kennedy's Center for Reclaiming America for Christ reflects this sentiment. Although "there is a spiritual war raging in our culture right now,"[1] the culture's roots lie in a Christian heritage. Conversely, many Christian groups still employ the rhetoric that Christians are "in the world but not of it." This slogan reveals a different sensibility. Culture, by and large, is hostile to Christians. Indeed, faithful Christians should anticipate resistance. This less optimistic view of culture transcends denominational and political tendencies. It manifests itself in liberal Protestant Christians who oppose militarism and economic exploitation just as it does among conservative Baptists who decry the amount of sex and violence in the media. Although some Christians would identify their social identity in respectable terms, others emphasize the distance between themselves and "the world."

The values in question, to adapt language from sociology, are deviance and legitimacy. Societies develop mechanisms for creating a meaningful order. Those mutually reinforcing mechanisms create values and practices that are legitimate. Even to question such a "self-evident" value is to challenge the order of things, thus posing a threat to conventional wisdom. Those who emphasize a self-evident continuity between church values and cultural norms speak the language of legitimacy. Most who are more suspicious of society would never call themselves "deviant," yet their celebration of Christian distinctiveness leads in precisely that direction. The truth is, many Christians, including religious leaders, switch back and forth from legitimacy to deviance talk without seriously reflecting on the apparent contradiction.

For example, imagine the reaction to someone who works in a large office and does not acknowledge the value of private property. Leaving work on a cold day, he borrows a colleague's coat without asking permission. He frequently munches on other people's snacks. Even if this person freely shares his own things, he would immediately provoke hostility. If, in response, he denies the legitimacy of private property, people would totally fail to comprehend him or worse, they would see him as deviant, a threat to good social order. Yet in some societies this person's behavior would seem perfectly ordinary. What is perfectly legitimate in one society amounts to deviance in another.

Now when a group sees itself as deviating from the larger social order—or when its neighbors so perceive it—tension arises. Does the group continue in its deviance, building its own norms in direct opposition to the society in which it finds itself? Or does the group acknowledge its distinctiveness, emphasizing that it is different only in some respects but perfectly legitimate in others? Even if they differ in their responses, contemporary U.S. Christians negotiate these difficult issues on a routine basis. Some appeal to traditional values, claiming their values as the "true" or legitimate U.S. values. Others, although still seeing their values as "true," regard the larger society as sinful or deluded. They may seem deviant in the eyes of others, even as they hold to the legitimacy of their own norms and behaviors.[2]

Unlike Christians in the United States, second- and third-generation Christians did not enjoy cultural privilege or respectability, at least, not as a result of their religious profession. Yet their literature reflects a similar struggle. Should Jesus' followers seek cultural legitimacy, or should they rejoice in being different from the rest? Some early Christian documents favor one side, and some the other, but most documents reflect a tension between a desire to fit in safely and their core values. This chapter will look into the tension between seeming odd (deviance) and fitting in (legitimacy) in Luke and Acts, 1 Corinthians, and 1 Peter. We will briefly consider the book of Revelation, which stands out because it seems free from this tension.

THE GOSPEL OF LUKE AND THE BOOK OF ACTS

Composed by the same author, Luke portrays Jesus' career, whereas Acts narrates the expansion of the Jesus movement in its first few decades. With an explicit interest in the missionary progress of "the Way," Acts in particular must negotiate how Jesus' disciples relate to their neighbors. We might expect such a self-conscious pair of documents to put forth a clear program concerning Jesus' followers and their place in society, yet this is precisely one of the most contested areas in New Testament scholarship.[3] The balance between legitimacy and deviance in Luke and Acts is far from clear. In general, one might say that Luke presents a more deviant Jesus, whereas Acts emphasizes the early church's legitimacy. Even that claim, however, gives the impression that things are fairly simple. They are not.

Many interpreters find a "Great Reversal" in Luke and Acts. That is, Luke and Acts explicitly attribute a reversal of status between the rich and the poor and the powerful and the oppressed to Jesus' ministry. This theme surfaces even before Jesus' birth, as Mary sings:

> [God] has shown strength with his arm; he has scattered the proud in the thoughts of their hearts. He has brought down the powerful from their thrones, and lifted up the lowly; he has filled the hungry with good things, and sent the rich away empty. (1:51-53 NRSV)

When his parents present the infant Jesus in the temple, the righteous Simeon proclaims:

> This child is destined for the falling and the rising of many in Israel. (2:34 NRSV)

And when Jesus inaugurates his ministry in his hometown synagogue, he reads from the prophet Isaiah.

> The Spirit of the Lord is upon me, because he has anointed me to bring good news to the poor. He has sent me to proclaim release to the captives and recovery of sight to the blind, to let the oppressed go free, to proclaim the year of the Lord's favor. (4:18-19 NRSV)

Luke and Acts never get around to showing how Jesus accomplishes this revolutionary program. People remain poor and oppressed at the end of both books. Yet Luke's Gospel repeatedly returns to this theme. Many such passages occur only in Luke among the Gospels, which is an indicator that they represent Luke's distinctive concerns. The most stunning example of this pattern is the parable of the rich man and Lazarus (16:19-31). While the rich man enjoys a life of feasting, Lazarus wastes away outside the gates of the mansion. In one of Scripture's most poignant images, Lazarus' condition has so deteriorated that the dogs lick his sores while the rich man feasts. In the afterlife, however, Lazarus reclines in Abraham's bosom while the rich man is tormented in Hades. Perhaps it is going too far to translate this parable into a doctrine: in the afterlife rich people who fail to show compassion or do justice will all be condemned to torment. Nevertheless, it is hard to avoid the conclusion that the primary reason for their opposing fates lies in their economic differences and how the rich man deals with his wealth. Indeed, the parable merely confirms what Jesus has proclaimed previously: "Blessed are you who are poor, . . ." but "woe to you who are rich"; "Blessed are you who are hungry now, . . ." but "Woe to you who are full now" (6:20-26; see 12:16-21; 18:25).

The book of Acts takes a slightly different tack on the matter of reversal. The first cluster of Jesus followers in Jerusalem shares their possessions with one another, as each has need (2:44-45; 4:34-35). This pattern does not continue throughout the book, even though the community cares for its widows (6:1-6; and perhaps 9:36-43). Economics plays a more limited role in Acts, largely because Acts is committed to a different kind of reversal. Whereas Jesus and his ministry almost exclusively served Jewish populations in Galilee and Judea, after his death the movement will serve Gentiles and the participation of Jews will decrease (28:23-28; see 18:6). In Acts, reversal has more to do with the inclusion of Gentiles than with status and poverty.

In chapter 3, we saw how Luke emphasizes Jesus' companionship with sinners. Luke shares this theme with Matthew and Mark, yet several passages in Luke amplify it. There is the sinful woman who anoints Jesus' feet (7:36-50), the parables in Luke 15 that respond to criticism about the company Jesus keeps (15:1-2), Jesus' invitation to Zacchaeus (19:1-10), and his pardon of the thief on the cross (23:43). Again, however, Acts takes this fairly radical emphasis and touches it with an air of respectability. Although Luke's Jesus is notorious for his disreputable associates, Acts emphasizes the respectability of new converts to the Way. The most likely exceptions are Saul/Paul and the Ethiopian eunuch (8:26-39). Saul persecutes the church, but he does so out of his own zeal for righteousness. Luke reminds us that, before Paul's encounter with the risen Jesus, he was a Roman citizen, a righteous Jew, and a student of the prominent rabbi Gamaliel (22:3). And although eunuchs carried significant social stigma (see Deut 23:1), this particular eunuch carries both status (as an official of the Candace, queen of the Ethiopians) and religious zeal (as a pilgrim).

Otherwise, the converts in Acts are a fairly impressive lot. The first converts are drawn from people pious enough to make pilgrimage at Pentecost (2:1-42). These people have both the money and the desire to make a major trip to worship in Jerusalem. Dorcas devotes herself to good works and charity (9:36). Cornelius, the first Gentile convert, is "a devout man who fear[s] God," one who gives generously to the people and prays constantly (10:1-2). Lydia is already a "worshiper of God" when she opens her heart to the gospel (16:14-15). Crispus is an official of the synagogue in Corinth (18:8). Cornelius, Lydia, and Crispus all lead "households," indicating their relative affluence. Apollos the missionary was already well instructed in the Scriptures before his conversion (18:24). Although Jesus' followers in Luke win more scorn than admiration, the converts in Acts conform to a more respectable mold.[4]

On the matters of possessions and the people who participate in the Jesus movement, then, Acts follows a far more conventional path than does Luke's Gospel. Luke's Gospel presents several other dimensions of a deviant Jesus, some of which we have already encountered. For example, Jesus' pattern of itinerancy would have hardly enhanced the status of his movement. He has no home, takes no wife, and produces no progeny; by conventional standards he fails to contribute to society's material welfare. This image is common to the gospel stories. Yet only Luke spells out just how far this pattern removes Jesus' followers from traditional life obligations. Just as Jesus "sets his face" for his journey to Jerusalem, he encounters three potential disciples. The first promises to follow Jesus wherever he goes, but Jesus stings him with a rebuke: "Foxes have holes, and birds of the air have nests; but the Son of Man has nowhere to lay his head." Jesus commands the second, "Follow me." Yet when this candidate requests leave to bury his father, Jesus retorts: "Let the dead bury their own dead." And when the third candidate seeks to say farewell to his homefolk Jesus replies, "No one who puts a hand to the plow and turns back is fit for the kingdom of God" (Luke 9:57-62). These confrontations leave the impression that traditional values like household and kinship have no place in Jesus' company.

Luke also develops a distinctive presentation of Jesus' relationship to the political authorities. Luke takes pains to situate Jesus' birth during the registration for an imperial tax that forces even pregnant women to travel (2:1-2). Luke also names the imperial authorities in power in the period of Jesus' birth (1:5; 3:1-2), and a member of Herod Antipas' household supports Jesus' ministry (8:2-3). One might think Luke takes a relatively "soft" approach to Pilate and Herod Antipas. After all, Pilate agonizes more over Jesus' fate than he does in the other Gospels, whereas Luke does not tell the grisly story of how Herod murders John the Baptizer (see Luke 9:9). Yet Luke adds some material in which Herod and Pilate look like the tyrants they were. Luke alludes to a story that Pilate had mingled the blood of some Galileans with their sacrifices (13:1). This story cannot be verified, so one cannot know its full context, but it lends itself to the image of Pilate as a bloodthirsty tyrant. Luke also relates a rumor that Herod is looking to kill Jesus — along with Jesus' reply to "that fox" Herod that Jesus has no plans to suspend his activities (13:31-33). Luke is the only Gospel to describe an alliance between Herod and Pilate. Pilate, hoping to distance himself from Jesus' trial, hands Jesus over to Herod. Herod returns Jesus to Pilate, but only after beating and mocking his prisoner. Neither Pilate nor Herod has the integrity to handle the case on his own. That, and perhaps Herod's brutality, creates a friendship between Pilate and Herod (23:1-12).

Although Luke paints Pilate and Herod in unflattering tones, Roman authorities come off somewhat better in the book of Acts. Herod Agrippa I, son of Herod Antipas, claims divine status. As a result, an angel of the Lord causes his grisly death (12:1-4, 20-25). Otherwise, although Jewish religious officials and local magistrates come off poorly in Acts, high level political authorities fare much better. The proconsul Gallio resists a bloodthirsty crowd in Corinth (18:12-17). In Jerusalem, the Roman tribune Claudias Lysias gives Paul permission to address the crowd (21:37-40), acknowledges Paul's citizenship (22:22-29), and protects Paul from authorities and mobs in Jerusalem (22:10-35). Taken to Caesarea, Paul appears before the governor, Felix. Felix protects Paul and listens to him avidly, but he also hopes Paul will offer a bribe (24:22-26). Felix' successor Festus not only sends Paul along to the emperor but allows Paul an audience with Herod Agrippa II and Bernice. Apparently Festus and Agrippa agree that Paul is innocent and should go free, except that Paul has already appealed for an imperial hearing (25:1-26:32). In Rome Paul is allowed to live by himself with a soldier guarding him. The diverse behaviors of the Roman authorities implicitly model an ambiguous disposition toward the state. Acts presents not an oppositional stance toward the empire, as Luke seems to, but a more discriminating one. Some authorities are corrupt, but others are just. Nothing controversial there.

Luke's literary style is well suited for respectability. In many respects one does not need to know Greek to appreciate it. Both Luke and Acts begin with fairly literary prefaces — this is unique among the Gospels — that imitate the historical writing of the period. Luke routinely links his stories with the political powers of the day. This technique evokes historical prose, while it also portrays Jesus and his followers as significant players on the historical stage. In the book of Acts, Jesus' followers — especially Peter, Stephen, and Paul — are extremely eloquent. The disciples' effective speaking "amazes" the Jerusalem authorities (4:13). Likewise, Paul holds his own when he receives an invitation to speak on the Areopagus in Athens, the seat of philosophy (17:16-34). Commentators have long noted how the speeches of Peter, Stephen, and Paul are basically similar in style and content — not to mention that the Paul of Acts sounds nothing like Paul in his own letters! Luke develops his speeches not so much to teach us about Peter, Stephen, and Paul as to tell us something about Jesus' first followers. In this regard consider the advice from the Roman historiographer Lucian:

> If you have to introduce a character making a speech, let the content of it be, first, suitable to the speaker and the situation, secondly (like the rest of the book) as lucid as possible — though you do indeed have licence to be rhetorical here and to demonstrate your stylistic ingenuity. (*How to Write History* 58)[5]

Acts presents Peter, Stephen and Paul as eloquent speakers who, given a fair hearing, can convince the most respectable audiences. No wonder Agrippa II replies to Paul, "Would you persuade me to become a Christian so quickly?" (26:28).[6]

Another means by which Acts legitimates the church's respectability comes through its description of church procedures. Time after time, the early believers grapple with emergent problems. Nearly always they develop smooth institutional responses. Facing the perceived need to replace the traitor Judas among the Twelve, they pray and cast lots (1:15-26). The apostles manage the community's shared property (4:34). When one group complains about unfairness in the care of widows, the apostles choose seven respectable men ("men of good standing") to administer the problem (6:1-6). When Gentiles find their way into the new movement, church leaders deliberate in Jerusalem and find common ground (11:1-18; 15:1-21). Things do not always go smoothly. One couple tries to deceive the apostles concerning their contribution of property, and God strikes them dead (5:1-11). Paul and Barnabas separate over whether to include John Mark in their missionary team (15:36-41). Indeed, sometimes things do not work out as the apostles imagine they will. For example, they appoint the seven respectable men to do administration while they preach, but the next two major preaching acts in Acts are performed not by apostles but by Stephen and Philip, two of the seven.[7] Yet on the whole the processes in the early church are well ordered and respectable.

Finally, to take on a controversial subject, there is the matter of how Luke and Acts portray gender, particularly the status of women. Luke and Acts often receive credit for featuring more women than most biblical books. In fact, one of Luke's most common techniques is to complement stories involving men with stories featuring women.[8] More recently, feminist scholars have noticed that Luke may include women, but typically limits them to traditional roles. In Luke and Acts, women follow, serve, listen, and support. They do not preach, nor do they lead.[9] The most familiar text in this discussion is the story of Martha and Mary from Luke 10:38-42. Martha, distracted by much ministry (the Greek word is *diakonia*), complains that Mary sits at Jesus' feet and listens to Jesus' speech while she performs her less glamorous ministry alone. Jesus, however, praises Mary for "choosing the better part." Optimistic interpreters have insisted on the story's liberating potential. Jesus, they say, includes Mary among his disciples, those who listen to him, and he implicitly frees Martha from her work in the kitchen. Yet the story never says Martha is in the kitchen; it says she is doing ministry. And even if she is in the kitchen or in some similar domestic role, that is precisely where Martha as a woman does her ministry, Jesus is taking that away from her. Mary has chosen the "better part" by sitting in silence.

This less optimistic interpretation gains credibility in the larger flow of Luke and Acts. Luke does include women and their contributions. Sometimes the women demonstrate strength, solidarity, and initiative. The widow insists on justice (Luke 18:1-8), Dorcas develops a local industry and cares for widows (Acts 9:36-43), and Lydia opens her house to the missionaries (Acts 16:11-15). All of these are solid, conventional roles. Yet councils of men make all the decisions in Acts, and men do all the preaching. Luke and Acts emphasize the contributions of women, but they limit those contributions to respectable, non-threatening roles.[10]

Opponents of the "Way," Luke tells us, accused Paul and his companions of turning the world upside down (Acts 17:6). This is consistent with the beginning of Luke's Gospel, which introduces Jesus as an upside-downer, the agent of a great social reversal. Yet Luke and Acts, especially Acts, go to great lengths to present the Jesus movement as respectable. It converts respectable people, Jews and Gentiles. It finds orderly ways of resolving conflict. Even the Roman authorities, presented by leaders of the Way, acknowledge their innocence. Luke and Acts tiptoe the fine line between deviance and legitimacy.

1 CORINTHIANS

Paul's first Epistle to the Corinthians provides precious insight into the wild goings-on among the earliest churches. Writing some time after his tenure in Corinth, Paul tries to fix problems that have emerged since his departure. As Richard A. Horsely speculates, Paul was building "an international counter-imperial (alternative) society."[11] This mission implied a strategy of resocializing these fledgling communities, moving them to adopt values of egalitarianism and mutuality in a patriarchal, hierarchical society. Paul would naturally have anticipated that his new converts might resist these new values—or at least back away from them.[12]

So problems popped up in Corinth. Among them, divisions regarding people's allegiance to various missionaries—Paul included; debates concerning specific sexual practices, including celibacy; church members taking other church members to court; inappropriate behavior when the group gathered; and tensions between believers of higher and lower social status.

Paul's letter reveals a double-minded relationship to the larger society. Sometimes Paul appeals to the Corinthians' deviance by emphasizing their distinctiveness from social norms. In other cases he clings to legitimacy, particularly when he calls on social values such as honor and shame.

Apparently the Corinthian congregation included at least a few people of fairly high status and some of more humble circumstances. People have made much of Paul's famous line,

> not many of you were wise by human standards, not many were powerful, not many were of noble birth, (1:26 NRSV)

and taken that as proof that early Christianity flourished among the poor. However, "not many" people held high status in any ancient city. In other words, Paul's comment reveals not that the Corinthians were particularly humble. On the contrary, social diversity among the Corinthian Christians likely mirrored the diversity that prevailed among their neighbors.

Other aspects of 1 Corinthians attest to this diversity. Through her "people," a Corinthian woman named Chloe has sent word to Paul in Ephesus, a distance of about 236 miles (1:10). We cannot tell whether Chloe has sent her people just to communicate with Paul, or whether she had them communicate as they went about other business. Nor do we know whether Chloe's people are slaves, friends, or business associates. Yet apparently Chloe is a person of means because she has people through whom she can communicate by sea. On the other hand, some of the Corinthians are apparently quite poor. The Lord's Supper in the ancient church hardly resembles the scene in a modern church, where communicants receive a morsel—or a wafer—of bread and a sip of wine or juice. Instead, it is a real meal, a celebration of the gathered community. In Corinth, however, some of the more prosperous believers go on with their own meals, filling themselves and getting drunk while others go away hungry. Acknowledging how differences in status can lead to division in the church, Paul censures the Corinthians for humiliating "those who have nothing" (11:17-22).

Paul plays on this diversity by appealing largely to a deviant mentality. According to "the flesh," or conventional measures, "not many" of the Corinthians were wise, powerful, or "well born." As a result, "their" wisdom does not conform to worldly wisdom. Rather, God has chosen the foolish—that includes the Corinthians—in order to bring shame on the wise. Paul takes this model to its logical conclusion: God has chosen lowly things such as the Corinthian believers, and God's wisdom values do not conform to conventional wisdom. "Hasn't God made foolish the wisdom of the world?" (1:18-31). Ordinary people cannot discern the spiritual wisdom available to the "simple" Corinthian believers (2:14).

Bold talk, this. According to Paul, God's wisdom contradicts conventional wisdom, so much so that salvation comes through the crucifixion of a legitimately condemned criminal. If one takes Paul seriously, following Jesus makes for a dangerous folly. Jesus' way leads to condemnation.

Yet at other points social respectability seems to motivate Paul a great deal. We see this when he considers how the Corinthians appear in the eyes of their neighbors and when he employs the language of honor and shame. For example, Paul scolds the Corinthians because some believers are taking up their complaints against others in the public courts (6:1-8). Calling those outside the church the "unrighteous," Paul asks how can the church fail to identify qualified arbitrators among themselves, rather than air their dirty laundry before dirty people (see 6:9-11). Their behavior is "shameful," Paul says. One gets the impression Paul does not want to offer outsiders any reason to hold the churches in contempt.

Paul also considers how the Corinthian worship gatherings might influence others' opinions. To the modern eye, Corinthian gatherings must have been wild affairs with individual believers expressing their spiritual ecstasy in a variety of ways. This topic takes up a major portion of 1 Corinthians, from chapter 11 to 14. In particular, some would be speaking in tongues (mystical heavenly languages), whereas others were prophesying (speaking through divine inspiration). All this chattering, much of it unintelligible to ordinary persons, would be going on simultaneously. "If," Paul asks, "the whole church gathers and every-one speaks in tongues, and outsiders or unbelievers come in, will they not say that you are all crazy?" (14:23). However, the same unbelievers or outsiders might find themselves confronted by the divine presence if they hear intelligible prophecy. After all, how can an outsider say "Amen" to unintelligible babble, even babble inspired by the Holy Spirit (14:16)?

Gender and sexuality particularly arouse Paul's sense of propriety. In one instance Paul addresses "someone who has his father's wife" (5:1). The NRSV translates this as "a man is living with his father's wife," though the exact circumstances Paul has in mind are far from obvious. The source of Paul's objection to this situation is easier to dis-cern: the law clearly forbids uncovering the nakedness of one's father's woman or that of other women in one's family circle (Lev 18:7-19). Paul's objection transcends his Jewish background, however. "Even among the Gentiles" people do not act like this (5:1). So Paul does not stand alone in his disapproval. His primary concern is moral. Yet his appeal to Gentile morality also reveals that to some degree Paul is look-ing over his shoulder at the broader society.

Paul is not the only one concerned with sexuality. Among other things, the Corinthians have written to him concerning whether unmar-ried persons should marry, married persons should abstain from inter-course, widows should remarry, and believing persons should divorce their partners (1 Corinthians 7). In each case Paul's advice is fairly moderate. Generally persons should hold on to their present status because "God has called us to peace" (7:15). On occasion Paul offers exceptions, as for persons who cannot restrain themselves from passion unless they marry—Paul thinks marriage will eliminate passion!—for persons whose unbelieving spouses seek divorce, and for slaves who have the opportunity to gain their freedom (7:21-23). Nothing unusual there, except that on the matter of sexual relations within marriage Paul advocates mutuality rather than domination by the husband. Paul is not the only ancient thinker to take this position, but he is relatively progressive.

So it surprises us when Paul's concern over sexuality surfaces again in a discussion concerning worship. The question involves how women should appear when they pray or prophesy in church, and Paul's response stands among the most impenetrable passages of Scripture (11:2-16).[13] For one thing, it is not clear exactly what the issue is. It seems Paul wants women to wear veils when they pray or prophesy, but some verses speak to women's hairstyles. Even if we can agree that veils are at issue, Paul's logic apparently contradicts itself. Twice he appeals to men's authority over women.

> For every man Christ is the head, and the head for a woman is a man, and the head of Christ is God. (11:3; see 11:7-9)

Yet Paul seems to undermine this logic.

> However, neither woman is independent of man nor man independent of woman in the Lord, for just as woman [proceeds] from man, even so does man [proceed] through woman—at any rate, all things [proceed] from God. (11:11-12)

"Women should be silent"
—1 Corinthians 14:33b-36

One cannot discuss gender in 1 Corinthians without mentioning 1 Cor 14:33b-36, the notorious passage that says in part,

> women should be silent in the churches. For they are not permitted to speak, but should be subordinate, as the law also says. . . . For it is shameful for a woman to speak in church. (NRSV)

At first glance this passage appears to apply legitimatizing language to the question of women's vocal participation. Paul is worried about how things look to outsiders. It is shameful for women to speak. However, I agree with many scholars who do not believe these words represent Paul's voice. Some of the earliest surviving copies of 1 Corinthians place these verses not after verse 33 but after verse

40. This suggests that a copyist inserted verses 34-35, probably in the margins of the Epistle, early in the process of copying and passing it on. Then one or more copyists, thinking they were providing an accurate text, tried to fit them within the text itself.

Besides the manuscript evidence, there are good reasons for thinking this is so. First, Paul has just instructed women on what to wear while they are speaking in church (11:2-16). How could he then tell them to be silent? Second, if one skips verses 34-35, the transition from verse 33 to verse 36 and then to verse 37 moves more smoothly than if we include verses 34-35. (Try it!)

(14:32-33b) And the spirits of *prophets* are subject to the *prophets*, for God is a God not of disorder but of peace, as in all the churches of the saints. (14:36-37) What?! Did the word of God originate with you? Or are you the only ones it has reached? Anyone who claims to be a *prophet* . . . must acknowledge that what I am writing to you is a command of the Lord. (Emphasis mine)

In short, I believe we should not include 1 Cor 14:33b-36 in assessing Paul's concern for how Jesus people should relate to the larger world.

As tortuous as Paul's logic is, he also betrays a concern with appearances and respectability. Again the cultural logic of shame appears. Just as it is shameful for a man to pray or prophesy with his head covered—a common custom in Roman religion—it is shameful for a woman to do so without a veil (11:4-5). After all, "It is shameful for a woman to be shorn or shaved" (11:6). At the end of the passage, Paul returns to this cultural logic. It is not "proper" for a woman to pray uncovered (11:13). "Nature" itself shows that it's a "shame" for a man to wear long hair, while a woman's hair is her "glory" (11:14-15).

It seems Paul's concern regarding women's veils emerges at least as much from appearances as from (strictly) theological considerations. By appealing to propriety, honor, shame, and "nature," he invokes ancient

Mediterranean social convention. In public respectable women kept their hair up and covered. "Loose" women—women without proper social attachments—might unbind their hair. What might a visitor think, encountering Corinthian Christian women in states of spiritual ecstasy with uncovered heads? Hearing of it, what might outsiders say?

First Corinthians is an especially rich document for exploring how some early Christians negotiated their precarious identity. On the one hand, they celebrated their distinctiveness, their deviance as some might call it. Knowing they lacked conventional social status, they claimed a countercultural wisdom. Their divine wisdom contradicted worldly wisdom, so much so that worldly persons would either fail to understand or call it scandalous. On the other hand, the letter reveals quite a bit of anxiety concerning legitimacy. Sex and gender issues emerge at the forefront of those concerns, but Paul also sought to keep disputes among believers out of the public eye and to promote orderly public assemblies. Finding the proper balance between distinctiveness and respectability proved a major challenge in Corinth.

1 PETER

Few interpreters believe 1 Peter was actually penned by Peter, the apostle of Jesus. Instead, it emerges from a period some time in the latter third of the first century.[14] Although it does not address itself to a particular congregation of Christians, it addresses concerns such as impending persecution and alienation from the larger society. Like Luke and Acts, and like 1 Corinthians, 1 Peter dances along the edges that divide deviance from legitimacy. Because the "real Peter" probably did not write 1 Peter, the letter may or may not address a "real audience." We may, however, consider the letter's implied audience, the image of the audience we derive from reading 1 Peter.

First Peter makes much of Christians' exalted spiritual status. Their inheritance resides in heaven (1:4-5). So great is this heavenly promise that it evokes even the angels' curiosity (1:12)! Once living among ordinary, misguided mortals, now the believers comprise "a chosen race, a royal priesthood, a holy nation," the very people of God (2:9-10).

Yet the letter plays on the tension between this spiritual exaltation, to be fully realized in the future, and present alienation. While anticipating this heavenly inheritance, 1 Peter emphasizes its audience's present alienation from the rest of society through exile language. This conflict surfaces right from the letter's beginning (1:1-2), which addresses "the exiles of the diaspora" who are scattered around large areas of Asia Minor, what today we would call Turkey. The phrase, "exiles of the diaspora," may suggest a Jewish Christian audience, but 1 Peter 2:10 clearly indicates an audience composed of Gentiles. As dispersed exiles, these persons are not "home," even if they live within steps of their own birthplaces. Presumably their alienation largely results from their allegiance to Christ. In this light the audience's true spiritual status functions as a compensation. Aliens and exiles, perhaps, but chosen, destined, and sanctified by God.[15] As Reinhard Feldmeier writes, 1 Peter "interpret[s] this foreignness as a mark of the essence of being Christian."[16]

Like many who live as strangers in foreign lands, 1 Peter's implied audience must keep up appearances. The epistle exhorts them "as aliens and exiles" to avoid fleshly passions, particularly by keeping good conduct among their Gentile neighbors. It expresses a fear that these neighbors might slander Christians, hoping to counter these accusations through the believers' good deeds (2:11-12).[17]

At this point 1 Peter calls its audience to build a good reputation by upholding conventional social norms. This call takes up a lengthy section of the letter (2:11-3:7). The exiles should submit to every human authority, from the emperor down through local governors.

> Honor everyone. Love the community of believers. Fear God. Honor the emperor. (2:17)

Consistent with this affirmation of the status quo, 1 Peter exhorts household servants, probably slaves, to submit to their masters, even the most unfair (2:18-25). Horrific as it may sound to modern readers, the letter blesses those innocent servants who endure violence. Their suffering unites them with the suffering Jesus. "Likewise"—because wives were subordinate to men in the conventional social order—wives should submit to their husbands, hoping that their obedience may win the husbands to faith (3:1-7). Women should embody the classical virtue of humility, repudiating elaborate hairstyles, jewelry, and dress, whereas men should be considerate of their "weaker" wives.

Perhaps the author of 1 Peter sincerely endorses such conventional—indeed, oppressive—social values. Certainly the letter never brings them to criticism. At the same time, careful attention to the letter's arrangement shows that such submissive allegiance is tied to the fear of persecution. After all, this section on submission (2:13-3:7) follows immediately on the admonition to good conduct among the Gentiles in fear that they might speak evil of the "aliens and exiles" (2:11-12).

The larger flow of the letter intensifies this concern over appearances by invoking the fear of persecution. It seems 1 Peter's implied audience already has some experience with persecution. Early in the letter we hear of "suffering various tests" (1:6), and the letter's call for respectable behavior aims to mitigate that threat. Following soon after the submission section, we encounter the question, "Who is doing evil to you if you are zealous for what is good?" (3:14). Indeed, blessing attends those who suffer for righteousness' sake. The ultimate hope is that if believers do what is right, their persecutors will incur shame on themselves (3:13-22). In the meantime the persecuted ones participate in Jesus' own suffering. Similar logic occurs in 1 Peter 4:12-19 and 5:10. Thus, innocence in the face of persecution poses a pressing concern in 1 Peter. Perhaps that concern influences the degree of social conformity promoted by the letter.

We know little about persecution of the earliest Christians. Apart from Nero's notorious suppression of Christians after Rome's great fire in the year 64, no hard evidence exists for widespread persecution of Christians around the Mediterranean in the first century. Thus, we can only speculate about the nature and extent of the persecution reflected by 1 Peter—if there was any. On the other hand, concern regarding persecution is scattered throughout nearly all layers of the New Testament, from Paul through the Gospels, Acts, and Revelation. So when 1 Peter 4:12 suggests believers not be surprised by the "fiery temptation" coming on them, we judge that at least the letter reflects a high degree of tension with the larger society.[18]

On closer inspection, we see that 1 Peter is not entirely devoted to conformity. Beyond its emphasis on the audience as exiles and aliens, the letter repeatedly insists that its audience no longer conform to its previous ways. Those practices are "the former desires of [your] ignorance" (1:14), the "ineffectual conduct of [your] ancestors" (1:8), and "the intentions of the Gentiles," marked mainly by wild partying (4:3).[19]

Passages like these reflect what social scientists would call a sectarian outlook. Simply, a sect is a religious group that lives in a "relatively high state of tension with their environment."[20] The sect organizes a cognitive minority against its larger environment, interpreting its environment as unbelieving or even hostile.[21] Thus, although 1 Peter recognizes—even celebrates—the deviance of its audience, it also pursues social legitimacy by promoting conventional behavior. If that deportment does not win public admiration, at least it will serve believers well when they face persecution.

REVELATION

Luke and Acts, 1 Corinthians, and 1 Peter all attest to the tension early Christians faced. Celebrating their distinctiveness, they recognized how that virtue marked them as deviants within the larger society. As a result, they tried to balance their gospel-motivated deviance with a healthy dose of social legitimacy. All of these texts—Luke and Acts, 1 Corinthians, and 1 Peter—reflect these tensions. The book of Revelation, on the other hand, does not. It thoroughly rejects cultural accommodation in favor of a dramatically sectarian, or deviant, outlook.[22]

Revelation addresses itself to seven churches in Asia Minor, all located in what today we would call southwestern Turkey. The first three chapters of the book address those churches directly, whereas the body of the book, chapters 4–21, tells the story of John's mystical vision into the heavenly realms. Like the book of Daniel, the Bible's only other literary apocalypse, Revelation's visions address the specific historical circumstances of its audience.

Revelation's primary concern involves cultural conformity. In their day, Revelation's seven cities were famous for their loyalty to Rome. Ephesus, the metropolis of Asia Minor, housed a temple to the goddess Roma and Julius Caesar and a temple for Domitian.[23] Pergamum housed a temple to Rome and Augustus, whereas Smyrna erected one for Tiberius, Livia, and the Senate. These demonstrations of loyalty and gratitude were not imposed on the cities by Rome; instead, they provided a focus for civic pride. Indeed, provinces and cities in Asia Minor often competed for the privilege of hosting temples or festivals in honor of the emperors. Provinces, for example, would submit proposals to the Roman Senate, which would discuss them and confer a decision. As a province Asia hosted three imperial temples by the end of the first century.[24]

READING REVELATION HISTORICALLY

Revelation sets forth "what [has been] seen, what is, and what will occur after these things" (1:19). It narrates the fall of one world order, the defeat of the forces of evil, and the descent of the New Jerusalem, where death and mourning, crying and pain, will be absent. There is no denying that Revelation is a future-oriented book. Yet evil continues to ravage the world, and the New Jerusalem has yet to appear. For these reasons, many readers naturally interpret Revelation as a prediction of our future.

Revelation also engages the specific concerns of ancient Christian people. It directly addresses seven churches in ancient Asia Minor, and it speaks to their circumstances. It further says its vision involves things that would happen soon, a point it emphasizes both at the beginning and end of the book (1:1, 3; 22:6, 10). Read in its own historical context, it addresses the imperial realities of its own day. For these reasons, scholars interpret Revelation not as a prediction of *our* future but as an address to *ancient* Christian communities.

This is how we naturally interpret other New Testament literature, such as Paul's Epistles. Their present significance is tied to the ancient audiences and circumstances they addressed. Revelation may seem different because it is an apocalypse, a work of visionary literature. But Revelation is just one of many other ancient Jewish and Christian apocalypses. The canonical book of Daniel is one. Others include 1 Enoch, 2 and 3 Baruch, 4 Ezra, the Shepherd of Hermas, and the Apocalypse of Peter.[1] All of these works also addressed the historical circumstances in which they were written. Few modern readers would think to predict the future on the basis of those books, and scholars interpret Revelation accordingly.[2]

[1] Some early Christian communities treated 1 Enoch, Hermas, and the Apocalypse of Peter as Scripture.
[2] For popular presentations of Revelation's contemporary relevance, see Craig C. Hill, *In God's Time: The Bible and the Future* (Grand Rapids: Eerdmans, 2002); and Barbara Rossing, *The Rapture Exposed* (New York: Perseus/Westview, 2004).

Though Revelation is notorious for its bizarre images and symbols, almost all interpreters agree that two of them, the Beast and the Whore, refer to Roman imperial authority. Revelation's opposition to the Beast and the Whore takes up a big chunk of John's vision, dominating chapters 13–19. The Beast first emerges in chapter 13, whereas the Whore dominates the section from 17:1–19:5.

The Beast rises out of the sea to make war against God's people (13:1). It is conventional in Israel's Scriptures and in Jewish apocalyptic literature to depict Israel's enemies coming from across the sea (see esp. Dan 7:3 and 4 Ezra 11:1; also Isa 51:9-11; Ezek 29:3-5; 32:2-8; Jer 51:34-37).[25] The Beast's crowns suggest its power. In response to its might, the earth's inhabitants cry out, "Who is like the Beast, and who is able to fight against it?" (13:4). How eerily one contemporary think tank's agenda echoes the acclamation of the Beast.

The United States is the world's only superpower, combining preeminent military power, global technological leadership, and the world's largest economy. Moreover, America stands at the head of a system of alliances which includes the world's other leading democratic powers. At present the United States faces *no global rival*. America's grand strategy should aim to preserve and extend this advantageous position as far into the future as possible. (emphasis mine)[26]

Though we might say much about the Beast, for now we may focus on two other details.[27] First, the Beast receives its power from the Dragon, Satan, who supervises its activities (Rev 12:9; 13:4). In other words, Revelation associates Roman imperial power with the dominion of the devil. Second, the Beast receives worship from all the people of the earth (13:4, 12-15). This detail is aimed against the Roman imperial cult, in which provinces, cities, and people did actually devote themselves to Rome and its emperors. The imperial cults raised a direct challenge for monotheistic Christians. How could one demonstrate one's loyalty to one's empire and city without compromising one's commitment to the one true God? According to Revelation, the two values—loyalty to Rome and loyalty to the God of Jesus—are thoroughly incompatible. For this reason, the Beast makes war against God's people and conquers them.

One more thing about the Beast: the Whore rides on its back. Clothed in purple and scarlet, arrayed in gold, jewels, and pearls, the Whore rides onto the scene on the back of the Beast. She, like the Beast, persecutes the saints, intoxicating herself with their blood (17:6). This vision confirms our impression that Revelation's target is Rome: the Beast's seven heads represent seven mountains, and Rome was known then as it is now as the city on seven hills (17:9). The Whore adds nuance to Revelation's anti-Rome program by emphasizing Rome's political and cultural reach. All the rulers of the earth have visited her bed (18:9). All the merchants of the earth have gained wealth by means of her, selling luxury items such as precious metals, jewels, fine textiles, military goods, and even slaves (18:11-17). Likewise, all who do commerce on the sea depend on the Whore for their wealth (18:17-19). Together, the Beast and the Whore embody the whole imperial system—cultic propaganda, political integration, military might, and commercial exploitation. All these John rejects: "Come out from her, my people, lest you participate in her sins and receive some of her plagues" (18:4).

It is one thing to condemn the broader political and cultural climate, but Revelation presses even farther. Everyone outside John's faithful circle, all the "inhabitants of the earth," participate in the work of the Beast and the Whore (13:8-17; 17:2-8). They even contribute to the martyrdom of the saints (6:10; 11:10). As a result, they receive the full brunt of the coming judgment (3:10; 8:13). Still, they do not—or cannot—repent (9:20-21; 16:9-11). Revelation takes an absolutely negative view toward the larger society, describing all contact with it as soiling one's garments (3:4; 19:8)!

Why the overt hostility to the Roman imperial system and its populace? What is at stake for the churches Revelation addresses? Chapters 2 and 3 of Revelation provide some hints. Here we find individual letters from the risen Jesus to each of the seven churches, beginning with the church in Ephesus. Each letter addresses the particular circumstances of those churches, revealing diverse conditions and debates among and within them. For example, some of the churches have already experienced a measure of persecution (Smyrna, 2:8-11; Pergamum, 2:12-17; perhaps Ephesus, 2:1-7). Some churches are relatively well off (Laodicea, 3:14-22), whereas others are struggling (Smyrna; Philadelphia, 3:7-13). And while some churches are clearly demonstrating their faithfulness (Smyrna and Philadelphia), others are doing poorly (Sardis 3:1-6; Laodicea). Still others receive mixed reports (Ephesus; Pergamum; Thyatira, 3:18-29).[28]

Beyond the churches' diverse circumstances, the letters also reveal intramural conflict among Christians in the seven cities. John condemns four other competing Christian movements. He attacks false apostles (2:2) and "Balaam" (2:14), the "Nicolaitans" (2:6, 15), and "Jezebel" (2:20-24)—all of whom appear to be in cahoots with one another. The pseudonyms Balaam and Jezebel associate John's opponents with persons notorious for leading Israel into idolatry, whereas the Greek term *Nicolaitans* (conquerors of the people) is nearly synonymous with the Semitic *Baalam* (lord of the people). Revelation accuses Balaam, the Nicolaitans, and Jezebel with encouraging believers to eat idol meat and participate in prostitution. For most commentators, these charges boil down to one thing: cultural accommodation. Most meat available in the public markets or in private banquets had already been dedicated to one god or another, whereas the Jewish Scriptures frequently depict idolatry in terms of sexual crimes such as adultery or prostitution.

Siding with John, many commentators assume that John's opponents were false teachers. If we can imagine ourselves among John's audience, however, we might imagine things differently. Of course John takes on these teachers because he disagrees with them. But in doing so he gives away something else. Some of his Christian colleagues found Balaam, the Nicolaitans, and Jezebel persuasive. They, too, were Christian leaders, but their diagnosis of the cultural context conflicted with John's. Their arguments made sense to a few, some, or perhaps most of their fellow believers.

Revelation's polemic against these other Christian teachers revolves around an obvious but tremendously important question: To what degree may followers of Jesus participate in the trappings of pagan imperial culture? Revelation calls its audience to avoid all such contact, including the act of eating meat. To forego meat would effectively remove people from the larger flow of society. One could not participate in public festivals or private meals in the homes of friends. One could not even attend the banquets of one's trade guild, burial society, or other club. Apparently, John's opponents are promoting a more moderate strategy. But John will have nothing of it.

Ironically, the struggles of Revelation's audience resemble that of 1 Corinthians in some important respects. Both Revelation and 1 Corinthians indicate communities of diverse social status. Some persons are more prosperous than others. Moreover, the question of idol food proves divisive in both communities because the more prosperous ones have quite a bit at stake in the question of cultural accommodation. In 1 Corinthians (and Romans), Paul agrees with the more prosperous that what one eats does not defile a person. Paul also believes that association with one's pagan neighbors is a good thing (1 Cor 5:9-11). Revelation takes a more severe path. It despises social respectability in favor of absolute devotion, knowing that such practices will incur wrath from neighbors.

CONCLUSION

It must have been tough trying to forge an early Christian identity.

Luke and Acts, 1 Corinthians, 1 Peter, and Revelation all reflect an acute consciousness that Jesus' followers differ from their neighbors. They are deviants. They have turned the world upside down (Acts 17:6), their wisdom confounds the wisdom of the world (1 Cor 1:18-25; 2:12-15), they are aliens in a hostile culture (1 Pet 1:1-2; 2:11-12), and they must avoid pollution from their larger cultural system (Rev 3:4; 18:4).

Among these books, Revelation alone refuses to qualify this deviant identity by seeking a measure of social legitimacy. Luke and Acts place Jesus and his followers among prominent persons, who offer them praise. In 1 Corinthians, Paul agonizes concerning how the Corinthians' behavior—both in public and within the worshiping community—might look to outsiders. Facing the specter of persecution, 1 Peter advocates cultural conformity and admonishes believers to do nothing that might intensify public disapproval.

This tension between deviance and legitimacy, so prominent in these texts, continues to shape Christian discourse, especially in the United States. Whereas some Christians christen the United States a "Christian" nation, others insist that they must live "in the world but not of it." Ironically, we often find the same persons and groups promoting both of these apparently contradictory claims. The New Testament itself attests to this tension, celebrating Christian distinctiveness while seeking social legitimacy.

Chapter 8

PERSECUTED

The prospect of persecution appears in every major layer of the New Testament. From intense to modest levels of concern, we observe this preoccupation in all four Gospels, Acts, the letters of Paul, Hebrews, 1 Peter, the Johannine Epistles, and Revelation. Beyond the canon, it is attested in writings as diverse as 1 Clement, the Shepherd of Hermas, the Acts of Paul and Thecla, the letters of Ignatius of Antioch, the Ascension of Isaiah, and the Apocalypse of Peter. Persecution figured prominently in the imaginations of early Christians.

The problem is, almost all of our evidence for persecution for the hundred years after Jesus' death comes from Christian sources. Our Greco-Roman sources indicate no systematic, empire-wide persecution of Christians, certainly not on a scale that corresponds to the impression we get from the New Testament. Historians now judge that over the church's first three centuries, perhaps less than 1,000 Christians faced a martyr's end. For the first ten decades of the movement, we possess less evidence of persecution than we do for, say, the third and fourth centuries. We cannot find laws or official policies that discriminated against Christians directly. Thus, our best historical data do not match the picture sketched by the earliest Christian documents. We want to understand how the earliest Christians provoked enough hostility that their neighbors occasionally attacked them. If we want to know that, we have to look beyond the surface.

PERVASIVE VIBES

Every significant layer of the New Testament, along with numerous other early Christian texts, addresses the fear of persecution. The Synoptic Gospels—Matthew, Mark, and Luke—feature Jesus warning his disciples to expect persecution, including persecution from local Jewish communities and from the Gentile authorities, even from their own families.

> Now you watch yourselves. They will hand you over in councils; you will be beaten in synagogues; you will stand before governors and rulers for my sake as a testimony to them. But first the gospel must be proclaimed to all peoples. When they hand you over and bring you in, do not worry in advance concerning what you will say; rather, it will be given to you in that hour what you will say—for it will not be you speaking but the Holy Spirit. Then a brother will hand over his brother to death, and a father his child, and children will rise up against their parents and put them to death. You will be hated by everyone on account of my name; but the one who endures until the end, that one will be saved. (Mark 13:9-13; cf. Matt 24:9-14; Luke 21:12-19)

There are strong grounds for suspecting that this passage expresses the perceptions of some first- and second-generation Jesus followers. Jesus and his disciples were Jewish, but within decades the Jesus movement had grown increasingly Gentile in composition. This passage reflects an earlier moment in which Jesus' [Jewish] followers experienced conflict with their [Jewish] neighbors, in which [Jewish] authorities could determine their fate. It reflects a frequent emphasis in early Christian literature: opposition on account of Jesus' very name. Moreover, the passage occurs in Matthew and Luke because those Gospels draw much of their material from Mark. However, we also encounter similar words only in other passages from Matthew and Luke, suggesting that they circulated not only in Mark but in at least one other early source.[1]

> But when they bring you in to the synagogues and the rulers and their authorities, do not worry concerning how you will defend yourself or what you will say. For the Holy Spirit will teach you in that hour what you must say. (Luke 12:11-12)

> But when they hand you over, do not worry concerning what you will say. For it will be given to you in that hour what you will say. (Matt 10:19)

Paul's letters, the earliest Christian writings that survive today, reflect similar dynamics. He does not mention it in all his letters, but Paul explicitly acknowledges his own participation in the persecution of Jesus followers (Gal 1:13; Phil 3:6). He also notes his own suffering for the gospel, including this catalogue from 2 Corinthians.

> Are they servants of Christ? I speak foolishly. More so am I! In greater labors, in more imprisonments, in countless more beatings. Often near death. Five times I received from Jews forty lashes, minus one; three times I was beaten with a rod; once I was stoned. Three times I have been shipwrecked. For a day and a night I have been adrift at sea. In many journeys, in danger from rivers, in danger from bandits, in danger from my own people, in danger from Gentiles, in danger in the city, in danger in the desert, in danger at sea, in danger from false brothers. . . . (11:23-26)

Paul's list includes natural risks, bandits, and shipwreck. Elsewhere he mentions beatings, imprisonments, and riots (6:5). His catalogue also includes persecution from fellow Jews, from Gentiles, and—what do we make of this?—danger even from other Jesus people. In other letters, Paul alludes to his imprisonment (Rom 16:7; Phil 1:7-17; many instances in Philemon), once (Phil 1:13) clearly indicating imprisonment by Roman authorities. Paul also mentions the suffering one church has experienced at the hands of their Gentile neighbors, even as he mentions opposition from Jewish communities that hinders his Gentile mission (1 Thess 2:14-16).[2]

The book of Acts relates both to the Gospel of Luke and to Paul's letters. The same person authored both Luke and Acts, devoting about half of Acts to a sketch of Paul's ministry. Among several themes Acts develops, one of the most prominent is persecution. Some resistance results simply from the invocation of Jesus' name (4:17-18; 5:28, 40-41; 9:16; 21:13). Persecution can be a scourge on the Jesus people, as Acts narrates not only imprisonments and beatings but the outright martyrdoms of Stephen (6:8-8:1) and James the brother of John (12:1-5). Acts depicts Paul as both a perpetrator and a victim of this violence. At the same time, Acts portrays persecution as an unwelcome—and painful—blessing. Persecution calls attention to the movement. Perhaps more important, it contributes to the spread of the gospel. As Acts 8:4 puts it, after one period of persecution, "Therefore, those who were scattered went about proclaiming the word."

The Johannine literature places its own distinctive spin on relations with "the world." Though God loves the world, the world fails to comprehend God's revelation (John 3:16; 1:5, 10; 1 John 3:1; 5:19). More to the point, Jesus' followers know the world hates them and persecutes them (John 15:18-21; 17:14; 1 John 3:13). As in the Gospel of Mark and Acts, the world persecutes Jesus' followers on account of his name—simply as a result of their allegiance to him. Despite the world's animosity, however, the Johannine literature insists that Jesus' followers may "conquer" the world, even as Jesus has done (John 16:33; 1 John 4:4; 5:4-5).

Problems with the world suggest that Johannine Christianity's struggles extend beyond conflict between Jews who believe in Jesus and Jews who do not. However, a couple of passages also suggest alienation between the Johannine people and the larger Jewish community. Just before his death, Jesus warns that people will cast his followers out of synagogues, believing it a service to God even to kill them (John 16:2). When Jesus restores vision to a blind man, we hear that "the Jews" had determined to cast from the synagogue anyone who confessed Jesus as messiah (9:22). Indeed, John's language concerning "the Jews"—which is prominent throughout the Gospel—strongly suggests hostility between the (probably Jewish) followers of Jesus and their Jewish neighbors. In the Epistles of John, this tension with "the Jews" is absent, suggesting that the movement has moved entirely away from its Jewish roots. Clearly, tensions remain.[3]

Among the remaining New Testament literature, in chapter 7 we noted how heavily persecution weighs in 1 Peter. Addressing Christians as "exiles," "aliens," and "exiles" in the world (1:1; 2:11), 1 Peter exhorts them to behave admirably "among the Gentiles" (2:12) so as to minimize their exposure to the coming persecution (3:13-17; 4:12-16). Again we notice the theme of suffering "on account of the name of Christ" (4:14). We also notice something unique in the New Testament: the title "Christian" linked to the fear of persecution (4:16). (The term "Christian" occurs elsewhere only in Acts 11:26; 26:28.) First Peter indicates a concern that simply being identified as a Christian could expose believers to persecution from their Gentile neighbors.

When the Epistle to the Hebrews exhorts its audience to "hold fast" to their confession without wavering (10:23), one wonders how much the fear of persecution contributes to this concern. The letter warns against neglecting group assemblies, reminding believers of the dangers of slipping back into sin (10:25-31). It then reminds them of "earlier days" when they endured a "difficult struggle" that included reproach, persecution, imprisonment, and the confiscation of property (10:32-34). Hebrews does not warn that persecution will return to the audience, but it draws on their endurance through past persecution as a source of endurance (*hypomonē*) in the present (10:36). However, other passages suggest the potential that persecution may return. Hebrews draws on the example of Moses, who—a millennium before Jesus—suffered abuse for Christ (11:24-26). And it encourages believers to "go outside the camp" and participate in the same abuse Jesus endured (13:13).

Hebrews' account of past persecution is instructive. Although local, sporadic persecution could lead to abuse, violence, and the seizure of property, imprisonment required action on the part of the local authorities. As Craig R. Koester notes, Christians may have been subject to violence from their neighbors, yet it was they—and not those who assaulted them—who were imprisoned.[4]

We turn to the Epistle of James, where the references to persecution are ambiguous. For example, the letter begins by encouraging its audience to consider it all joy when they encounter testing of any kind (1:2). One could easily read this as general pastoral advice, perhaps even dangerous pastoral advice: no matter what hardships one faces, they all contribute to spiritual virtue (1:3-4). Yet two signs suggest that James has persecution, not general hard times, in view. First, the spiritual fruit produced by such hardships is endurance (*hypomonē*; cf. 5:11), a virtue attributed to the Jewish martyrs in 4 Maccabees (1:11; 7:22; 9:30; 17:4, 12).[5] The book of Revelation also employs *hypomonē* to indicate steadfast faithfulness in the face of cultural pressure (Rev 1:9; 2:2-3, 19; 3:10; 13:10; 14:12; Heb 10:36). Second, James further warns against double-mindedness (1:6-8). The Christian apocalypse Shepherd of Hermas specifically identifies the dangers of double-mindedness in the face of persecution (esp. 22:1-10; 23:4; see 6:7; 97:3). In this light, James 2:6 suggests opposition from beyond the church because rich persons both slander "the good name" by which believers are called and drag them into court. Clearly, one cannot argue that endurance and double-mindedness prove a preoccupation with persecution in James. The literary relationships between James, 4 Maccabees, Revelation, and Hermas will not bear that weight. They are suggestive, however. William F. Brosend, II offers similar arguments in *James and Jude*.[6] Luke Timothy Johnson has drawn particular attention to the relationships between James and 4 Maccabees and the Shepherd of Hermas, though to my knowledge Johnson does not draw the potential connection with persecution.[7] For these reasons I conclude that this epistle begins with advice concerning faithful response to persecution.

Finally, there is the book of Revelation. So prominent are Revelation's references to persecution that many interpreters have assumed the book must have been written in response to a serious outbreak of violence. More recent scholarship shows that Revelation may have been written in anticipation of persecution, not in response to a major crisis.

Revelation 6:9-11, for example envisions a host of martyrs—Revelation is the first Greek work to employ the word *martyrs* to denote persons who die for their faith—crying out for vengeance. At the same time, the passage points ahead toward future persecution, when even more would meet death. Likewise, Revelation explicitly names only one martyr, a man named Antipas (2:13). Nevertheless, conflict with the outside world simply dominates the Apocalypse. The Beast and the Whore, Revelation's twin icons of imperial evil, make war on the saints and drink their blood (13:7, 15; 17:6, 24). At a couple of points Revelation even appeals to memories of Nero, notorious as the first emperor to execute Christians.[8] At the local level, Revelation depicts conflict with neighboring non-Christian Jews, calling them the "synagogue of Satan" and accusing them of slandering the churches and perhaps fomenting persecution (2:9-10; 3:9).[9] However we evaluate the nature and extent of actual (as opposed to anticipated) persecution reflected in Revelation, a persecution mindset dominates the book.

This brief survey reveals how concern with persecution permeates the overwhelming majority of New Testament documents. This preoccupation extends beyond the New Testament to other early Christian documents. First Clement, perhaps written contemporaneously with some New Testament books, refers to the martyrdoms of Peter and Paul and persecution against "a great multitude of the elect" (6:1; LCL translation). First Clement may reflect an outbreak of persecution in Rome.[10] The Acts of Paul and Thecla, written perhaps by 150 C.E., portrays persecution as a result of Thecla's refusal to marry her betrothed and her public rebuke of another man who seeks to take her by force. Among early Christian apocalypses, the Shepherd of Hermas calls for courage and single-mindedness in the face of persecution, the Apocalypse of Peter envisions postmortem torture for those who hand over and persecute Christians, and the Ascension of Isaiah predicts Nero's return to persecute the church. Both Hermas and the Apocalypse of Peter offer hard news for Christians who fall away in the face of persecution. The *Apologies* of Justin, who earned the appellation Martyr in about 165, attempt to persuade the emperor and the senate that Christians are innocent of moral and religious crimes. Two ancient documents provide eyewitness martyrdom accounts. Around 110 C.E., Ignatius, the bishop of Antioch in Syria, was transported to Rome for his martyrdom. He wrote a series of letters to churches introduced to him along the way. His prayer that he might "be allowed to fight the beasts in Rome" (to the Ephesians 1:2) suggests awareness that some Christians have already met a similar end (12:2; see to the Romans 4:1-2; 5:2-3). In 156, Bishop Polycarp came before the proconsul as an "atheist"; the church in Smyrna published an account of his martyrdom. Clearly, persecution posed a major concern for the first three to five generations of Christians, though corroborating evidence is scarce at best.

I have surveyed a wide range of early Christian texts, all reflecting the threat of persecution. Some depict the persecution of Jewish followers of Jesus by other Jews, some perhaps the persecution of Jewish Christians by Gentiles, still others the persecution of Gentile Christians by their Gentile neighbors. Clearly, many Christians worried over how their neighbors might treat them.

Yet can we flip the script? Can we enter the minds of ancient persons and imagine, What motivated some people to single out Christians for persecution? What made persecution seem a sensible thing to do? Two things frustrate the historian in this respect. First, "external" evidence—accounts of persecution from outside the churches—is both rare and spotty. They do not confirm that sense that persecution was pervasive or intense during the first 100 or so years of the Jesus movement. Second, we have only two "inside views" of a persecutor's thoughts, leaving us guessing as to what motivated them to punish Christians. Paul is the sole author who records both persecuting Jesus people and then experiencing persecution as a Christian, but he does not explain *why* he persecuted the church. Our sole other primary source is Pliny the Younger, governor of Bithynia (a region in Asia Minor) in the early first century. On the basis of such slender evidence, one will have to work quite hard—and use some imagination—to guess how their neighbors regarded the first Christians.

JEWISH PERSECUTION AGAINST
JEWISH FOLLOWERS OF JESUS

I approach Jewish persecution against Jesus followers with sensitivity. History is filled with Christian persecution of Jews, often on the pretenses that "Jews killed Jesus" or that "the Jews rejected Jesus." Indeed, *some* Jews played a role in Jesus' death, and *some* Jews did persecute his early followers. However, blanket assessments about how Jews related to the Jesus movements are both historically misleading and ethically dangerous (to say the least). The traditional reconstruction often participates in anti-Semitic discourse. We find such reconstructions even in serious academic publications. Such accounts ultimately blame Jews for their aggressive resistance to Christianity, as if the issue were simply a matter of religious intolerance. It participates in the myth that a nonviolent Christianity emerged through conflict with a deadly Judaism. Clearly, such a reconstruction leaves little room for articulating a plausible motivation for Jewish resistance to the churches.

After all, the early Jesus movements emerged from within Judaism, not beyond it. The movement continued to attract Jews for many decades; in fact, it probably fared better among Jews than among Gentiles. Paul grieves that "The very thing Israel sought, it did not obtain" (Rom 11:7) and acknowledges Israel's "rejection" of the gospel (11:15), fully aware that his audience includes both Jewish and Gentile Christians.[11] As a result, most of the earliest documents from the Jesus movements are blissfully ignorant of a distinction between "Judaism" and "Christianity."[12] This applies even to texts that address Gentile audiences or acknowledge alienation between Jesus' followers and the synagogue.

Three considerations guide our approach. First, Jesus' earliest followers included many Jews who never understood themselves to have abandoned "Judaism" for "Christianity." Thus, we cannot speak simply of "Jews" and "Christians" as if those were distinct groups. Second, the Jesus movements attracted adherents from among both Jewish and Gentile circles. Thus, we have no room for the idea that "Jews" persecuted "Christians." Third, we must acknowledge that early followers of

Jesus, many of them Jewish, experienced persecution from other Jews. Our task is not to condemn "Jews" for persecuting "Christians," nor to explain away their motives, but to understand why it made sense to some Jews to suppress emerging Jesus movements.

Perhaps we glean insight from Paul, who provides our earliest literary source for Jewish persecution of Jesus followers.[13] Not only does Acts portray Paul as imprisoning and beating Jesus followers (8:3; 22:4, 19; 26:10), even participating as a consenting witness in Stephen's martyrdom, Paul himself mentions his persecution "of the church" when it serves his purposes to do so (1 Cor 15:9; Gal 1:13-14; Phil 3:6).[14]

Unfortunately, Paul does not explain his motives for this activity, nor does Acts. But he does offer a couple of clues. First, in two of the three passages in which Paul names his activity as a persecutor, Paul is actually boasting. Persecution is one of the activities that qualifies Paul as a faithful Jew (Gal 1:13-14; Phil 3:6).[15] Second, Philippians 3:6 explicitly links persecution with zeal in such a way as to suggest that Paul's religious zeal motivated him to participate in persecution: "as for zeal, a persecutor of the church." Galatians 1:13-14 also mentions both persecution and names Paul himself a Zealot, though it does not link the two explicitly as does Philippians 3:6.[16] Acts 22:3-4 makes the same association, linking Paul's zeal with persecution.

How would Paul's zeal compel him to track down members of the emergent Jesus movements? Some interpreters believe zeal functioned in ancient Judaism as a code word for a specific type of behavior. It indicated such complete devotion to the ways of Israel's God that zealous Jews employed violence against anyone, Jew or Gentile, who threatened what Paul calls "the traditions of my ancestors" (Gal 1:14). When Phineas the priest kills a man and his Midianite wife for transgressing the boundaries of Israel, he demonstrates zeal (Num 25:6-14). Elijah's zeal manifests itself when he brings about the execution of the prophets of Baal and Asherah (1 Kgs 19:10, 14). When a Jew worships at a pagan altar, zeal motivates Mattathias to kill him and a pagan military officer (1 Macc 2:24-26). The eminent Jewish scholar Philo of Alexandra, whose lifespan overlapped Paul's, describes "thousands . . . full of zeal for the laws, strictest guardians of the ancestral traditions, merciless to who do anything to subvert them" (*De specialibus legibus* 2.253, LCL). As N. T. Wright describes it, "for the first-century Jew 'zeal' was something you did with a knife."[17] We're guessing, of course, but the conjunction of zeal with violence against those who threaten Israel's faithfulness suggests that Paul's zeal involved the judgment that those who followed Jesus were somehow compromising the integrity and faithfulness of the Jewish community.[18]

Now we come to the hard part. What was it about early Christ followers that motivated Paul and some other Jews to oppose the movement with violence? We are talking about violence on the part of some Jews against other Jews who believed in Jesus. When discussing zeal and violence, perhaps a logically compelling reconstruction is more than we have a right to expect. Yet a simple judgment that "they were renegade Jews, leading Israel astray from true loyalty to the one true God" lacks the specificity we need.[19]

Explanations abound. Perhaps Paul regarded the confession of Jesus just theologically wrong and dangerous. Perhaps he regarded Jesus as a deceiver, whose followers would lead Israel astray. Perhaps he regarded the Jesus movements as compromising the Jewish law. Perhaps he opposed the inclusion of Gentiles in the Jesus movements or at least the terms of their inclusion. Perhaps, because Jesus died a convicted seditionist, Paul regarded the Christ followers a threat to Jewish security.[20] All of these explanations have liabilities. In my view, a less specific explanation provides adequate satisfaction. I think the Jesus followers threatened Jewish solidarity. Their confession of Jesus was divisive. Not only did the crucifixion scandalize the imagination, Jesus' followers insisted that the crucified Jesus was Israel's Messiah, that he demanded people's absolute loyalty. In a time when Jewish identity constantly bore the pressure of Roman hegemony and Hellenistic culture, anything less than a pure adherence to "the traditions of the ancestors" posed a threat. Perhaps that is enough. But it tells us precious little concerning how the Christ followers who were Jewish appeared in the eyes of their Jewish neighbors.

The common colonial environment in which Judaism and the Jesus movements interacted presents a plausible context in which persecution

might make sense. Roman imperialism placed minority Jewish communities under significant pressure from time to time and place to place.
Whereas Rome granted Jews exemption from the imperial cult and
military conscription, Jews were by no means secure in the imperial
cities. Twice Jews had been expelled from Rome during the past century, the Alexandrian riot of 38 C.E. revealed the potential dangers of
anti-Jewish sentiment, and the public suspicion of Jews could only
have worsened after the Jewish Revolt of 66–70. Suetonius records that
during Domitian's reign Roman authorities began to seek out persons of
Jewish identity who may not have made that identity public (*Domitian*
12.2), while Dio reports that Domitian executed members of the imperial household for adopting Jewish practices (*Roman History* 67.14.1-
2). Despite the Roman historians' bias against Domitian, their accounts
reveal the tenuous security of Jews in the empire. In short, although
many Gentiles were attracted to the synagogue, and although Jews in
Asia Minor apparently participated actively in public life, anti-Jewish
sentiment was also widely known and dangerous.[21]

One might imagine that such widespread pressure would cause
Jewish communities to monitor their boundaries closely. Any troublesome behavior by persons identifying themselves with Jewish communities posed a threat to those communities. And early followers of
Jesus likely represented just such a threat. Sharing a common deity and
common Scriptures, and competing for the legacy of Abraham, these
early churches could easily call negative attention to the synagogues.
And because they worshiped a failed Jewish king (i.e., a messiah),
the churches could be regarded as seditious. With porous boundaries
between churches and synagogues, this relative intimacy only increased
potential tensions.

In such a context, how might synagogue persons have created trouble for church persons? Two responses make sense, getting them out
and pointing them out. Paul's activities suggest the first response: that
Paul sought to drive out Jesus followers from within Jewish communities. So do those sayings of Jesus involving being brought before councils. No evidence suggests a concerted Jewish movement against the
churches during this period, but some of our early Christian material

suggests opposition on a local level in some places. As for the second response, our evidence for that is extremely limited, primarily to Acts and Revelation. Acts presents local Jewish persons stirring up conflict between the Jesus followers and their Gentile neighbors (13:48-52; 14:2-7, 19-20; 17:1-15; 18:12-17; and perhaps 20:3). Revelation accuses the "synagogue of Satan" with "slandering" the churches, making them vulnerable to persecution (2:9; 3:9). Acts and Revelation hardly constitute solid sources for understanding the behaviors of non-Christian Jews, much less their motives. Nevertheless, one can imagine why some Jews might point out early Jesus followers to their Gentile neighbors. With Jewish identity and security under constant cultural pressure and more than occasional hostility, the presence of a new, suspicious, and potentially subversive sect posed a genuine threat. One possible way to protect the boundaries and reputations of Jewish communities in particular cities would involve pointing out the distinctions between themselves and the Jesus movements.[22]

A PAGAN POINT OF VIEW

When Jesus people walked down the streets, the vast majority of their neighbors were pagans. That is, they worshiped many supernatural forces, including ancestral and household deities, local deities, empire-wide gods, and occasionally gods imported from other lands. For the most part, ancient people did not argue over which gods were better than others. On moving from one city to another, one might very well expect to leave behind old gods and worship new ones. For most people the point of religion was *Pietàs*, the appropriate service to the gods, which insured a harmonious relationship with the powerful forces of life. Religious competition was not the norm.

However, new religious movements aroused some suspicion. Such movements often came from far-flung regions, with little or no connection with the empire's traditional centers. In the eyes of some, foreign religious movements represented the low culture of the hinterlands, and as such, merited little respect. Frightened that secret societies might prove seditious or that foreign influence might undermine solidarity in the capital city, Rome often banned secret gatherings—even those that were not explicitly religious, but especially those that were. The same applied to professional astrologers and other deviant movements. Although some imported religions attracted many followers, most people remained ignorant of their practices and rituals, a situation that almost guaranteed suspicion and rumor. Those new movements that gathered in secret, created unusually strong bonds among their adherents, or developed sophisticated rituals of initiation atttracted particularly high levels of resentment.[23]

Unfortunately, we possess nearly no evidence concerning what ordinary pagans said about their Christian neighbors in the first ten decades after Jesus' career. Three reports from Roman sources do survive. Because they derive from elite sources, however, they offer little information concerning popular attitudes during the period.

Suetonius describes how in the year 49 C.E. the emperor Claudius expelled (some? all?) Jews from Rome resulting from constant disturbances instigated by Chrestus (*Claudius* 25). Suetonius is writing several decades after these events, of course, and it is not obvious he has Christians in view. Yet if this incident actually involves Christians, it tells us two things. First, Christians had already attracted the emperor's attention within twenty years of Jesus' death. And second, they made their first impression as troublemakers. Suetonius describes the movement as a "new and wicked [*maleficus*] superstition."[24] The word *maleficus*, translated wicked, conveys the connotation that early Christians participated in maleficent magic, though it may simply reflect diverse and unspecified accusations against Christians.[25]

Our second account derives from the historian Tacitus, whose literary activity precedes that of Suetonius by a few years (Annales 15.44). Tacitus reports that Nero blamed—and then tortured—Christians as the cause of Rome's devastating fire in the year 64 C.E. Describing Christians as "a class hated for their abominations," Tacitus points out that their founder had suffered "the extreme penalty" at Pilate's hands. He goes on to describe the Jesus movement as a "pernicious superstition" that had spread evil all the way from Judea to Rome and suggests that its adherents were "criminals" who deserved the brutal tortures Nero devised for them. Tacitus does not criticize Nero for punishing

Christians, only for doing so for the sake of political expediency and for torturing them to such a degree that they elicited public sympathy.

Because it is more detailed, Tacitus' account suggests just a little more information than does Suetonius'. Again, we see that Christians are known to the Roman populace and to the authorities. Whether or not people in Nero's day would have seen it as Tacitus does, he suggests that Christians would have been derided for adopting a "superstition," that is, an inferior religious import. And although we cannot achieve precision in understanding this, his account suggests that, in Nero's opinion if not in fact, it seemed plausible to accuse Christians of criminal activity.

Our third record relates events that occurred five decades after Nero's reign. Unlike Suetonius and Tacitus, however, they are primary sources, composed by participants in the events in question. Around the years 111 to 113, the Roman governor Pliny (the Younger) consulted the emperor Trajan concerning how to deal with anonymous accusations concerning Christians in Bithynia and Pontus, Roman provinces in modern day Turkey. (Pliny the Younger, *Letters* 10.96 and 10.97. These letters are widely available in translation, both in print and online.) Pliny's letter, together with Trajan's response, reveals a great deal about the status of Christians toward the close of the New Testament period.

Pliny writes because he has been confronted with anonymous accusations against Christians. Having never attended a trial of Christians, he is unsure how to proceed with their interrogation and punishment. His procedure has been simply to ask accused persons whether they were Christians. If they confessed this identity, he would ask them again and again, adding the threat of capital punishment.[26] A person who denied Christianity, confirming their denial by worshiping Trajan's image and the gods and by cursing Christ, would be acquitted. Because the accusations involve large numbers of people from all social stations, Pliny feels obliged to consult with the emperor. Trajan's reply essentially congratulates Pliny for his wisdom, though it insists that anonymous accusations ought never be acted on.

What can we learn from this correspondence? Though Pliny has never seen Christians tried, his letter demonstrates awareness that such events have taken place. Moreover, he and Trajan agree that worshiping the Roman gods is sufficient grounds for pardon or exoneration. However, one also gets the impression that Christians have become quite a nuisance in Bithynia. Not only have some been moved to publish an anonymous accusation, but the influence of Christians has adversely affected participation in local temples and festivals and in the trade for sacrificial animals.[27] Pliny affirms that Christians derive from every age and class (he mentions two female slaves as deacons), and that it has extended from urban to rural, even remote, locations. Pliny's report of their activities seems entirely innocent. They gather, they sing, they pledge to lead moral lives, and they eat. When Pliny forbade secret associations, they suspended their meetings. Nevertheless, Pliny describes them as a "distorted and excessive superstition," not to mention a contagious one.

The Christians' refusal to worship the imperial gods presented Pliny with a serious dilemma on two accounts. For one thing, people looked to the gods for blessing and security. That some persons opted out from participation in local religion—apparently with some measurable effect—placed the region at risk. The gods might withdraw their protection and beneficence; worse, they might even punish the inhabitants of the provinces. Pliny's concerns addressed not only "religion" but politics. By refusing to acknowledge the imperial gods, or more particularly to worship before the emperor's image, these Christians demonstrated disloyalty to Rome.[28] Not only were they deficient religiously, they were traitors.

Pliny seems ignorant of the more sensational charges faced by later generations of Christians. He ponders whether he should weigh punishment only for "the name" itself, or for the "crimes" associated with the name. This suggests that Pliny knows of some allegations weighed against Christians, yet he betrays no sense that they are guilty of anything in particular. Unfortunately, the nature and origin of those accusations is lost to us.

In one remarkable way Pliny's letter coincides with some early Christian references to persecution: "the name." Several New Testament documents mention "the name," or "my name" as the basis for persecution against Jesus' followers, suggesting that simply confessing to the Jesus movement mounted sufficient grounds for persecution.[29] One might explain away this pattern by suggesting that Christians interpreted their persecution as resulting simply from their allegiance to Jesus, while in fact their persecutors had other reasons. Yet Pliny mentions "the name" alone as a potential ground for prosecution. It seems that the mere confession of Jesus' name provoked persecution from a very early period—as far back as our sources will allow us to go.

In later decades, early Christians faced more specific charges. They ate flesh and drank blood; they committed lewd acts with one another; and they practiced magic. The accounts of Suetonius, Tacitus, and Pliny all suggest that some such charges were in the air in the movement's first few decades, yet none of these sources spell out the specific offenses Christians were supposed to commit. We recall 1 Peter's admonition that it is one thing to suffer while innocent, but entirely another to suffer for evil one has actually committed (3:13-22; 4:12-19; 5:10).

CONCLUSION

Within two centuries of Jesus' death all kinds of accusations flew through the air with Christians as their target. Cannibalism, incest, bizarre sexualized rituals, even animal abuse—you name it, people said it. By the fourth century Christians stood apart for their endurance of official persecution on an empire-wide scale. One easily imagines that similar accusations appeared in the movement's first hundred years, and perhaps they did, but no such evidence survives. Moreover, although local and sporadic persecution did break out from time to time and place to place, no empire-wide persecutions occurred during this period. Thus, we cannot assume that the wild charges weighed against Christians from the middle of the second century on apply to the first few generations. Yet we do know that even then Christians suffered at the hands of their neighbors. Why?

On what grounds did Jesus' earliest followers face persecution? According to one explanation, attested by Pliny and by Christians, they faced trouble simply on account of the name of Jesus. This should be no surprise because Jesus himself endured an execution of the most severe kind, a public shaming and a demonstration of his guilt. Moreover, Jesus was crucified as a seditionist, a threat to public order. His followers praised him with names that properly belonged to the emperor: lord, savior, and son of God were all applied to the emperors before their association with Jesus. In calling Jesus "Messiah" (or "Christ"), early Christians invoked a Jewish revolutionary motif. Identification with Jesus, a notorious rebel, likely posed sufficient grounds for persecution.

Early persecution included opposition from Jews outside the (at first Jewish) Jesus movements. We may only guess at their motives, but the precarious status of Jewish communities in the Roman world suggests one set of explanations. Whatever their "theological" differences concerning early Christian claims about Jesus' messianic identity or the resurrection, Jews outside the Jesus movements fully appreciated that association with a crucified rebel threatened their own communities. Moreover, as the Jesus movements grew and attracted Gentile adherents, they posed a threat to Jewish identity and Jewish security. By pushing out Jesus followers and pointing them out to local and imperial authorities, Jewish communities were maintaining their own social boundaries and securing themselves from outside suspicion.

And what of the local and imperial authorities themselves? Romans were suspicious of both imported religions and secret societies. Suetonius, Tacitus, and Pliny all regard emerging Christianity as a superstition, that is, an inferior and barbaric religious movement bad for society. Without accusing Christians of specific crimes, they do suggest that some accusations were in the air. Most of all, however, the early Christians rejected the common religious obligations acknowledged by everyone. As such, they posed a threat to both civic morale and public order. (Decades later, the Bishop Polycarp would be executed as an "atheist.")[30] Their impiety (a term Romans used to describe those who did not fulfill their religious obligations) extended to the point of treason, in that they refused to worship the imperial gods and the emperor himself.[31] In the eyes of their pagan neighbors, Christians suffered persecution because of their antisocial and treasonous behavior.

Epilogue

SINNERS IN THE LIFE OF THE CHURCH

This book traces several neglected aspects of early Christian identity. I begin by the troubling identification of "sinners." Social understandings of sin and sinners change over time in response to a variety of social stresses. From a sociological point of view, a sinner is a person who transgresses the norms of their own context. The first generations of Jesus' followers remembered him for identifying himself among sinners, sharing table with them, and appealing to them as heroes in some of his teachings. They recalled how people confronted Jesus with their social impurity, and how Jesus (even if reluctantly) crossed the boundaries that divided the pure from the impure. They described Jesus as a man who resisted the conventional expectations of men in his own day, and they experimented with appropriate gender roles in their own communities. They understood that Jesus met a public execution as a predictable consequence of his disruptive behavior, and they accepted that his crucifixion posed an obstacle or embarrassment for their own proclamation. As time passed, early Christian communities struggled to define their place in the world, often promoting respectable behavior even as they recognized their distinctiveness as "aliens and exiles" in the world (1 Pet 2:11). Nevertheless, we find persecution language scattered throughout early Christian literature, in part because Christians were considered disruptive of Jewish identity or subversive of Roman imperial values. In important ways, early Christians remembered Jesus and understood themselves as sinners, that is, people who stood outside the approved norms of their social contexts.

To engage these concepts in contemporary contexts requires us to exercise our imaginations. One helpful path leads us to story and film. One ought not to expect direct parallels to the social and religious dynamics explored in early Christian literature, yet critical moments—fictional or otherwise—provide resources to conceptualize some of the questions faced.

WHAT IS A SINNER?

Chapter 1 explores what it means to be a sinner. In a theological sense, one might say that all people are sinners; that is, we all do bad things or participate in unjust systems. Yet the Gospels describe only some persons, and not others, as sinners. We see this with the woman who anoints Jesus in Luke 7:36-50, when people recognize her as a sinner as soon as she enters the room. She provides an example of what it means to be a sinner in a sociological sense. How is it that societies come to label persons and groups as deviant in one way or another?

To illustrate this point, I will use selected scenes from the film *Stand By Me*, which is based on a Stephen King novel. The story line has four young men—boys just entering adolescence—who go on an overnight adventure. The boys smoke, cuss, play cards, and generally experiment with a variety of transgressive "adult" behaviors. Each of the boys has his own complicated life story, but we focus on their leader, Chris. He is cool and articulate, but he also lives with the stigma of being a "bad" kid, partly because his older brother is a notorious hoodlum.

Stand By Me reveals Chris' character as a leader. He rescues one of his friends. He reconciles differences. He takes risks first. You would never know Chris is vulnerable to anyone but his big brother. Camped out at night, however, Chris reveals his soul. He knows that he and his best friend, Gordie, will be separated in middle school. Gordie's bound for college, but no way Chris will get into the college track. Gordie tries to convince Chris that he can do the same work, but Chris retorts,

"They won't let me in. . . . It's the way people think of my family in this town. It's the way they think of me. Just one of those low-life Chambers kids."

When Gordie persists, "That's not true."

Chris replies, "Oh, it *is*. No one even asked me if I took the milk money that time. I just got a three-day vacation."

"*Did* you take it?"

"Yeah, I took it. You knew I took it. . . . Everyone knew I took it. . . . But maybe I was sorry, and I tried to give it back."

"You tried to give it back?"

"Maybe, just maybe—and maybe I took it to old lady Simons and told her, and all the money was there. But I still got a three-day vacation because it never showed up. And maybe the next week old lady Simons had a brand new skirt on when she came to school. . . . Yeah, so let's just say that I stole the milk money, but old lady Simons stole it back from me. Just suppose that I told this story. Me, Chris Chambers, kid brother to Eyeball Chambers. Do you think that anybody would have believed it?"

Chris' story illustrates the complicated relationship between labeling and deviance. Chris did steal the lunch money, thus living up to his bad reputation. In the public eye, that's who he is: "Me, Chris Chambers, kid brother to Eyeball Chambers." Stealing the lunch money hardly represents the whole of who Chris is, but in society's eyes that does not really matter.

FRIEND OF SINNERS

Chapter 2 traces how the Gospels depict Jesus befriending the sinners of his day, often joining them at table. Early Christians recalled how this practice identified Jesus with sinners in the eyes of his adversaries. Film offers an ideal medium for communicating the power of the table—to build walls or to build community. Likewise, films often establish friendships between persons who ought not be friends, in particular between insiders and outsiders. I find these motifs developed beautifully in the classic adaptation of Harper Lee's novel, *To Kill a Mockingbird*. The Finch family, Atticus and his children Jeb and his little sister Scout, supply the film's primary protagonists. In the highly stratified society of the Depression-era Deep South, Atticus, a single father and an attorney, honors everyone, regardless of race or class.

Early in the film, the audience encounters Walter Cunningham, a poor farmer who simply cannot pay his legal fees in cash. Instead, Cunningham pays in collards and hickory nuts, trying to deliver his goods without the shame of a face-to-face encounter with Atticus. Totally innocent of such things, Scout calls Atticus to meet Cunningham, who leaves after a brief exchange. On Cunningham's departure, Atticus suggests,

"Scout, next time, uh, next time Mr. Cunningham comes, you better not call me."
"I thought you'd want to thank him."
"Oh, I do. I think it embarrasses him to be thanked."

Poor Scout tries, but she still does not grasp the complicated social code. On the first day of school she attempts to explain to her teacher why Walter Cunningham Junior, lacks lunch money. This exchange leads to a playground fight, which ends only with Jeb's intervention. Demonstrating his more advanced awareness, Jeb shocks Scout by inviting Walter over for lunch. For his part, Walter so enjoys his lunch that he pours syrup over the entire plate. This astounds Scout, who begins — but just begins — to voice her scorn. Atticus calls her outside.

"Come out here. I want to talk to you. That boy is your company. If he wants to eat that tablecloth, you'll let him. If you can't act fit to eat like folks, you can just sit here and eat in the kitchen."

If Jeb demonstrates the power of the table to put an end to conflict, Atticus teaches Scout how the table can bridge the greatest social distances.

Mockingbird's plot turns primarily around the trial of Tom Robinson, a black man falsely accused of sexual assault on a white woman. Robinson has only the most remote chance of a fair trial, yet Atticus takes on his case. This decision poses a grave risk to Atticus. By making him the ally of a black man over against a white family, and by putting this conflict in the public eye, the Robinson case exposes Atticus to guilt by identification.

The film never dramatizes public scorn directed toward Atticus. If anything, his prestige rises during the trial, even when Robinson receives his inevitable conviction. Twice, however, Atticus does face the possibility of assault. In the first case, Bob Ewell, the alleged victim's father, confronts Atticus in the courthouse and challenges his intention to defend Tom Robinson. Later one night, Ewell finds Atticus outside the Robinsons' home and spits in Atticus' face. But Bob Ewell is a coward, and Atticus disregards his threat.

A greater threat materializes on the night scheduled for Tom Robinson's removal to a safer jail. Having heard about a plot to snatch Tom from the jail and lynch him, Atticus camps out at the jailhouse door. Meanwhile, Jeb, Scout, and their friend Dill trail Atticus to spy on him. The lynch mob indeed materializes, commanding Atticus to step aside. Here the threat is more than symbolic, but the children intervene. Again, Jeb discerns what is at stake, but it is Scout who turns the tide. Standing by Atticus' side, she spots Walter Cunningham, who hides beneath the brim of his hat.

"Hey, Mr. Cunningham.
He ignores her. "I said, Hey Mr. Cunningham."
Scout goes on to remind Mr. Cunningham of their previous encounter and of her friendship with Walter Junior. She forges ahead.
"I go to school with your boy. I go to school with Walter. He's a nice boy. Tell him 'hey' for me, won't you?"
Still he ignores her as she goes on, the mood growing intensely awkward. Scout finally acknowledges the tension, perhaps because she remembers Mr. Cunningham's social shame.

"What's the matter? I sure meant no harm, Mr. Cunningham."

Finally, an answer. "No harm taken, young lady. I tell Walter you said hey." Then, to the mob, "Let's clear outta here. Let's go, boys."

The twin trajectories of Walter Cunningham and Tom Robinson come together at this crucial moment. Atticus' fidelity to Tom instigates this grave threat. Guilty by association, Atticus possesses no guarantee of his own security. Who knows how things will turn out at the jail? Yet his previous act of table hospitality, embodied in the welcome Jeb extended to Walter Junior, has built a bond that Walter Senior—an outcast in his own right—cannot deny. The audience sees similar dynamics at play in early Christian memories of Jesus. His embrace of sinners effected reconciliation, although it also provided his enemies with one more excuse to despise him.

JESUS AND IMPURITY

Though many people credit Jesus with violating the purity codes of his society, in chapter 3 I maintain that is not exactly how early Christians told the story. Jesus himself does not violate the law in his interaction with impure persons. Moreover, the Gospels do not depict Jesus reaching out to lepers and Gentiles; rather, they come to him. Early Christians remembered Jesus for responding to impure persons and for overcoming impurity with the power of God's blessing.

We moderns do not experience purity issues in the same way as did ancient persons. When we hear the language of purity, instantly our imaginations gravitate toward what is morally or socially taboo. We do this in a couple of ways. In some circles we hear of sexual purity, which implies abstinence outside of marriage and the absence of lustful thoughts toward anyone besides one's spouse. More commonly, we think of behaviors that violate our sense of what is acceptable, sometimes with hygiene in mind. Here I recall the *Seinfeld* episode in which George is visiting a bookstore. Caught having taken a book into the men's room, he is forced to pay for the book. After all, who wants a book that has been to the toilet?

As we have seen, biblical purity does not correspond neatly to either notion of purity. Though biblical purity may involve morality, it often does not. Persons become impure through perfectly normal acts such as childbirth, seminal emission, and burial preparation. It generally has nothing to do with hygiene, either, or even with what is considered socially acceptable in a generic sense.

These cultural differences require an act of interpretive imagination for us to appropriate anything from early Christian stories about Jesus and purity. In chapter 3, I argued that according to most of the gospels Jesus does not transgress the law of Israel but he does contact impure persons. Moreover, I suggested that in most such encounters Jesus does not initiate these moments. Instead, his virtue consists mainly in his response to persons who confront him.

I have found the HBO film *Normal* extremely helpful in generating conversations about how contemporary groups might respond to people whose presence is met with aversion. In *Normal*, Roy (later Ruth) Applewood grapples with his sexual identity. He is, he says, a woman trapped in a man's body. Faithful church members, Roy and his wife Irma approach their pastor for marital counseling when Roy finally brings forth the entire truth. Pastor Dale tries—very hard—to maintain his professional and compassionate demeanor, but this revelation is more than he can sustain. He picks up his Bible, starts to open it, then simply places it on his desk and suggests a later meeting. In the meantime he will study up. My students love this scene because it so beautifully illustrates how one cannot expect to find direct answers for every emergent situation by finding the "right" text from Scripture. Pastor Dale's theological training has not prepared him for this one.

The film traces Roy and his family as they struggle through all sorts of problems, some amusing, others almost too painful to watch. Irma's fashion advice is worth the rental fee. But we find a telling scene at church. Irma watches from the choir while Ruth (formerly Roy) and her daughter Patty Ann sit near the back. As the offering plate comes by, Ruth begins to place an envelope in it, but the usher ignores her. Immediately thereafter, the usher makes eye contact with Pastor Dale, who weakly nods back as the usher invites Ruth and Patty Ann to leave the church. Irma steps down from the choir loft and follows them out.

Transgender concerns do not correspond to biblical purity concerns, but *Normal* does present an important question for contemporary church persons. Many persons in our society live under the cloud of ostracism, simply as a result of some aspects of their identity. (The closest parallel to this case would be the biblical lepers, who were supposed to live apart from the rest of society.) Their stigma only intensifies in religious communities. However, their presence confronts religious communities with a moment of decision. *Normal* dramatizes this process, which repeats itself over and over again. Will the church respond with blessing or with additional condemnation?

DEADBEATS

Chapter 4 attends to ancient gender values, particularly what behaviors and dispositions marked one as masculine. In some ways Jesus and Paul fulfilled conventional expectations of men, but in other respects they transgressed those roles. Neither Jesus nor Paul established a household, gained wealth, or contributed to the civic welfare. Indeed, both Jesus and Paul apparently critiqued or discouraged conventional marriage. Although they endured suffering, neither exerted physical power over other men.

One episode of *The Simpsons* episode, *Lisa v. Malibu Stacy*, experiments with gender roles in a contemporary setting. A transparent stand-in for Barbie, Malibu Stacy has long blonde hair and big eyelashes, among other attributes. Lisa and her classmates are huge fans until a new *talking* Malibu Stacy hits the shelves. Then Lisa hears "the remarkably sexist drivel" Malibu Stacy has to offer.

I wish they taught shopping in school!
Let's bake some cookies for the boys!
And the coup de grace: *Don't ask me; I'm just a girl!* To which Bart replies, "Right on! Say it sister!"

To this Lisa offers her full critique.

It's not funny, Bart. Millions of girls will grow up thinking that this is the right way to act—that they can never be more than vacuous ninnies whose only goal is to look pretty, land a rich husband, and spend all day on the phone with their equally vacuous friends talking about how damn terrific it is to look pretty and have a rich husband!

Finding her friends playing with their dolls on the school playground—*Let's buy makeup so the boys will like us!*—Lisa objects that "the things she says are sexist." That does not go well at all; the girls giggle, "Lisa said a dirty word!"

Lisa springs into action. She calls the Malibu Stacy factory and arranges a tour. At the end of the tour she asks, "Is the remarkably sexist drivel spouted by Malibu Stacy intentional, or is it just a horrible mistake?" Her female tour guide assures Lisa that the Malibu Stacy company is sensitive to "such concerns," just in time for a male colleague to whistle, "Hey Jiggles, grab a pad and back that gorgeous butt in here!"

Finally Lisa gets a brilliant idea. She finds Malibu Stacy's creator and persuades her to market a totally new doll, Lisa Lionheart.

She'll have the wisdom of Gertrude Stein and the wit of Cathy Guisewite, the tenacity of Nina Totenberg, and the common sense of Elizabeth Cady Stanton! And to top it off, the down-to-earth good looks of Eleanor Roosevelt.

As Lisa Lionheart begins getting some press, Lisa finally encounters resistance from the Malibu Stacy culture. In an after-hours meeting, Stacy's manufacturers determine "to reinvent Malibu Stacy for the nineties." One might hope that Lisa's activism has had an effect. Who knows, even if the new Stacy crushes Lisa Lionheart for a share of the market, maybe the new Malibu Stacy will fill alternative roles? Imagine Malibu Stacy in a lab coat!

But that is not the way things work. The final scene depicts Lisa Lionheart's rollout at the local toy store. A crowd of kids lines up for the store opening, eager to get their hands on Lisa Lionheart. The doors open, and they rush to the Lisa Lionheart display. But just as they get there a huge new pallet rolls out in front of them: Malibu Stacy—"with NEW hat!" Lisa points out that the new hat has not changed anything, but Mr. Smithers strikes down that objection: "But she's got a new hat!" The Malibu Stacys sell out immediately, and then Lisa observes a little girl playing with the Lisa Lionheart doll. *Trust in yourself, and you can do anything!* And the little girl smiles.

Lisa v. Malibu Stacy strikes a nerve because of the kinds of resistance Lisa does—and does not—receive. Lisa aims to challenge conventional gender codes that are supported by an enormous marketing and entertainment industry. Family and friends dismiss her. (In another episode, her own teacher complains, "It's girls like you that keep the rest of us from landing a husband!") Corporate America strikes back at her. Perhaps more importantly, however, the resistance she receives is largely quiet, entirely noncoercive. Her little attempt to imagine things differently has some successes, but it never poses a serious threat to the basic order of things. It is simply one experiment by one girl and the people she influences directly.

JESUS THE CONVICTED SEDITIONIST AND THE SCANDAL OF THE CROSS

Chapters 5 and 6 look into how Jesus died and what that meant for early Christian identity. Among the least expedient forms of execution, crucifixion aimed to inflict both suffering and humiliation on its victims. The gospel stories of Jesus' death relate two apparently conflicting values. On the one hand, Jesus is God's righteous one, who does not deserve his fate. On the other, Jesus' crucifixion is the predictable result of his disruptive behavior during Passover week. After Jesus' death, his followers could not ignore the implications. Jesus died as a criminal, and this represented a "scandal" or embarrassment for early Christian identity. Although Christians insisted that Jesus' faithfulness demonstrated the righteousness of God (Rom 3:21-26), they understood that he died because of acts he actually committed.

Public verdicts of guilt and shame have not always deterred people from following the way of Christ. In *God's Long Summer: Stories of*

Faith and Civil Rights, Charles Marsh, son of a white Mississippi Baptist pastor, recounts stories of faith from the voting rights struggles of that state.[1] The story of Fannie Lou Hamer exemplifies how faithfulness can lead to condemnation.

Fannie Lou Hamer grew up in grinding poverty. She picked cotton for white plantation owners from the age of 6, a job that kept her and her family in debt for years. Poverty and humiliation dominated her entire life. One night she attended an organizational meeting in a local church, when she heard the call of civil rights. The next day, she got on a bus, rode to the county courthouse, and tried, unsuccessfully, to register to vote.

This was Fannie Lou Hamer's first experience with the consequences of violating the Southern race code. Fear gripped the new activists when the bus arrived at the courthouse, but Fannie Lou Hamer just marched right on in. Men with hunting rifles happened to pass by—in the courthouse—while she took her voting test, the test itself requiring her to divulge her employer's name and her own address—implicit threats of retaliation that were soon to be fulfilled. On the ride home police stopped the bus driver for driving a bus that was "too yellow." While the activists sat on the bus, pondering the fearsome walk home, Fannie Lou Hamer broke into song: "Have a little talk with Jesus, Tell him all about our troubles. . . ." The group joined in, and Fannie Lou Hamer gained a reputation for singing in the face of danger.

Eventually, the driver was allowed to convey the group home, but trouble was not over for Fannie Lou Hamer. Her landlord and boss stopped by and threatened to evict her if she would not remove her name from the voting application. She moved out to stay in a friend's house, but the consequences followed her. Days later, she moved out to join relatives in another county, fearing that her presence would endanger her friend. The next week the room in which she had stayed was riddled with 16 bullets.

Hamer persisted. She eventually won her right to vote, but this caused more suffering. Her husband and family lost their jobs and their home. Still, when she received an invitation to travel to Charleston for civil rights training, she started packing immediately. This is how the passion of Fannie Lou Hamer took place. On the ride back to Mississippi, the activists attempted to eat in the Winona, Mississippi transit station. Police were called, arrests were made, and Fannie Lou Hamer was recognized. In her jail cell she heard the sounds and screams of torture. She saw her colleagues parade by, faces misshapen by beatings. Then her own turn came. Beaten repeatedly with a truncheon, Fannie Lou Hamer's entire body hardened from the swelling. One of her kidneys permanently damaged, and with a huge clot over her left eye, Fannie Lou Hamer heard her captors plotting her murder. When she returned to her cell, she could not even sit down for the pain. Yet the next day something happened, as Fannie Lou Hamer began to sing.

> Paul and Silas was bound in jail, let my people go.
> Had no money for to go their bail, let my people go.
> Paul and Silas began to shout, let my people go.
> Jail doors open and they walked out, let my people go.

The song's genius, blending imprisonment with Israel's deliverance from slavery, caught on with the jailed activists. From one cell to another, they joined in the song. As things turned out, her suffering in the Winona jail led to her leadership among activists in Mississippi. As vice chair of the Mississippi Freedom Democratic Party, she attended the 1964 Democratic National Convention. Yet no one could foresee that during her torture and imprisonment, and even her elevation to leadership was qualified by the expediencies of white politicians, who excluded her troublesome presence from key conversations. Fannie Lou Hamer's faithfulness made her a hero, but it also led her through great suffering.

RESPECTABILITY AND PERSECUTION

Chapters 7 and 8 look into how early Christians positioned themselves within society. Most of the time, they celebrated their distinctiveness, yet they usually kept an eye on how they represented themselves to their neighbors. This mix of deviance and respectability makes sense in a context marked by the fear of persecution. Although we cannot know the full nature, extent, or motivations of persecution against Christians, we can tell that the fear of persecution marks the vast majority of early Christian literature.

In 2007 participants in Lancaster Seminary's youth leadership program, in which I participate, experienced this tension in a relatively mild form. The program's annual summer global experience took young people and their mentors to the Arizona-Mexico borderlands to learn about both Mexican culture and the current immigration crisis. Almost immediately on their return to Lancaster, they learned that a local Rotary Club had invited a prominent politician to voice his opinions on the issue, opinions the students and their leaders regarded as both unjust and racist.

Seminary students, staff, and young people began preparing a response. They contacted the Rotary Club to initiate a conversation, but that overture was rebuffed. In a culture suspicious of protests, and in a region where they held a distinctively minority opinion, how might they voice their concerns in a manner that would win positive, and not negative, attention? The group developed a carefully measured approach. They contacted the Rotary Club leadership and local media outlets to share their intentions. They determined not to disrupt the Rotary Club meeting, but rather to stand outside with signs and informational materials. In the end, their "respectable" approach to a controversial issue led to surprising success. Not only did they gain favorable media coverage, they won invitations from other local Rotary Clubs to present their point of view.

The youth leadership program drew its inspiration from familiar civil rights strategies. Charles Marsh recounts the career of Ed King, a white Methodist minister active in the civil rights struggles of 1964 Mississippi.[2] A child of privilege, King grew up largely unaware of the severe poverty that so humiliated people like Fannie Lou Hamer and her family. When he became aware, his discomfort led to action. During his seminary career, he had been arrested twice in Montgomery, once in a café for the "disorderly conduct" of meeting with a racially mixed group and again for inviting an African American minister to share lunch at his boarding house.

These experiences and others prepared King for his prophetic ministry of 1963 and 1964. In 1963, King organized visits by mixed-race groups to Jackson's First Baptist Church and Galloway Memorial Methodist Church, both prominent white congregations. The visit to Galloway led to the pastor's request for another appointment because he could not serve a congregation that denied admission to people on the grounds of color. Some of his visits forced white ushers to form themselves into human walls, forbidding visitors from receiving communion. In one case, the visitors literally reached across the ushers' arms to knock on the closed chapel doors while parishioners received the sacrament. Eventually, the police began arresting the church visitors, and the escalating conflicts provided King with a platform. His public actions condemned Mississippi Christianity for its hypocrisy.

The brilliance of King's strategy lay in a combination of shamelessness and respectability. Knowing the consequences of his initiatives, knowing that they would bring arrests and accusations of treason, King and his colleagues appeared to take the moral high ground. They dressed up for church, King in clerical stole, showed up on time, and conducted themselves peaceably. But their actions were calculated to provoke hostile reactions that revealed segregationist Christianity's moral bankruptcy. At one church, a black woman engaged an usher-guard in conversation, eliciting the comments, "Please don't try to appeal to my conscience," "Just leave Jesus out of this," and "This is a Christian church and we intend to keep it that way."[3] King's efforts, undeniably successful in making their point, never succeeded in opening white churches. That would happen much later. The summer of 1964 saw the notorious murders of James Chaney, Andrew Goodman, and Mickey Schwerner, along with a spate of church burnings. The veil of respectability did not guarantee success.

CONCLUSION

The holy combination of shamelessness and respectability signals a distinctive way of keeping the memory of Jesus. One of my heroes in the faith, Clarence Jordan, embodied these tensions in his daily life.[4] Jordan is perhaps most famous for his *Cotton Patch* translations of much of the New Testament into Southern idiom, leading to the musical, *Cotton Patch Gospel*. Foreshadowings of his future activism emerged while he was a student at the Southern Baptist Theological Seminary in Louisville. His ministry in a poor black neighborhood drew complaints that Jordan encouraged whites and blacks to share covered dish dinners. He gained a reputation for pleading the cause of racial justice in white Baptist churches through the 1930s and early 1940s. In 1942 Jordan founded Koinonia Farm, an intentional farming community in Georgia from which the Habitat for Humanity Movement eventually emerged. The Koinonia Farm drew antagonism from the beginning, in part because Jordan and his white colleagues shared table with black employees. The farm community participated in a local Baptist congregation, but tension there eventually led to the dismissal of Koinonia residents from congregational membership. The official letter attributed the action to "differences of opinion on the race issue, devotion to our government, and proper relationship to the church."[5]

A certain mischievousness empowered Jordan to deal with his antagonists. Once when Jordan was speaking, a man accused him of being a Communist. "Sir," Jordan asked, "why do you say I'm a Communist?"

"Well, you fraternize with Myles Horton . . . and everybody knows Myles Horton is a Communist. Birds of a feather flock together. So, I know you're a Communist."

Jordan: "Well, I'll readily admit that Myles Horton has been to Koinonia. I think he's a fine man, and we've given him hospitality at Koinonia. But, sir, if you showed up at Koinonia, we'd give you hospitality too. But you know, I really have trouble with your logic. I don't think my talking to Myles Horton makes me a Communist any more than talking to you right now makes me a jackass."

Likewise, the Koinonia farm sold produce through a roadside stand. But some locals burned down the stand one night. Not to be deterred, Jordan built another, but someone blew up that one with dynamite. Now Koinonia gave up on the roadside stand. They started selling pecans through the mail, with Jordan's advertizing slogan, "Help Us Ship the Nuts Out of Georgia."[6]

Those examples are entertaining, but another may be more edifying. In Koinonia's first year, Klan representatives confronted Jordan at his home, warning him that they would not let the sun set on a white man who shared table with black people. Jordan paused, breathed deeply, offered a broad smile, and began shaking the man's hand. "I'm a Baptist preacher and I just graduated from the Southern Baptist Seminary. I've heard about people who had power over the sun, but I never hoped to meet one." After a long pause, the man replied, "I'm a son of a—I'm a son of a Baptist preacher myself." As the story goes, "so they talked and laughed and the old sun went right on down."[7] If only it always worked out like that.

NOTES

Chapter 1

1. Carol F. Karlsen, *The Devil in the Shape of a Woman: Witchcraft in Colonial New England* (New York: Norton, 1987), xiv.
2. Karlsen, *Devil in the Shape of a Woman*, 225.
3. Karlsen, *Devil in the Shape of a Woman*, 122.
4. John Demos, "Underlying Themes in the Witchcraft of Seventeenth Century New England," in *Religion in American History: Interpretive Essays* (ed. John M. Mulder and John F. Wilson; Englewood Cliffs, N.J.: Prentice-Hall, 1978), 87; see John Demos, *Entertaining Satan: Witchcraft and the Culture of Early New England* (New York: Oxford University Press, 1982).
5. Demos, "Underlying Themes," 93–94, 99–100.
6. Demos, "Underlying Themes," 92.
7. James M. Morone, *Hellfire Nation: The Politics of Sin in American History* (New Haven: Yale University Press, 2003), 82–83.
8. Jerome H. Neyrey, *Paul, in Other Words* (Louisville: Westminster John Knox, 1990), 184–86. Neyrey relies on the work of Mary Douglas, "Thirty Years After Witchcraft, Oracles, and Magic," in *Witchcraft Confessions and Accusations* (ed. Mary Douglas; New York: Tavistock Publications, 1970), xiii–xxxviii. See *The HarperCollins Dictionary of Religion* (ed. Jonathan Z. Smith; San Francisco: HarperSanFrancisco, 1995), 1133–34.

9. Jeff Robinson, "Mohler Message on Family Life Today: Don't Put Off Marriage," *Baptist Press*. www.bpnews.net/bpnews.asp?ID=18611. Accessed 30 June 2004.

10. Sharon Ringe has suggested that the woman's loose hair and her jar of ointment [for massage?] might suggest that she is a sex worker (*Luke* [*Westminster Bible Companion*]; Louisville: Westminster John Knox, 1992), 108.

11. Joachim Jeremias, *Jerusalem in the Time of Jesus* (Philadelphia: Fortress, 1969), 105.

12. See the classic discussion in E. P. Sanders, *Jesus and Judaism* (Philadelphia: Fortress, 1985), 174–211; and E. P. Sanders, "Sin, Sinners (NT)," *ABD* 6.40–47. Some historians have suggested that Torah observance would have meant far different things in Galilee than in Judea, but that point is irrelevant to this discussion.

13. In addition to the works by E. P. Sanders, see Richard Bauckham, "Apocalypses," in *Justification and Variegated Nomism*, vol. 1: *The Complexities of Second Temple Judaism* (ed. D. A. Carson, et al.; Grand Rapids: Baker, 2001), 135–87, esp. 142–51; David A. Neale, *None but the Sinners: Religious Categories in the Gospel of Luke* (JSNT Sup 58; Sheffield, UK: Sheffield Academic, 1991), esp. 68–97; George W. E. Nickelsburg, *Ancient Judaism and Christian Origins* (Minneapolis: Fortress, 2003), 42–43. For a sophisticated alternative, see James D. G. Dunn, *Jesus Remembered* (Grand Rapids: Eerdmans, 2003), 526–32.

14. Bauckham, "Apocalypses," 146.

15. Elisabeth Schüssler Fiorenza, *In Memory of Her: A Feminist Theological Reconstruction of Christian Origins* (New York: Crossroad, 1985), 128; cited in Mitzi Minor, *The Spirituality of Mark: Responding to God* (Louisville: Westminster John Knox, 1996), 125, n. 15.

16. See Patrick Mullen, *Dining with Pharisees* (Interfaces; Collegeville, Minn.: Liturgical Press, 2004), 115.

17. Barbara E. Reid, *Choosing the Better Part? Women in the Gospel of Luke* (Collegeville, Minn.: Liturgical Press, 1996), 115.

18. F. Scott Spencer, *Dancing Girls, "Loose" Ladies, and Women of "the Cloth": The Women in Jesus' Life* (New York: Continuum, 2004), 109.

19. This conclusion finds detailed support in a wide range of scholarship. See Kathleen E. Corley, *Private Women, Public Meals: Social Conflict in the Synoptic Tradition* (Peabody, Mass.: Hendrickson, 1993); Charles H. Cosgrove, "A Woman's Unbound Hair in the Greco-Roman World, with Special Reference to the Story of the 'Sinful Woman' in Luke 7:38-50," *JBL* 124 (2005): 675–92.

20. Corley, *Private Women, Public Meals*, esp. 24–79, 128; Reid, *Choosing the Better Part?*, 122.

21. Reid, *Choosing the Better Part?*, 110–11.
22. Mullen, *Dining with Pharisees*, 110. See Jane Schaberg, "Luke" in *Women's Bible Commentary* (expanded edition; ed. Carol A. Newsom and Sharon H. Ringe; Louisville: Westminster John Knox, 1998), 374.
23. Cosgrove, "A Woman's Unbound Hair." Summary.
24. Tal Ilan, *Jewish Women in Greco-Roman Palestine* (Peabody, Mass.: Hendrickson, 1996), 219.
25. Gale A. Yee, "Gomer," in *Women in Scripture* (ed. Carol Meyers, Toni Craven, and Ross S. Kraemer; Grand Rapids: Eerdmans, 2001), 84–86.
26. Melissa Farley et al., "Prostitution in Five Countries: Violence and Post-Traumatic Stress Disorder," *Feminism & Psychology* 8 (1998): 405–26.
27. I am grateful to Lancaster Theological Seminary alumnus David de Jesus Bowles who referred me to Andrew Bard Schmookler, *The Parable of the Tribes: The Problem of Power in Social Evolution* (2nd ed.; Albany: SUNY Press, 1995). Schmookler suggests that violence is an inevitable outcome of civilizations encroaching on one another's limited resources. In this view violence—with all its symptoms—is simply an outcome of human civilization. Sin, then, would be unavoidable. It is a most provocative book.
28. Rodney Stark and William Sims Bainbridge, *Religion, Deviance, and Social Control* (New York: Routledge, 1996), 2.
29. Classic literature on deviance includes John Hagan and Alberto Palloni, "The Social Production of a Criminal Class in Working-Class London, circa 1950–1980," *American Journal of Sociology* 96 (1990): 265–99; Robert J. Sampson and John H. Laub, "Crime and Deviance over the Life Course: The Salience of Adult Social Bonds," *American Sociological Review* 55 (1990): 609–27; Howard Becker, *Outsiders: Studies in the Sociology of Deviance* (Boston: Free Press, 1963); Walter Gove, ed., *The Labelling of Deviance: Evaluating a Perspective* (2nd ed.; New York: Sage, 1980); David Matza, *Becoming Deviant* (Englewood Cliffs, N.J.: Prentice-Hall, 1969). See Lloyd Pietersen, "Despicable Deviants: Labelling Theory and the Polemic of the Pastorals," *Sociology of Religion* 58 (1997): 343–52. See Spencer, *Dancing Girls*, 111–16, for treatment of the woman in Luke 7:36-50 as a deviant and her behavior as confirming the basic categories ascribed to female deviants.
30. Morone, *Hellfire Nation*, 485–87.
31. Morone, *Hellfire Nation*, 485–87.
32. Stark and Bainbridge, *Religion, Deviance, and Social Control*, 5.
33. We will pay more careful attention to this question in chapter 3. E. P. Sanders is especially noteworthy for the argument that Jesus did not call sinners to repent (*The Historical Figure of Jesus* [New York: Penguin, 1993], 226–37; *Jesus and Judaism*, 174–211), whereas Craig L. Blomberg argues

that Jesus did (*Contagious Holiness: Jesus' Meals with Sinners* (NSBT 19; Downers Grove, Ill.: InterVarsity, 2005).

Chapter 2

1. Unless otherwise noted, all biblical translations are mine.
2. See Alan Beardsworth and Teresa Keil, *Sociology on the Menu: An Invitation to the Study of Food and Society* (New York: Routledge, 1997).
3. The following discussion draws heavily on several authoritative sources, including: Peter Garnsey, *Food and Society in Classical Antiquity* (Key Themes in Ancient History; New York: Cambridge University Press, 1999); Dennis E. Smith, *From Symposium to Eucharist: The Banquet in the Early Christian World* (Minneapolis: Fortress, 2003); Corley, *Private Women, Public Meals*; and Robert J. Karris, *Eating Your Way through Luke's Gospel* (Collegeville, Minn.: Liturgical Press, 2006).
4. Mary Douglas, "Deciphering a Meal," in *Myth, Symbol, and Culture* (ed. Clifford Geertz; New York: Norton, 1971), 61; quoted in Corley, *Private Women, Public Meals*, 20.
5. Corley, *Private Woman, Public Meals*. Book argument.
6. *Epistulae* 2:6; cited with discussion in Gerd Theissen, *The Social Setting of Pauline Christianity: Essays on Corinth* (Philadelphia: Fortress, 1982), 155–58. See the discussion on distribution of food in Garnsey, *Food and Society in Classical Antiquity*, 135–38.
7. Sanders, *Jesus and Judaism*, 208.
8. We discussed Luke's version, the story of the sinful woman (7:36-50), in chapter 1. It also occurs at a meal.
9. Halvor Moxnes lists these scenes as Luke 5:29-32; 7:36-50; 10:38-42; 15:1-2, 6, 9, 22-25; 16:19-25; 19:6-10; 22:14-22; 24:30-31; 24:41-43 (*The Economy of the Kingdom: Social Conflict and Economic Relations in Luke's Gospel* [OBT; Philadelphia: Fortress, 1988], 87, n. 29). I would not necessarily include 10:38-42.
10. Karris, *Eating Your Way through Luke's Gospel*, 97.
11. For an extremely concise discussion, see Dunn, *Jesus Remembered*, 599–600.
12. Cited in Robert W. Funk, *Honest to Jesus: Jesus for a New Millennium* (New York: HarperCollins, 1996), 208-9.
13. For discussion with extended reflection on the tension between Jesus' moral teachings and his immoral company, see Richard A. Burridge, *Imitating Jesus: An Inclusive Approach to New Testament Ethics* (Grand Rapids: Eerdmans, 2007), esp. 33–79. Though both erudite and insightful, Burridge's discussion perhaps underappreciates the Gospels' diverse testimonies and overestimates their direct representation of the historical Jesus.

14. For a discussion of the main lines of argument, see Fernando Méndez-Moratalla, *The Paradigm of Conversion in Luke* (New York: T&T Clark, 2004), 153–80.
15. S. Scott Bartchy, "The Historical Jesus and Honor Reversal at the Table," in *The Social Setting of Jesus and the Gospels* (ed. Wolfgang Stegemann, Bruce J. Malina, and Gerd Theissen; Minneapolis: Fortress, 2002), 177.
16. The most influential case for this view is expressed by Sanders, *The Historical Figure of Jesus*, 226–37; and Sanders, *Jesus and Judaism*, 174–211.
17. Note, however, that he says this only in Luke. The versions in Matthew and Mark differ.
18. See Sanders, *Historical Figure of Jesus*, 230–32. Arguing against Sanders, see Blomberg, *Contagious Holiness*, 26.
19. Claudia Setzer, *Jewish Responses to Early Christians: History and Polemics, 30–150 C.E.* (Minneapolis: Fortress, 1994), 137.
20. See the summary of these accusations—and Christian defenses—in Jane Schaberg, *The Illegitimacy of Jesus: A Feminist Theological Interpretation of the Infancy Narratives* (San Francisco: Harper & Row, 1987), 165–78.
21. The translation is that of M. A. Knibb, "Martyrdom and Ascension of Isaiah," in *Old Testament Pseudepigrapha: Volume 2* (ed. James H. Charlesworth; New York: Doubleday, 1984), 143–76.
22. See similar but distinctive discussions in Schaberg, *Illegitimacy of Jesus*, 32–34; and Amy-Jill Levine, "Matthew," in *Women's Bible Commentary* (expanded edition; ed. Carol A. Newsom and Sharon A. Ringe; Louisville: Westminster John Knox, 1998), 339–49. For each of these characters, see *Women in Scripture: A Dictionary of Named and Unnamed Women in the Hebrew Bible, the Apocryphal/Deuterocanonical Books, and the New Testament* (ed. Carol Meyers, Tony Craven, and Ross S. Kraemer; Grand Rapids: Eerdmans, 2000).
23. Some have understood *lestēs* as a category of social bandit like Robin Hood. The use of the term elsewhere in the Gospels, however, does not encourage that interpretation. See Mark 11:17, paralleled by Matthew 21:13 and Luke 19:46; and Luke 10:30, 36.
24. Arland Hultgren, *The Parables of Jesus: A Commentary* (Grand Rapids: Eerdmans, 2000), 147.
25. Dan O. Via, *The Parables: Their Literary and Existential Dimension* (Philadelphia: Fortress, 1967), 161.
26. Bernard Brandon Scott, *Re-Imagine the World: An Introduction to the Parables of Jesus* (Santa Rosa, Calif.: Polebridge Press, 2001), 51. For Scott's more detailed exegesis, see his *Hear Then the Parable: A Commentary on the Parables of Jesus* (Minneapolis: Fortress, 1989), 389–403.

27. Charles W. Hedrick, *Many Things in Parables: Jesus and His Modern Critics* (Louisville: Westminster John Knox, 2004), 39.
28. Scott agrees (*Re-imagine the World*, 53).
29. I think at least two other characters might qualify as sinner-heroes: the Landowner in the parable of the vineyard (Matt 20:1-16) and the Landowner in the parable of the pounds/talents (Matt 25:14-30; Luke 19:12-27).

Chapter 3

1. Two decades ago, E. P. Sanders observed a growing trend among Christian scholars to regard Jesus as transgressing the law, but a "remarkable consistency" among Jewish historians to see Jesus as living in continuity with it (*Jesus and Judaism*, 51–55).
2. See the discussion in E. P. Sanders, *Judaism: Practice and Belief, 63 BCE–66 CE* (Philadelphia: Trinity Press International, 1992), 71–72.
3. Sanders, *Judaism*, 220.
4. Bruce J. Malina, *The New Testament World: Insights from Cultural Anthropology* (Atlanta: John Knox, 1981), 125.
5. Sanders, *Judaism*, 214.
6. Paula Fredrickson, *Jesus of Nazareth, King of the Jews: A Jewish Life and the Emergence of Christianity* (New York: Random House, 1999), 197.
7. Sanders, *Judaism*, 218.
8. For fascinating assessments of Jewish material culture in ancient Rome, see the essays by L. Michael White, "Synagogue and Society in Imperial Ostia: Archaeological and Epigraphic Evidence," in *Judaism and Christianity in First-Century Rome* (ed. Karl P. Donfried and Peter Richardson; Eugene, Ore.: Wipf & Stock, 1998), 30–68, and Graydon F. Snyder, "The Interaction of Jews with Non-Jews in Rome," in *Judaism and Christianity in First-Century Rome* (ed. Karl P. Donfried and Peter Richardson; Eugene, Ore.: Wipf & Stock, 1998), 69–90.
9. See John P. Meier, *A Marginal Jew*, vol. 3: *Companions and Competitors* (ABRL; New York: Doubleday, 2001), 322.
10. Anthony J. Saldarini, *Pharisees, Scribes and Sadducees in Palestinian Society* (Grand Rapids: Eerdmans, 1988), 214–15.
11 So suggests N. T. Wright, *The New Testament and the People of God* (Minneapolis: Fortress, 1992), 187–88.
12. Shaye J. D. Cohen, *From the Maccabees to the Mishnah* (Library of Early Christianity; Philadelphia: Westminster, 1987), 74.
13. See Meier, *Marginal Jew*, 3: 549–60.
14. The book of Acts includes a sympathetic portrait of the Pharisee Gamaliel (5:34-40).

15. Mark Allan Powell, "Characterization on the Phraseological Plane in the Gospel of Matthew," in *Treasures Old and New: Contributions to Matthean Studies* (ed. David R. Bauer and Mark Allan Powell; SBLSymS 1; Atlanta: Scholars Press, 1996), 161–77.
16. Meier, *A Marginal Jew*, 3: 314–15, 373, n. 114.
17. See Isaiah 58:1-14; Micah 6:6-8.
18. So also Sanders, *Jesus and Judaism*, 245–69 and Fredriksen, *Jesus of Nazareth*, 197–214.
19. The most articulate such case of which I am aware is David Rhoads, *Reading Mark: Engaging the Gospel* (Minneapolis: Fortress, 2004), 140–75. Although I have learned a great deal from Rhoads' discussion, I think he misses the point with respect to his evaluation of Jesus' behavior as described by Mark on some important points.
20. Bart D. Ehrman discusses this textual problem at some length in *Misquoting Jesus: The Story Behind Who Changed the Bible and Why* (San Francisco: HarperSanFransciso, 2005), 133–39.
21. Ehrman's suggestion.
22. So I recall learning from one of my teachers, Amy-Jill Levine. For a sample of her thought, see "Discharging Responsibility: Matthean Jesus, Biblical Law, and Hemorrhaging Woman," in *Treasures Old and New: Contributions to Matthean Studies* (ed. David R. Bauer and Mark Allan Powell; SBLSymS 1; Atlanta: Scholars Press, 1996), 379–97 and *The Misunderstood Jew: The Church and the Scandal of the Jewish Jesus* (San Francisco: HarperOne, 2006), which I have not yet reviewed.
23. Theodore W. Jennings Jr., and Tat-Siong Benny Liew, "Mistaken Identities But Model Faith: Rereading the Centurion, the Chap, and the Christ in Matthew 8:5-13," *JBL* 123 (2004): 467–94.
24. Rhoads, *Reading Mark*, 167. I particularly resonate with Blomberg's phrase, "contagious holiness," as a way of describing this pattern, though I disagree with some of his conclusions (*Contagious Holiness*, esp. 93–96).

Chapter 4

1. The landmark publication in this area is an anthology: Stephen D. Moore and Janice Capel Anderson, eds., *New Testament Masculinities* (Semeia Studies; Atlanta: Society of Biblical Literature, 2003).
2. This chapter is heavily influenced by Halvor Moxnes, *Putting Jesus in His Place: A Radical Vision of Household and Kingdom* (Louisville: Westminster John Knox, 2003). It is one of those books that fundamentally changes how one thinks about things.
3. For those who are interested, Lee Wardlaw, *101 Ways to Bug Your Parents* (New York: Penguin, 2003).

4. Virginia Burrus, *"Begotten, Not Made": Conceiving Manhood in Late Antiquity* (Figurae: Reading Medieval Culture; Stanford, Calif.: Stanford University Press, 2000), 19; Jennifer A. Glancy, "Protocols of Masculinity in the Pastoral Epistles," in *New Testament Masculinities* (ed. Stephen D. Moore and Janice Capel Anderson; Semeia Studies; Atlanta: Society of Biblical Literature, 2003), 237; Maud W. Gleason, "Elite Male Identity in the Roman Empire," in *Life, Death, and Entertainment in the Roman Empire* (ed. D. S. Potter and D. J. Mattingly; Ann Arbor: University of Michigan Press, 1999), 67–70; Moisés Mayordomo Marín, "Construction of Masculinity in Antiquity and Early Christianity," *lectio difficilior* 2 (2006), www.lectio.unibe.ch, 3; Craig A. Williams, *Roman Homosexuality: Ideologies of Masculinity in Classical Antiquity* (New York: Oxford University Press, 1999), 153–59.

5. Dale B. Martin, *The Corinthian Body* (New Haven: Yale University Press, 1995), 32–34. See also Dale B. Martin, *Sex and the Single Savior: Gender and Sexuality in Biblical Interpretation* (Louisville: Westminster John Knox, 2006), 46–47; Gleason, "Elite Male Identity," 70, Marín, "Construction," 4.

6. Tat-siong Benny Liew, "Re-Mark-able Masculinities: Jesus, the Son of Man, and the (Sad) Sum of Manhood?" in Moore and Anderson, *New Testament Masculinities*, 96.

7. Janice Capel Anderson and Stephen D. Moore, "Matthew and Masculinity," in Moore and Anderson, *New Testament Masculinities*, 69; Williams, *Roman Homosexuality*, 154; Marín, "Construction," 7.

8. A great deal of research investigates honor in the ancient world and in biblical texts. The first and most influential treatment in New Testament studies is Malina, *The New Testament World*, esp. 25–50. For an early feminist assessment, see Karen Jo Torjeson, "Reconstruction of Women's Early Christian History," in *Searching the Scriptures: A Feminist Introduction* (ed. Elisabeth Schüssler Fiorenza; New York: Crossroad, 1993), 290–91, 302–3. Somewhat more recently, see Bruce J. Malina and Jerome H. Neyrey, *Portraits of Paul: An Archaeology of Ancient Personality* (Louisville: Westminster John Knox, 1996), 176–83; Carolyn Osiek and David L. Balch, *Families in the New Testament World: Households and House Churches* (Louisville: Westminster John Knox, 1997), 38–41.

9. See the helpful discussion in Ekkehard W. Stegemann and Wolfgang Stegemann, *The Jesus Movement: A Social History of Its First Century* (Minneapolis: Fortress, 1999), 24–27.

10. On common working space for women and men in Galilean and Palestinian households, see Moxnes, *Putting Jesus in His Place*, 41.

11. Jerome H. Neyrey, "Jesus, Gender, and the Gospel of Matthew," in Moore and Anderson, *New Testament Masculinities*, 44–45. See Osiek and Balch, *Families in the New Testament World*, 43–45.

12. Cited, with discussion in Erik Gunderson, *Declamation, Paternity, and Roman Identity: Authority and the Rhetorical Self* (New York: Cambridge University Press, 2003), esp. 35–41.
13. Gleason, "Elite Male Identity," 74–82.
14. See Carolyn Osiek and Margaret Y. MacDonald, *A Woman's Place: House Churches in Earliest Christianity* (Minneapolis: Fortress, 2006), 194–219.
15. I assume, but cannot prove, that the ratio would have been more balanced for Galilee and Judea, where abortion and infanticide would have been less prevalent.
16. Rodney Stark provides a fascinating discussion of these dynamics in *The Rise of Christianity* (San Francisco: HarperCollins, 1996), esp. 95–128.
17. See Mary Rose D'Angelo, "'Knowing How to Preside over His Own Household': Imperial Masculinity and Christian Asceticism in the Pastorals, Hermas, and Luke-Acts," in Moore and Anderson, *New Testament Masculinities*, esp. 265–71.
18. See Gail Corrington Streete, "Outrageous (Speech) Acts and Everyday (Performative) Rebellions: A Response to Rhetorics of Resistance," *Semeia* 79 (1997): 97–105; see Moxnes, *Putting Jesus in His Place*, 73.
19. See Stephen D. Moore and Janice Capel Anderson, "Taking It Like a Man: Masculinity in 4 Maccabees," *JBL* 117 (1998): 249–73.
20. The most helpful discussion of Jesus and marriage of which I am aware is, John P. Meier, *A Marginal Jew*, vol. 1: *The Roots of the Problem and the Person* (ABRL; New York: Doubleday, 1991), 332–45.
21. Luke softens this story, saying the brothers "left everything" (5:11).
22. John's Gospel famously has Jesus arranging care for his mother on his death (19:25-27).
23. For example, William R. Herzog, II, *Jesus, Justice, and the Reign of God* (Louisville: Westminster John Knox, 2000), 215; Richard A. Horsley, *Jesus and Empire: The Kingdom of God and the New World Disorder* (Minneapolis: Fortress, 2003), 110–11. More recent research seems to undermine this model, as in Morten Hoerning Jensen, "Family Life and Family Dwellings in First-Century Rural Galilee," unpublished paper presented to the Early Christian Families Section, Society of Biblical Literature Annual Meeting, San Diego, November 18, 2007.
24. I first encountered this argument in Schüssler Fiorenza, *In Memory of Her*, 147–48.
25. This array of passages, it seems to me, indicates why the more moderate/conventional view fails to persuade. Stephen C. Barton surveys a wide range of Jewish and Greco-Roman traditions that subordinate family loyalty to the service of God; thus, Jesus is not dismissing family or promoting impiety but calling people to a "greater piety" ("The Relativisation of Family Ties in the Jewish and Greco-Roman Traditions," in *Reconstructing*

Early Christian Families: Family as Social Reality and Metaphor [New York: Routledge, 1997], 81–100). In my view, Barton emphasizes the cultural comparisons to the degree that he does not take the more provocative Jesus traditions as serious evidence that Jesus (in early Christian memory) disregards the conventional family piety of his day. This is true as well in his *Discipleship and Family Ties in Mark and Matthew* (SNTSMS 80; New York: Cambridge University Press, 1994).

26. See Malina and Neyrey, *Portraits of Paul*, 154–64.
27. F. Scott Spencer, *What Did Jesus Do? Gospel Profiles of Jesus' Personal Conduct* (Harrisburg: Trinity Press International, 2003), 43.
28. Meier, *A Marginal Jew*, 3: 247.
29. Moxnes, *Putting Jesus in His Place*, 96–97.
30. See Seán Freyne, *Galilee from Alexander the Great to Hadrian, 323 BCE to 135 CE* (Edinburgh: T&T Clark, 1998), 155–207. See also Seán Freyne, *Jesus, A Jewish Galilean: A New Reading of the Jesus-Story* (New York: Continuum, 2004), 141; Richard A. Horsley, *Galilee: History, Politics, People* (Harrisburg: Trinity Press International, 1995), 202–21. For Jesus' disciples, see Stegemann and Stegemann, *The Jesus Movement*, 197–203.
31. John Dominic Crossan's work has most famously developed these images. See John Dominic Crossan, *The Historical Jesus: The Life of a Mediterranean Jewish Peasant* (San Francisco: HarperSanFrancisco, 1991) and John Dominic Crossan, *Jesus: A Revolutionary Biography* (San Francisco: HarperSanFrancisco, 1994).
32. Moxnes, *Putting Jesus in His Place*, 74–75.
33. See Moxnes' account of eunuchs in the ancient world (*Putting Jesus in His Place*, 78–80).
34. See Anderson and Moore, "Matthew and Masculinity," 87–91; Moxnes, *Putting Jesus in His Place*, 74–84.
35. Cited in Anderson and Moore, "Matthew and Masculinity," 89.
36. Moxnes, *Putting Jesus in His Place*, 80.
37. This may represent a case of overinterpretation. Pheme Perkins notes how this passage embodies the folklore technique in which signs identify a prominent person ("Mark," *NIB* 8.658). On the other hand, Marcus J. Borg and John Dominic Crossan regard the triumphal entry as a staged event (*The Last Week: A Day-by-Day Account of Jesus' Final Week in Jerusalem* [San Francisco: HarperSanFrancisco, 2007], 3).
38. Whether Peter actually finds this coin, Matthew does not relate.
39. Spencer, *What Did Jesus Do?*, 138–39. Spencer provides a fairly exhaustive survey of gospel traditions concerning Jesus and money (pp. 129–59).
40. The classic work to this effect is Wayne A. Meeks, *The First Urban Christians: The Social World of the Apostle Paul* (New Haven: Yale

University Press, 1983). For a more recent summary of research, see Stegemann and Stegemann, *The Jesus Movement*, 288–316.

41. David J. A. Clines judges that Paul "is more of a man than we have been inclined to notice" ("Paul, the Invisible Man," in Moore and Anderson, *New Testament Masculinities*, 181–92), though I am inclined to see things differently.

42. Ironically, the King James Version's translation of *malakoi* as "effeminate" represents the most accurate rendering of any modern English translation. Greeks frequently used *malakos* to refer to men who acted as the passive or "bottom" partners in homoerotic sex. The New American Standard Bible (NASB) keeps "effeminate," whereas other major translations use "male prostitutes" [NRSV and NIV; cf. NAB], "the self-indulgent" [NJB], and "sexual perverts" [a fascinating choice for two Greek words in the RSV]. See John J. Winkler, *The Constraints of Desire: The Anthropology of Sex and Gender in Ancient Greece* (The New Ancient World; New York: Routledge, 1990), 50–52; and Martin, *Sex and the Single Savior*, 37–50.

43. See the discussion and bibliography in Reidar Aasgaard, "Paul as a Child: Children and Childhood in the Letters of the Apostle," *JBL* 126 (2007): 130–31, 156.

44. Beverly Roberts Gaventa, "Our Mother St. Paul: Toward the Recovery of a Neglected Theme," in *A Feminist Companion to Paul* (ed. Amy-Jill Levine; Cleveland: Pilgrim Press, 2004), 89–90. Cf. Gaventa's forthcoming *Our Mother Saint Paul* (Louisville: Westminster John Knox, 2007.)

45. Sandra Hack Polaski, *A Feminist Companion to Paul* (St. Louis: Chalice, 2005), 25.

46. This is the proposal of Daniel Boyarin, "Paul and the Genealogy of Gender," in *A Feminist Companion to Paul* (ed. Amy-Jill Levine; Cleveland: Pilgrim Press, 2004), 13–41.

47. See the helpful discussion in Ralph P. Martin, *2 Corinthians* (WBC 40; Waco, Tex.: Word Books, 1986), 344.

48. See the brief summary in Osiek and Balch, *Families in the New Testament World*, 148–55.

49. Moxnes, *Putting Jesus in His Place*, 73.

50. See the scathing assessment by Dale B. Martin: "Modern Protestant attempts to enlist Paul as an advocate of marriage, family, and heterosexual intercourse entail, from a historical point of view, ideological misconstruals. Even more misleading are claims that Paul supports a healthy [or pathological, Martin later writes] view of human sexuality. . . ." (*The Corinthian Body*, 211).

Chapter 5

1. The terms *messiah* and *christ* both mean anointed one. Their primary association involved Jewish hopes that a divinely appointed king would lead the nation to a new age of freedom and righteousness.

2. Raymond E. Brown, *The Death of the Messiah* (ABRL; New York: Doubleday, 1994), 1: 729–30.

3. N. T. Wright suggests that both the temple authorities and Pilate knew Jesus was no revolutionary (*Jesus and the Victory of God* [Minneapolis: Fortress, 1996], 544).

4. The most helpful resource for understanding crucifixion is Martin Hengel, *Crucifixion in the Ancient World and the Folly of the Cross* (Philadelphia: Fortress, 1977).

5. Jesus was executed outside the walls of Jerusalem, in a place where, according to the Gospels, a crowd gathered.

6. Sanders, *The Historical Figure of Jesus*, 249–50. I use "less than 30,000" in deference to the table of urban populations in Stark, *The Rise of Christianity*, 131–32. Stark, in turn, relies on Tertius Chandler and Gerald Fox, *Three Thousand Years of Urban Growth* (New York: Academic Press, 1974). Jeremias estimated Jerusalem's population as 25,000 (*Jerusalem in the Time of Jesus*), 27.

7. Two influential scholars, who interpret Jesus' final week in different ways, agree on this basic assessment. See Sanders, *Historical Figure of Jesus*, 249–50; Crossan, *Jesus*, 127–28. I have had opportunity only to survey Borg and Crossan, *The Last Week*, which, despite its pretentious subtitle, sketches a similar scene.

8. Sanders, *Historical Figure of Jesus*, 23–24, 295, n. 17. See also the discussion by Richard A. Horsley, *Jesus and the Spiral of Violence: Popular Jewish Resistance in Roman Palestine* (Minneapolis: Fortress, 1993), 34–35, 50–54.

9. See the discussion in Craig A. Evans, *Jesus and His Contemporaries: Comparative Studies* (AGJU 25; New York: E. J. Brill, 1995), 353–54.

10. See the discussion in Crossan, *Jesus*, 127–28; Horsley, *Jesus and the Spiral of Violence*, 50–51.

11. Sanders, *Historical Figure of Jesus*, 22–32, 249–50.

12. I do not assume that Mark provides the "most accurate" Passion Narrative, but I do find Mark's passion account generally plausible until the scene of Jesus' arrest.

13. John attributes the scene to the Passover crowd's enthusiasm.

14. So determined is Matthew to make this point that he, misunderstanding Zechariah, notoriously and ridiculously places Jesus on two animals simultaneously!

15. See Julia O'Brien, *Nahum, Habakkuk, Zephaniah, Haggai, Zechariah, Malachi* (AOTC; Nashville: Abingdon, 2004), 242.
16. Borg and Crossan, *The Last Week*, 2–5.
17. "Interpreters have rightly sensed that this action, if understood correctly, potentially clarifies Jesus' mission with respect to Israel and makes intelligible his execution at the hands of the Romans, Israel's overlords" (Evans, *Jesus and His Contemporaries*, 345).
18. Richard A. Horsley, *Jesus and Empire: The Kingdom of God and the New World Disorder* (Minneapolis: Fortress, 2003), 92.
19. William R. Herzog, II, *Prophet and Teacher: An Introduction to the Historical Jesus* (Louisville: Westminster John Knox, 2005), 166: "Jesus . . . believed that the temple was beyond reformation and needed to be destroyed altogether."
20. Evans, *Jesus and His Contemporaries*, 319–80. For a concise discussion, see Ben Witherington, III, *The Gospel of Mark: A Socio-Rhetorical Commentary* (Grand Rapids: Eerdmans, 2001), 313–14.
21. So also John T. Carroll, *The Death of Jesus in Early Christianity* (Peabody, Mass.: Hendrickson, 1995), 32.
22. See the discussion in Ched Myers, *Binding the Strong Man: A Political Reading of Mark's Story of Jesus* (Maryknoll, N.Y.: Orbis, 1988), 297–98; Francis J. Moloney, *The Gospel of Mark: A Commentary* (Peabody, Mass.: Hendrickson, 2002), 222.
23. See the discussion in William R. Herzog, II, *Jesus, Justice, and the Reign of God: A Ministry of Liberation* (Louisville: Westminster John Knox, 2000), 227–28.
24. "Collision Course: Jesus' Final Week," *The Christian Century*, cited 20 March 2007, http://christiancentury.org/article.lasso?id=3091.
25. Even in the United States of 2008, someone would likely be arrested for those behaviors.

Interlude

1. Translation according to Richard P. McBrien, *Catholicism* (rev. ed.; San Francisco: HarperSanFrancisco, 1994), 547.
2. See Wolfhart Pannenberg, *Jesus—God and Man* (rev. ed.; Philadelphia: Westminster, 1977), 355–56.
3. Henry Chadwick, "Orthodoxy and Heresy from the Death of Constantine to the Eve of the First Council of Ephesus," in *The Cambridge Ancient History: XIII: The Late Empire, A.D. 337–425* (ed. Averil Cameron and Peter Garnsey; New York: Cambridge University Press, 1998), 579.
4. This is not an original claim. I am no doctrinal theologian, but I am particularly influenced in this proposal by the works of Wolfhart Pannenberg and Dietrich Bonhoeffer, cited throughout this piece.

5. Pannenberg, *Jesus—God and Man*, 362.
6. Cited in Pannenberg, *Jesus—God and Man*, 362.
7. Dietrich Bonhoeffer, *Ethics* (New York: Macmillan, 1965), 64–70.
8. Geffrey B. Kelly and F. Burton Nelson, *The Cost of Moral Leadership: The Spirituality of Dietrich Bonhoeffer* (Grand Rapids: Eerdmans, 2002), 114.
9. See Dietrich Bonhoeffer, *Letters and Papers from Prison* (enlarged ed.; New York: Macmillan, 1971), 341–42.
10. Dietrich Bonhoeffer, "After Ten Years," in *Letters and Papers from Prison* (enlarged ed.; New York: Macmillan, 1971), 3.
11. Bonhoeffer, "After Ten Years" 258.
12. Bonhoeffer, *Ethics*, 67.
13. Bonhoeffer, *Ethics*, 240.
14. Bonhoeffer, *Ethics*, 241.
15. Bonhoeffer, *Ethics*, 241.
16. Graham Neville, "Sinlessness and Uncertainty in Jesus," *ExpTimes* 116 (2005): 362.

Chapter 6

1. Martin Hengel, *Crucifixion in the Ancient World and the Folly of the Message of the Cross* (Philadelphia: Fortress, 1977), 90.
2. The definitive work remains Hengel, *Crucifixion*. See Craig A. Evans, "Crucifixion," *NIDB* 1: 806–7. The Web site for the PBS *Frontline* documentary, *From Jesus to Christ*, also features helpful information. Online: www.pbs.org/wgbh/pages/frontline/shows/religion/jesus/ crucifixion.html.
3. Gerard S. Sloyan, *Why Jesus Died* (Facets: Minneapolis: Fortress, 2004), 19.
4. Cited in Sloyan, *Why Jesus Died*, 15.
5. Evans, "Crucifixion," 807.
6. Cited in Hengel, *Crucifixion*, 25.
7. A small seat was usually affixed to the upright stake to support his body.
8. Luke's Greek suggests a crowd.
9. Cited in Hengel, *Crucifixion*, 35.
10. The translation of this passage is disputed. Are some crucified, and others used as torches? It makes sense to me to imagine crucifixion as the means by which bodies could function as torches. See Hengel, *Crucifixion* 26–27.
11. John Dominic Crossan and Jeffrey L. Reed, *Excavating Jesus: Beneath the Stones, Behind the Texts* (San Francisco: HarperSanFrancisco, 2001), 247.
12. Crossan, *Jesus*, 126.
13. Paul is not the only one who associates Deuteronomy 21:23 with crucifixion. A couple of the Dead Sea Scrolls do as well (see 4QpNah; 11QTemple

64.12). See Otto Betz, "Jesus and the Temple Scroll," in *Jesus and the Dead Sea Scrolls* (ed. James H. Charlesworth; ABRL; New York: Doubleday, 1992), 89–90.

14. Hengel, *Crucifixion*, 33.
15. Sloyan, *Why Jesus Died*, 15.
16. Hengel, *Crucifixion*, 36–38.
17. See Michel Foucault's classic *Discipline and Punish: The Birth of the Prison* (trans. Alan Sheridan; New York: Vintage, 1979).
18. As cited, with typographical errors and quoted in Evans, "Crucifixion," 807.
19. Hengel, *Crucifixion*, 47–48.
20. Quoting Eric J. Hobsbawm, *Bandits* (2nd ed.; Middlesex: Penguin, 1985), 17; as cited in Crossan, The *Historical Jesus*, 169.
21. Horsley, *Jesus and the Spiral of Violence*, 37.
22. As quoted in Horsley, *Jesus and the Spiral of Violence*, 38.
23. Cited in Hengel, *Crucifixion*, 42.
24. Sloyan, *Why Jesus Died*, 17.
25. David Barr, "The Lamb Who Looks Like a Dragon? Characterizing Jesus in John's Apocalypse," in *The Reality of Apocalypse: Rhetoric and Politics in the Book of Revelation* (SBLSymS 39; Atlanta: Society of Biblical Literature, 2006), 209. Barr provides the most compelling case for a nonviolent lamb of which I am aware, and from which I have learned a great deal. See David Barr, *Tales of the End: A Narrative Commentary on the Book of Revelation* (The Storytellers Bible 1; Sonoma, Calif.: Polebridge, 1998), esp. 137–38.
26. Scholars debate the composition history of 2 Corinthians, though they generally affirm that the contents of 1 Corinthians predate those of 2 Corinthians.
27. In a forthcoming essay for a volume edited by David Hester, I discuss "Paul and the Rhetoric of Ignorance."
28. See Hengel, *Crucifixion*, 5.
29. For the use of blending in biblical interpretation, see the emerging work of Vernon K. Robbins and the Rhetoric of Religious Antiquity project. It follows work in cognitive science. See Gilles Fauconnier and Mark Turner, *How We Think: Conceptual Blending and the Mind's Hidden Complexities* (New York: Basic, 2002).
30. Paul's logic is notoriously difficult here, and I am deviating from mainstream interpretation of this passage. Many commentators identify "the scandal of the cross" with the message of a law-free gospel, though this is not how Paul interprets the scandal in 1 Corinthians 1.
31. Michael J. Gorman, *Apostle of the Crucified Lord: A Theological Introduction to Paul and His Letters* (Grand Rapids: Eerdmans, 2004), 383.

32. See Robert Louis Wilken, *The Christians as the Romans Saw Them* (2nd ed.; New Haven: Yale University Press, 2003), 17–22.

33. Cited in Wilken, *Christians*, 45, 105.

34. Cited in Hengel, *Crucifixion*, 17.

35. Quoted in Wilken, *Christians*, 96.

36. Cited in Hengel, *Crucifixion*, 4.

37. Hengel, *Crucifixion*, 5.

38. Hengel anticipates this argument, though I believe I am taking it in a different direction than he does (*Crucifixion*, 15–21).

39. The newest introduction to Gnosticism—with other introductions somewhat dated—is Birger A. Pearson, *Ancient Gnosticism: Traditions and Literature* (Minneapolis: Fortress, 2007). For a brief popular introduction, see Bart D. Ehrman, *Lost Christianities* (New York: Oxford University Press, 2003), 113–34. For an advanced assessment of current research, see Karen L. King, *What Is Gnosticism?* (Cambridge, Mass.: Belknap, 2003).

40. Cited in Kurt Rudolph, *Gnosis: The Nature and History of Gnosticism* (San Francisco: HarperSanFrancisco, 1987), 167.

41. For discussion and references to primary texts, see Ehrman, *Lost Christianities*, 186–88; Elaine Pagels, *The Gnostic Gospels* (New York: Random House, 1979), 72–75, 82–98, 101; Rudolph, *Gnosis*, 153–71.

42. See the discussion in Pagels, *Gnostic Gospels*, 92–93.

43. See the translation in Andres Werner, "The Coptic Gnostic Apocalypse of Peter," in *NTA* 2: 700–12.

Chapter 7

1. Cited 9 January 2007, www.reclaimamerica.org.

2. This discussion depends heavily on Peter L. Berger and Thomas Luckmann, *The Social Construction of Reality: A Treatise in the Sociology of Knowledge* (New York: Anchor, 1989 [1966]), esp. 92–128, and its application by Iutisone Salevao, *Legitimation in the Letter to the Hebrews: The Construction and Maintenance of a Symbolic Universe* (JSNTSup 219; New York: Sheffield Academic, 2002), 50–69.

3. For a summary of recent work on this topic, see François Bovon, *Luke the Theologian: Fifty-Five Years of Research (1950–2005)* (2nd rev. ed.; Waco, Tex.: Baylor University, 2006), 543–53. Bovon describes "an *embarrass de richesses*" on the topic of wealth and poverty (549).

4. See the interesting discussion on conversion in Anthony B. Robinson and Robert W. Wall, *Called to Be Church: The Book of Acts for a New Day* (Grand Rapids: Eerdmans, 2006), 139–44.

5. Translation by D. A. Russell, in *Ancient Literary Criticism: The Principal Texts in New Translations* (ed. D. A. Russell and M. Winterbottom; Oxford: Oxford University Press, 1972), 546.

6. The translation of Acts 26:28 (and v. 29) poses a notorious problem. My point here is simply that, however one translates their interchange, Agrippa's wordplay with Paul suggests that Paul is a skilled orator.

7. For this pattern of surprises see Justo L. González, *Santa Biblia: The Bible through Hispanic Eyes* (Nashville: Abingdon, 1996), 35–42.

8. Consider Simeon and Anna in Luke 2 or the shepherd and the woman searching for a coin of Luke 15.

9. Chapters 1 and 2 of Luke do feature women's speech, though not as preaching.

10. On this topic, I have been especially influenced by Reid, *Choosing the Better Part?*; Schaberg, "Luke," in the *Women's Bible Commentary*, 363–80; Gail R. O'Day, "Acts," in the *Women's Bible Commentary* (rev. ed.; ed. Carol A. Newsom and Sharon H. Ringe; Louisville: Westminster John Knox, 1998), 394–402; and Loveday C. Alexander, "Sisters in Adversity: Retelling Martha's Story," in *A Feminist Companion to Luke* (ed. Amy-Jill Levine; Cleveland: Pilgrim Press, 2004), 197–213.

11. Richard A. Horsley, "Paul and Slavery: A Critical Alternative to Recent Readings," *Semeia* 83/84 (1998): 176.

12. Horsley, "Paul and Slavery," 178–80.

13. For an extraordinarily helpful and concise discussion, see Jouette M. Bassler, "1 Corinthians," in *Women's Bible Commentary* (rev. ed.; ed. Carol A. Newsom and Sharon H. Ringe; Louisville: Westminster John Knox, 1998), 416–19.

14. For a detailed treatment of 1 Peter's date, see John H. Elliott, *1 Peter* (AB 37B; New York: Doubleday, 2000), 134–38.

15. John H. Elliott spells out the legal, social, and religious dimensions of the terms translated here as *exiles* and *aliens* in *A Home for the Homeless: A Sociological Exegesis of 1 Peter, Its Situation and Strategy* (Philadelphia: Fortress, 1981), esp. 21–58. Elliott emphasizes actual geographical displacement, whereas I regard these terms in a more metaphorical sense. For this judgment see Paul J. Achtemeier, *1 Peter* (Hermeneia; Minneapolis: Fortress, 1996), 56; Donald P. Senior, *1 Peter, Jude, and 2 Peter* (Sacra Pagina 15; Collegeville, Minn.: Michael Glazier, 2003), 8–10.

16. Reinhard Feldmeier, *The First Letter of Peter* (Waco, Tex.: Baylor University Press, 2008).

17. First Peter 2:12 includes a significant translation problem. Are the Gentiles supposed to see the Christians' good deeds now, glorifying God on the last day, or will they see those good deeds and glorify God only at the judgment?

18. For an excellent historical discussion of persecution in early Christianity with a particular view toward 1 Peter, see Achtemeier, *1 Peter*, 23–36.

19. Achtemeier confirms this view, *1 Peter*, 53.
20. Stark, *The Rise of Christianity*, 25.
21. Peter L. Berger, *The Sacred Canopy: Elements of a Sociological Theory of Religion* (New York: Anchor, 1990 [1967]), 164.
22. This is only a mild overstatement. No text, including Revelation, thoroughly rejects the conventional values of its culture, but Revelation largely repudiates its society, the people in it, and the governing authorities.
23. The Ephesian temple of Artemis stood among the famous seven wonders of the ancient world.
24. Steven J. Friesen, *Imperial Cults and the Apocalypse of John: Reading Revelation in the Ruins* (New York: Oxford University Press, 2001), 25, 38.
25. Frederick J. Murphy, *Fallen Is Babylon: The Revelation to John* (The New Testament in Context; Harrisburg, Penn: Trinity Press International, 1998), 296–97; Friesen, *Imperial Cults*, 175.
26. The Project for the New American Century, *Rebuilding America's Defenses: Strategy, Forces, and Resources for a New Century*, Cited September 2007. www.newamericancentury.org/RebuildingAmericasDefenses.pdf, 8.
27. An excellent, concise discussion appears in Craig R. Koester, *Revelation and the End of All Things* (Grand Rapids: Eerdmans, 2001), 125–35. For a brief overview of Revelation, see Greg Carey, *Ultimate Things: An Introduction to Jewish and Christian Apocalyptic Literature* (St. Louis: Chalice Press, 2005), 179–92.
28. For the most compelling assessment of the seven churches and Revelation's response to them, see Paul B. Duff, *Who Rides the Beast? Prophetic Rivalry and the Rhetoric of Crisis in the Churches of the Apocalypse* (Oxford: Oxford University Press, 2001).

Chapter 8

1. Scholars believe Matthew and Luke shared a literary source other than Mark's Gospel. Most call this hypothetical source Q, short for the German *Quelle*, or "source," because it explains how Matthew and Luke share material, often word for word, that does not derive from Mark. We do not possess any ancient copies of this source, yet the overwhelming majority of interpreters believe it existed.
2. Some commentators judge this passage as a later interpolation into the text of Paul's letter. I understand why: The passage blames Jews for killing "the Lord Jesus and the prophets" and promising God's wrath on them. Nowhere else does Paul sound like this. Nevertheless, lacking any manuscript evidence for an interpolation, I attribute this passage to Paul.
3. Allen Dwight Callahan offers an alternative construction of the development of Johannine Christianity (*A Love Supreme: A History of the Johannine*

Tradition [Minneapolis: Fortress, 2005]). The proper understanding of "the Jews" has proven highly controversial among scholars. To translate *(h)oi Ioudaioi* as "the Jews" lends itself to Christian anti-Semitism, since this term so often figures negatively in John. However, the term does not always refer to the religious authorities (as some suggest), nor is it merely an ethnic designation that does not involve "Jewish" religious identity (as others do). In my view, the term requires the sort of historical context provided here: John's Gospel reflects divisions among co-religionists and cannot be taken as a commentary on Jews in Jesus' day or any other day, for that matter.

4. Craig R. Koester, *Hebrews* (AB 36; Garden City, N.Y.: Doubleday, 2001), 67–68.

5. Luke Timothy Johnson, *The Letter of James and Jude* (AB 37A; New York: Doubleday, 1995), 178.

6. William F. Brosend, II (*New Cambridge Bible Commentary*; New York: Cambridge University Press, 2004), 36–38.

7. See Luke Timothy Johnson, *Brother of Jesus, Friend of God: Studies in the Letter of James* (Grand Rapids: Eerdmans, 2004), 56–60; Johnson, *Letter of James*, 39–40, 75–80.

8. Though Nero committed suicide in 68 C.E., a generation or two later, some expected him to return from the dead to work evil. See Carey, *Ultimate Things*, 97–98, 184–85; David Aune, *Revelation 6–16* (WBC 52B; Nashville: Thomas Nelson, 1998), 737–40.

9. Several historians have suggested an alternative interpretation of these passages, according to which the "synagogue of Satan" indicates Gentile Christians posing as Jews: David Frankfurter, "Jews or Not: Reconstructing the 'Other' in Rev 2:9 and 3:9," *HTR* 94 (2001): 403–25; John W. Marshall, *Parables of War: Reading John's Jewish Apocalypse* (ESCJ 10; Waterloo, Ont.: Wilfrid Laurier University Press, 2001), 12–16, 124–48; Stephen G. Wilson, *Related Strangers: Jews and Christians, 70–170 C.E.* (Minneapolis: Fortress, 1995), 162–65. For an alternative view, see Paul B. Duff, "'The Synagogue of Satan': Crisis Mongering and the Apocalypse of John," in *The Reality of Apocalypse: Rhetoric and Politics in the Book of Revelation* (SBLSymS 39; ed. David L. Barr; Atlanta: Society of Biblical Literature, 2006), 147–68.

10. A key text is 1 Clement 1:1, which mentions "sudden and repeated misfortunes and setbacks" in Rome. Though Bart D. Ehrman judges the evidence for persecution unconvincing (*The Apostolic Fathers* [LCL 24; Cambridge, Mass.: Harvard University Press, 2003], 24.), in my view 1 Clement 7:1 suggests a contemporary concern with persecution. Having just enumerated those heroes who have endured persecution, Clement writes, "we are in the same arena and the same contest is set before us."

11. A minority of interpreters regards Romans as addressed to a Gentile audience. Among others, see Stanley K. Stowers, *A Rereading of Romans* (New Haven: Yale University Press, 1994); Neil Elliott, *Liberating Paul: The Justice of God and the Politics of the Apostle* (Maryknoll, N.Y.: Orbis, 1994), 66–72; John G. Gager, *Reinventing Paul* (New York: Oxford University Press, 2000).

12. Paul, for example says, "in Christ," whereas modern readers might say "Christian."

13. Often Paul is undervalued as a witness to the earliest Jesus movements. His letters and Acts both confirm that he encountered the movements soon after Jesus' death.

14. On Acts, see the brief discussion in Klaus Haacker, "Paul's Life," in *The Cambridge Companion to St. Paul* (ed. James D. G. Dunn; New York: Cambridge University Press, 2003), 22–23.

15. First Timothy 1:13 includes persecution among Paul's pre-Christian sins. I agree with the vast majority of scholars that Paul did not write 1 Timothy. This passage does not reflect Paul's point of view.

16. Most translations do not reflect that Paul uses "zealot" rather than the adverbial "zealous." See Mark R. Fairchild, "Paul's Pre-Christian Zealot Associations: A Re-examination of Gal 1.14 and Acts 22.3," *NTS* 45 (1999): 526–28.

17. N. T. Wright, *What Did St. Paul Really Say?* (Grand Rapids: Eerdmans, 1997), 25–35.

18. The most influential argument to this effect is Martin Hengel, *The Pre-Christian Paul* (Philadelphia: Trinity Press International, 1991), 63–86. See Haacker, "Paul's Life"; Fairchild, "Paul's Pre-Christian Zealot Associations," 514–32; N. T. Wright, *The New Testament and the People of God* (Minneapolis: Fortress, 1992), esp. 170–197; Wright, *What Did St. Paul Really Say?*, 25–35; Michael J. Gorman, *Apostle of the Crucified Lord: A Theological Introduction to Paul and His Letters* (Grand Rapids: Eerdmans, 2004), 52–56.

19. Wright, *What Did St. Paul Really Say?*, 35.

20. For helpful summaries of the options, Calvin J. Roetzel, *Paul: The Man and the Myth* (Studies on Personalities of the New Testament; Minneapolis: Fortress, 1999), 38–42; see Gorman, *Apostle of the Crucified Lord*, 55–56.

21. See Claudia Setzer, *Jewish Responses to Early Christians: History and Polemics, 30–150 C.E.* (Philadelphia: Fortress, 1994), 22–23.

22. See the cautionary assessment by Wilson, who maintains that Jews did take internal disciplinary actions against Jesus followers in some cases, but that our evidence is largely tainted by later Christian bias (*Related Strangers*, 172–76). Note also Jack T. Sanders' judgment that the anti-Jewish invective we find in texts like Luke, John, and Acts reflects the

defensive response of "deviants" (Jesus people) against those Jews who "labeled" them (*Schismatics, Sectarians, Dissidents, Deviants: The First One Hundred Years of Jewish-Christian Relations* [Harrisburg: Trinity Press International, 1993], 232–33).

23. For a classic treatment of the boundaries of Roman religion in the city of Rome, see Simeon L. Guterman, *Religious Toleration and Persecution in Ancient Rome* (Westport, Conn.: Greenwood Press, 1951).

24. So the translation by W. H. C. Frend in "Persecutions: Genesis and Legacy," in *The Cambridge History of Christianity*, vol. 1: *Origins to Constantine*, ed. Margaret M. Mitchell and Frances M. Young (New York: Cambridge University Press, 2006), 504.

25. Frend, "Persecutions," 504; Wilken, *The Christians as the Romans Saw Them* (2nd ed.; New Haven: Yale University Press, 2003), 98; L. F. Janssen, "'Superstitio' and the Persecution of the Christians," *Vigiliae Christianae* 33 (1979): 157. Janssen's article appears with others cited in this chapter in a valuable anthology, Everett Ferguson, ed., *Church and State in the Early Church* (Studies in Early Christianity 7; New York: Garland Publishing, 1993).

26. Roman citizens, he sent to Rome for trial.

27. Wilken speculates that perhaps the anonymous charges came from merchants whose trade had been adversely affected, *The Christians as the Romans Saw Them*, 15–16.

28. Pliny mentions requiring accused Christians to worship before the emperor's image. Trajan omits reference to worship of himself, thus demonstrating humility while agreeing with Pliny's assessment.

29. See Matt 10:22; 24:9; Mark 13:13; Luke 21:12, 17; John 15:21; Acts 4:7-18; 5:28, 40-41; 9:14-16, 21; 1 Pet 4:14-16; Rev 2:13; 3:8; possibly Mark 6:14; James 2:7; Rev 2:3. See also Achtemeier, *1 Peter*, 37.

30. Frend, "Persecutions," 509. This is the classic position articulated by G. E. M. de Ste. Croix, "Why Were the Early Christians Persecuted?" *Past and Present* 26 (1963): 6–38.

31. Thus, Gillian Clark: "Christians were executed because their refusal to worship the Roman gods entailed refusal to obey the Roman authorities, and because they aroused suspicions of anti-social behavior," *Christianity and Roman Society* (Key Themes in Ancient History; New York: Cambridge University Press, 2004), 39.

Epilogue

1. Charles Marsh, *God's Long Summer: Stories of Faith and Civil Rights* (Princeton: Princeton University Press, 1997).

2. Marsh, *God's Long Summer*, 116–51.

3. Marsh, *God's Long Summer*, 139.

4. Here I draw heavily from Ann Louise Coble, *Cotton Patch for the Kingdom: Clarence Jordan's Demonstration Plot at Koinonia Farm* (Scottdale, Penn.: Herald Press, 2001).
5. Coble, *Cotton Patch for the Kingdom*, 89.
6. Related by Millard Fuller in his Foreword to Coble's *Cotton Patch for the Kingdom*, 11.
7. Related by Dallas Lee and quoted in Coble, *Cotton Patch for the Kingdom*, 74–75.

INDEX OF ANCIENT SOURCES

AUTHOR INDEX

SUBJECT INDEX